NOTHING VENTURE NOTHING WIN

Dedication

To my dear wife, Hazel, who for over fifty years has shared with me the joys and sorrows of life.

Hazel has read the proofs with unremitting care and made many helpful suggestions.

NOTHING VENTURE NOTHING WIN

MICHAEL WOODRUFF

1996
SCOTTISH ACADEMIC PRESS
EDINBURGH

Published by
Scottish Academic Press Ltd.
56 Hanover Street, Edinburgh EH2 2DX

ISBN 0 7073 0737 6

British Library Cataloguing in Publication Data

A catalogue record for this book is available from
the British Library

Typeset by Trinity Typesetting
Printed in Great Britain by Antony Rowe Ltd, Chippenham, Wiltshire

Contents

v

Illustrations

Apologia

If the proper study of mankind is Man, then writing an autobiography is a proper activity, because everyone looks inwardly at their own life and outwardly at the world from a unique vantage point inaccessible to anyone else.

The aim of an autobiography should be to paint for others a picture of what the writer has seen in the course of the strange adventure on which, willy nilly, we all embark when we are born, and to record his reflections on what it all means.

This is what I have tried to do.

1

The Genetic Lottery

We cannot choose our parents, but what we are depends very much on who they were. They give us a set of genes which, unless we have an identical twin, is unique. Our mother provides the protected intra-uterine environment in which our antenatal development takes place, and together our parents may, or may not, provide us with a stable, loving and stimulating family environment during our childhood and adolescence. They may choose the schools we go to, and guide us in our choice of what we do after we leave school.

Parents can also decide how many, if any, children they are going to have and when to have them, and in recent times the choice has been extended by artificial insemination and *in vitro* fertilization. Within limits they can choose the kind of offspring they produce. Selective abortion is used increasingly to eliminate foetuses destined to develop into individuals who are seriously handicapped, mentally or physically, and while some feel, on ethical or religious grounds, that this is never justified, discussion centres mainly on the stage of pregnancy up to which termination is acceptable. Moreover, techniques have been developed in animals by which offspring can be selected for sex, and by which the genome of cells can be modified. These techniques are in principle applicable to man, and this possibility raises formidable ethical questions.[1] The possibility of correcting single-gene defects responsible for serious congenital disease is attractive, but once we have learned to do this in somatic (i.e. non-germ) cells there will be pressure to extend the technique to germ cells, as has already been done in animals. The question will then arise, 'Why stop there?' Should we not try to reduce the incidence of diseases

like atherosclerosis (which is largely responsible for coronary
thrombosis and strokes) and cancer, in which multiple genetic
factors appear to play a part, by eliminating as far as possible the
relevant genes from the human gene-pool? Again the question
arises, 'Why stop there?' Should we not try to create a new race
of people superior to present day humans in respect of physical
fitness, intelligence, and perhaps even goodness? As I have
written previously,[1] 'The notion of breeding supermen raises
disturbing memories for people of my generation, and prompts
the reflection that it is fortunate that molecular genetics did not
exist in Hitler's day. But it exists now, and we are soon going to
be faced with choices of decisive importance for the future of
mankind. It would be irresponsible not to begin thinking about
these choices now.'

Some physical characteristics are clearly inherited in animals
and man, and also in plants. Pure-bred bulldogs do not produce
Yorkshire terrier puppies, and the children of Caucasian, Black
and Chinese parents are easily distinguishable. Strangely, however, many people deny the existence of inherited differences in
ability, especially mental ability, between individuals, whether
they are members of the same, or different, families, social classes
or ethnic groups. Andrew Huxley,[2] addressing the British Association for the Advancement of Science in 1977, compared today's
controversy about the extent to which human ability is inherited
with the controversy about evolution in which his grandfather
was so heavily involved over a hundred years ago. In both cases
many people felt that ethical and religious principles were
involved, and that the self-respect of *homo sapiens* as a species, or
of some particular category of people, was threatened. Huxley
accepted that, whereas the evidence Darwin presented in the
Origin of Species is incontrovertible, the question of inheritance
of ability is complicated by the fact that there is a social
component in the determination of any aspect of human performance; what surprised and distressed him, as it does me, is
that many people, including some scientists, 'regard the assumption of equal inherited ability as something which does not
require experimental evidence to establish it and which it is
positively wicked to question because the conclusion might
disagree with their social and political preconceptions'. People
who challenge this are labelled racist, and held up to ridicule, but

surely the epithet racist, at least in a pejorative sense, should be reserved for those who hold that racial differences justify the subjugation of one race by another, which is a very different matter.

Some people feel that the genetic lottery is unfair, and, although they seldom say so explicitly, that society should set out to correct the inequality it gives rise to by designing an educational system that will not only help the less privileged but hold back those who are especially gifted. I cannot accept this, and if it be elitist to hold that the objective of education should be to develop to the fullest extent possible the potential of every child, I am indeed elitist.

I was perhaps lucky to have been born when I was, and certainly fortunate in my parents.

My father, Harold Addison Woodruff, was born in Sheffield on 10 July 1877. His father, Joseph Woodruff, was for many years the manager of the spring-making department of Cammel Laird and Company and invented a machine which made a lot of money for the company. He considered resigning and trying to exploit this himself but, with three children, decided not to do so, and was rewarded with a bonus of £5. Harold's parents were Wesleyan Methodists, and their two boys went to Wesley College, which later became King Edward VII Grammar School, Sheffield. After leaving school my father studied at the Royal Veterinary College (RVC), London, and qualified MRCVS in 1898. After a year as tutor in surgery at the RVC he joined the staff of the Royal Agricultural College in Cirencester. He was an excellent horseman and much enjoyed hunting, which was readily available in the vicinity. He returned to the RVC in 1900 as Professor of Veterinary Hygiene and Materia Medica, and in 1908 was appointed to the Chair of Veterinary Medicine. While occupying this post he managed to study human medicine at University College Hospital and qualified in 1912. He became fascinated by the similarity between auricular fibrillation in humans and a cardiac arrhythmia that was common in horses. One day, when a horse with this condition had to be put down, he invited Sir Thomas Lewis from UCH to the RVC and was able to demonstrate post-mortem the fibrillating auricle and irregular ventricular rhythm. Fifty years later I heard Sir George Pickering, who had been working with Lewis at the time, recount this story in a lecture he gave in Edinburgh, though he did not know until I told him that the Michael Woodruff in his audience was Harold Woodruff's son.

In 1908 my father married Margaret Ada Cooper (Fig 1), the eldest daughter of Charles Henry Cooper, a manufacturer engaged in the 'rag trade', and Mary Esther, *née* Scott. The Coopers had nine children, six girls and three boys. Like the Woodruffs, they had a strong Wesleyan Methodist connection, though I think that Charles Cooper was, at heart, a Unitarian. The girls went to the North London Collegiate School for Girls, the creation of a remarkable pioneer in education for girls, Miss Frances Mary Buss. My mother married soon after she left school. Sadly, I do not remember her clearly because she died when I was only five. From her photographs she must have been very beautiful, and, from the accounts of her family and friends, very talented. My father adored her. She was a keen tennis player and golfer but, unlike my father, not happy on horseback. Mary Cooper is reputed to have prayed that if her first child was a girl she would be beautiful, but had added 'if it did not lead her into temptation'. The next in the family, Violet, went to Cambridge, where she took a first in the Natural Sciences Tripos (though being a girl was not awarded a degree until many years later), and played hockey for Girton, and also for the University Women's team against Oxford.

My parents bought a house in Mill Hill, where I was born on 3 April 1911. I was christened Michael (because my parents liked the name), Francis (not, as it is tempting to imagine, after Frances Mary Buss but after my father's brother Frank, who married another of the Cooper girls, Stephanie), and Addison (the maiden name of my paternal grandmother).

London — Melbourne Return

In 1913 my father became Professor of Veterinary Pathology and Director of the Veterinary Institute in the University of Melbourne. At the time Australia must have seemed very remote, and it has never failed to amaze me that my father should have given up a secure chair in London for a post in the antipodes. Presumably my parents were moved by the challenge of a job to be done and the spirit of adventure. A clue pointing in this direction is provided by a story that my father delighted to tell about a young doctor who had been a contemporary of his at UCH. One day, just after he had qualified and had in his pocket some money with which he was planning to celebrate, this man was walking down Whitehall and felt moved to wander into one of the large government buildings, which turned out to be the Colonial Office. Here he saw a commissionaire go into a room, come out with a young man, and conduct him to another room from which he emerged a quarter of an hour later. After seeing this process repeated once or twice, he asked the commissionaire what was going on, and was told that applicants were being interviewed for a medical post in Australia. He took a sovereign out of his pocket, gave it to the commissionaire, and said 'Show me in next'. After some hesitation the man did so. To cut a long story short, he got the job. Years later I met him in Australia.

My father sailed for Melbourne in January 1913; my mother, my brother Philip, who had been born a few days after my father left, and I (Fig 2) followed in RMS *Orsova* soon afterwards. We were accompanied by my mother's sister, Stephanie, and a nurse. This must have been very nearly the ship's maiden voyage and, years later, I sailed in her again to Australia on her last voyage. In between I have travelled back and forth many times, spending more than a year at sea as a passenger or temporary ship's surgeon. How boring, some people say. Not at all. If you set your mind to it, you can do a great deal of work on a ship — I once wrote two scientific papers between Wellington and London — and still enjoy yourself very much.

We settled in the Melbourne suburb of Kew, in a house my parents named Mill Hill. Such was life in those days that two servants, Lettie and Katie Lemmon, who had been with us in England, came out to join us. The following year war broke out in Europe. Next day my mother wrote to her family:

Wednesday 5th Aug. 1914

Mill Hill, Fellows St
Kew, Melbourne

My dear ones all,

How terrible the war news is — It makes us feel terribly anxious about you all, and about Steph [who was on her way back to England] too, though I suppose she will really be quite safe. There is a censorship of all cables here now and of course the news we get is very meagre — but at midday the news came through that England had declared war on Germany because of not getting a satisfactory answer from them with regard to their respecting the integrity of Belgium. I had hoped that England could have kept peace with honour — particularly if Italy remained neutral, but on reading Sir Edward Grey's speech today, which was cabled out, one realises that we were bound to protect France in the Channel. It is a great thing to be able to endorse in one's mind all that he says — he is so dignified and obviously anxious for peace yet realises that we are bound to act for Britain's honour, interests and obligations. I am sure we can't be too thankful that we have such a man at the Foreign Office. But it all seems too awful, and we know so little here, comparatively ...'

My father wanted to join either the British or the Australian army as a Veterinary Officer, but was asked by the University not to do so until the Veterinary Institute was securely established. In 1915 he wrote to the Chief Veterinary Officer at the War Office (whom he knew) to offer his services but, after some correspondence between the British and Australian Commands, he was appointed ADVS to the Australian division with the rank of Major, and served in Egypt and then in France (Fig 3).

We had been in Australia less than two years and, although my parents had already made many friends, it was decided that my mother, my brother and I should return to London to live with my Cooper grandparents.

Soon after we arrived I contracted measles, complicated by *staphylococcal otitis media*, and, while nursing me, my mother developed staphylococcal septicaemia. My father was granted compassionate leave, but she died before he reached London. A few months later, my grandfather, Charles Cooper, died of a cerebral haemorrhage. Many children first encounter death when a pet animal dies and are, as a result, prepared to some extent for the death of a friend or member of the family, but this was not so with me. I have no recollection of my mother's death, probably because I was so ill when it happened, but I remember being taken to my grandfather's funeral in the church at Ballards Lane, where the Coopers had long been members, and where my parents had been married. With my father away in the army, the fact that I was able to come to terms with the situation speaks much for the wisdom and love of my grandmother and my aunts, especially Brenda and Elsie Cooper, who were unmarried and living at home at the time. My father's letter to my brother and me about our mother expresses his love for her and his Christian faith, and can still move me to tears whenever I read it.

My brother and I went to a kindergarten/primary school in Finchley run by two maiden ladies, the Misses Coatsworth. It was a wonderful place where we learned the three Rs properly, and were encouraged to ask questions. The Misses Coatsworth were, I suppose, in their forties, and are said to have been quite different in appearance, but my recollection is a composite picture of one elderly lady whom I revered. Many years later, when my wife and I were looking for a first school for our daughter, Margaret, we had the good fortune to find in Currie, on the outskirts of Edinburgh, a similar establishment, St Mungo's, run by Miss Christine Lovell, where Margaret too learned the three Rs properly, together with art, geography, history, and scripture (the order is alphabetical) and a little latin, and how to live with other children. Schools of this kind seem to be becoming increasingly rare; long may those that are left remain.

My grandmother's house was in Seymour Road, North Finchley, and not far away, in the direction of Highgate, an anti-aircraft battery was established to fight off zeppelins and other enemy aircraft. When an air raid was imminent, a red vehicle with a loud siren toured the streets and my brother and I were woken up — for this always seemed to happen at night — and taken down to a large cupboard underneath the stairs. Before we were whisked off, we could see the searchlights from our bedroom window, and this came back to me vividly when, as a young man, I saw the film of Noel Coward's play, Cavalcade. Half a century later my brother knocked on the door of my grandmother's old house and asked if he could see the cupboard underneath the stairs, if it was still there. It was, indeed, but I am not sure what moral, if any, is to be drawn from this tale.

Towards the end of 1917 my father was called back to Melbourne by the University. My brother and I followed on the SS *Thermistocles* with our youngest aunt, Elsie Cooper, and she kept house for us in Melbourne until, in 1919, my father married Isabella (Ella) Glaister, the eldest daughter of John Glaister, Professor of Medical Jurisprudence in Glasgow. The Woodruffs, Coopers and Glaisters had been friends for many years, but my father's courtship must have been conducted largely by correspondence. Soon after the wedding Elsie Cooper married Aubrey Holmes, a civil servant in the Navy Office in Melbourne, whose eldest sister had been one of my mother's closest friends.

Our trip on the *Thermistocles* was quite an adventure. The vessel was still functioning as a troopship, and we were the only civilians on board. We had a naval escort part of the way, and apparently sighted several German submarines, but I remember only two things: the daily lifeboat drills, and Christmas Day 1917, when the senior officer on board cut an enormous Christmas cake with his sword.

Before her marriage Ella Glaister had a busy life as Chief Inspector in the Scottish Department of Education for the teaching of Domestic Science. Like my own mother she must have had some misgivings about migrating to a new country, but she took to life in Australia like a duck to water — literally so when she learned to swim — and seemed to know instinctively how to mother two rather slap-dash small boys. We quickly came to love her dearly and accept her as our mother, and our love grew with the years. She retained her interest in the teaching of domestic science, and served as adviser to both the Emily

1. My parents wedding photograph.

2. Listening to my father's watch (aged 18 months).

MacPherson College of Domestic Economy, which was concerned with training girls seeking a career in this field, and the Invergowrie Hostel, which was established to teach girls before they married how to cope with the problems of managing a home. She quickly developed a wide circle of friends in Melbourne and the University, and derived much pleasure from her membership of the Lyceum Club.

Schooldays

Before I describe my schooling, readers unfamiliar with the Australian educational scene may like to know something of the organization of primary and secondary education in Australia when I was a boy. It has not changed much since except that nowadays the proportion of co-educational schools is much greater.

There were, as in Britain, schools that were free and schools that charged fees.

The non-fee paying schools were run by the State Government Education Departments, and consisted of primary schools, referred to in Victoria as *state schools* and in New South Wales as *public schools*, and secondary schools termed *high schools*. The primary schools, and some of the high schools, were co-educational.

The fee-paying schools were all church foundations: Anglican, Baptist, Methodist, Presbyterian, Quaker and Roman Catholic. Most of them were single-sex. In Victoria, the fee-paying schools for boys formed themselves into three main groups: the *Associated Public Schools* (consisting of Geelong College, Geelong Church of England Grammar School, Melbourne Church of England Grammar School, Scotch College, Xavier College and Wesley College); the *Associated Grammar Schools* (consisting of all the Church of England grammar schools except Geelong Grammar and Melbourne Grammar, and Carey Baptist Grammar School); and the Roman Catholic boys' schools (with the exception of Xavier College). In New South Wales, since the state schools were called public schools, the leading fee-paying schools were referred to as the Great Public Schools or GPS.

Many of the boys' schools had a close affiliation with a particular girls' school. Most of the fee-paying schools had a majority of day pupils with one boarding house. Some, like Geelong Grammar, where Prince Charles went for a term, and Clyde School for Girls, fairly easily identifiable as the setting for the novel, and film, *Picnic at Hanging Rock*, were essentially boarding schools, similar in character to their British counterparts.

All these schools prepared pupils for public examinations at three levels, called (in Victoria) *Intermediate, School Leaving Pass or Matriculation*, and *School Leaving Honours*. These were roughly similar to British O-levels, Scottish Highers, and English A-levels respectively. A pass in School Leaving in appropriate subjects sufficed for entrance to the university, but study at the honours level for at least a year made first year at the university much easier, and was essential for anyone trying for a College or University Entrance Scholarship. On average, in these examinations, pupils from the state high schools performed as well as, or only marginally less well than, those from the fee-paying schools, but the latter offered much more in the way of sporting facilities, music, and the opportunity to take part in plays and debates, as well as a strong religious background. The fee-paying schools were not subsidised but many of them offered competitive scholarships for entry to the senior school, and fees were deductible for income tax purposes.

When we returned to Melbourne in 1917 my father bought another house in Kew, in the same street as *Mill Hill*, and my brother and I went as day boys to the preparatory section of Trinity Church of England Grammar School. This was about two miles from home and we rode to school on a pony. My father had a larger horse, and for some years rode every day to the Veterinary School, a distance of just over four miles, more than half of it on main roads. My sole distinction at this school was to win a prize for mental arithmetic. The headmaster's son was a hot favourite and was expected to score 100 per cent. This he did, but I managed to do the same, and so shared the prize. This took the form of J. C. Smith's *A Book of Verse for Boys and Girls*,[1] which well illustrates the editor's claim that 'most short poems that are worth knowing are worth knowing by heart'.

Our summer holidays were spent in Tasmania in a little place called Dover, on Port Esperance Bay, some fifty miles south of

Hobart. To get there we went by overnight steamer across Bass Strait from Melbourne to Launceston, thence by train to Hobart and on, next day, by ferry steamer, the SS *Dover*, to our destination. The ship which took us across Bass Strait, the *Loongana*, was shallow draft because she had to be able to get up the River Tamar as far as Launceston, and the passage through the tide race at the entry to Port Philip Bay was often extremely rough. The ship's departure always seemed to be timed so that we would pass through the *rip*, as it is called, not at slack water but when it was at its roughest, and on the outward journey dinner was always served at this time. My father was not in the least put out by this, but the rest of the family usually retired to their bunks.

Port Esperance is a sheltered bay with several islands, the three most prominent ones being called Faith, Hope and Charity, and a river flowing in at its southwestern extremity. There was fishing and swimming in the bay, trout fishing in the river, and a fine surf beach about five miles away near the mouth of the River Huon. During one of our first holidays some men felling timber near a place called Hastings discovered the entrance to a stupendous limestone cave, and soon afterwards several more caves were found. Every holiday thereafter we went on a two-day expedition to the caves, armed with ropes, torches and candles. To reach them we set out by horse and trap, then walked perhaps ten miles along a disused timber 'tramway' that had been built for hauling out logs, and then through dense bush, guided by blaze marks cut in the bark of trees by the original discoverers of the caves and those who followed them (Fig 4). These caves have now been opened up as a tourist attraction, and illuminated electrically, but may have lost something of their excitement in the process. Another expedition we enjoyed was to climb Adamson's Peak, a mountain of just over 4000 feet. This too was a two day trip, which began in a horse-drawn vehicle or on horseback. Two thirds of the climb was through dense bush; the rest a trek over a swampy tableland and a scramble over rocks to the summit. The view was breathtaking: to the east the D'Entrecasteaux Channel and Bruny Island, and, on a very clear day, the Tasman Peninsula and Port Arthur; to the southwest and west, mile upon mile of mountain and bush, and then more sea. Today, one can go much of the way by car and then follow an easy path to the top, but for me something of the excitement of the trip has been lost. Why? Partly because of nostalgia for things past, but also, perhaps, because we don't want things to be made too easy for us:

> Not for ever in green pastures
>> Do we ask our way to be;
> But the steep and rugged pathway
>> May we tread rejoicingly.[2]

In 1924 my father was granted a year's sabbatical leave to work at the Pasteur Institute in Paris. It was decided that my brother and I should go as boarders to Queen's College, Taunton. To get there by the beginning of the English school year, we left Australia with our stepmother in the SS *Esperance Bay* in August 1923, and my father followed in December.

One of my contemporaries at the school was J. P. Widgery, who later became Lord Chief Justice of England. At that time soccer was played in the first term, followed by rugger in the next and cricket in the summer. A few years later it was decided to give up soccer and concentrate on rugby after the first fifteen had been soundly beaten by the Mill Hill second fifteen, but I remember Widgery as a decidedly useful soccer player. This was the only time I ever played soccer, and what I learned in my one term proved a useful introduction to hockey, which I took up as an undergraduate. I enjoyed many things during my year in Taunton, especially the cricket coaching from the sports master, 'Dapper' Chanon, who had played for Somerset, walks in the lovely Cheddar Gorge or Weston-super-mare with various aunts and uncles. I would have enjoyed myself more had I not been put in a form with boys who were older than I was but far from bright, because the headmaster believed, as he had the effrontery to tell my father, that 'colonial boys were backward'. I went up a form a term, but at the end of the year had barely reached the place where I should have begun. I think that my later suspicion of comprehensive schools probably stems from this frustrating experience.

We spent Christmas 1923 in London, and then went north by train to 'see in' the New Year with the Glaisters in Scotland. They had a town house in Glasgow, and a country house at Thornhill in Dumfriesshire, where we celebrated the New Year in Scottish style. For my brother and me, this was our first opportunity of getting to know our new grandparents, and some new uncles and aunts, including John Glaister Jnr., who later succeeded to his father's chair after some astonishing adventures as Professor of Forensic Medicine in Cairo.

Grandad Glaister was a formidable figure, but very tolerant of his new grandchildren. His wife, Granny Glaister, was a quiet, charming lady, with the sort of charisma we have come to associate with HM the Queen Mother. In those days, professors in the Scottish Universities lived in considerable style. For years John Glaister kept a carriage and horses, and employed a full-time coachman; unfortunately, the carriage had been replaced by a car just before our visit.

Our summer holiday was spent in Paris, and this went far to make up for my boredom at school. My parents were staying in a hotel on the left bank, within walking distance of the Pasteur Institute, and another room was found for my brother and me. We had lessons in French from a real Russian princess who had escaped during the revolution, spent hours seeing the sights of the city, and in the evening usually went to a small restaurant near the hotel for dinner, where I was allowed about a teaspoonful of wine in my mineral water. Two excursions stick vividly in my memory. The first was a trip by train from the Gare d'Orsay — now the Musée d'Orsay — to Versailles. The second took us to the battlefields of Northern France. Near Lille we located a house where my father had been billeted during the war. The old lady who owned it recognized my father instantly. She did not have a fatted calf to kill, but she did open a precious bottle of cognac.

Short holidays were spent in London with uncles, cousins and aunts. One of my mother's sisters, Dorothy, had married a solicitor, Leslie Burgin, and I have vivid memories of the 1924 general election in which Leslie stood as a Liberal in the London constituency of Hornsey. He was defeated by the Conservative candidate, Captain Euan Wallace, but later became MP for Luton, which he represented for many years, first as a Liberal and then as a National Liberal. He became Minister of Transport in Neville Chamberlain's government in succession to Hore-Belisha, and in 1939 Minister of Supply, but resigned when Chamberlain was succeeded by Churchill.

He had an extraordinary gift for foreign languages, and when, as Transport Minister, he had to speak at a dinner in honour of some Japanese visitors, he did a crash course in Japanese and was able to make his speech in that language. Leslie Burgin greatly admired Neville Chamberlain, and sincerely believed that Chamberlain's approach to Hitler was the right course to take at the time. After he resigned, he gave me a copy of Chamberlain's speeches,[3] and inscribed this as follows:

> To Michael from Leslie, 15/4/39
> The author of these speeches is the world's most commanding figure.

Sadly, Leslie Burgin died while I was a prisoner of war, so I never had a chance to discuss this with him.

We spent our last weeks in England in Duffield, just north of Derby, with my father's sister Ethel and her husband, Dr Herbert Mason, who was in general practice, and their three children, Philip, James and Pauline. Philip went on from Sedbergh school to take a first in Modern Greats at Oxford. He then topped the Civil Service Examination, but instead of opting for the Treasury, as he was expected to do, decided to enter the Indian Civil Service. He wrote several novels set in India, including *Call the Next Witness, The Wild Sweet Witch*, and *The Island of Chamba*; and a thoughtful history of the Indian Civil Service, *The Men Who Ruled India*.[4] Many of Philip's books were written under the pseudonym of Philip Woodruff, which somewhat irked my brother, whose real name this was.

We returned to Melbourne in a coal-burning cargo ship, the *Port Kembla*, which carried twelve passengers, and also, to my great delight, two dogs that my brother and I were allowed to exercise on the deck each day. After leaving Tilbury the engines were stopped only twice before we reached Melbourne: to disembark the Thames pilot and to pick up the pilot at the entrance to Port Philip Bay. There was not enough room in the bunkers for the coal needed for such a long journey, so more coal was carried in the hold and transferred to the bunkers after we had rounded the Cape of Good Hope. The flashing light on the Cape, which was the first sign of land since we left England, was reassuring, at least to the passengers. At Queen's we had had to wear stiff Eton collars on Sunday when the school went to church in Taunton, and my parents thought we should continue to wear them on Sunday in Melbourne. My brother and I were filled with dismay at the prospect, and at this point on the journey we finally plucked up enough courage to throw them out through our cabin porthole. Our parents were puzzled when, on reaching Melbourne, they were nowhere to be found.

Among the passengers on the *Port Kembla* was a New Zealander, Archdeacon Williams, with his wife and daughter. He was something of a mathematician, and was interested in problems of the kind to be found in Rouse Ball's *Mathematical Recreations and Essays*.[5] He introduced me to magic squares, and also to Kirkman's 'School-girls' problem, which he presented in the form of how to arrange fifteen girls in a crocodile consisting of five rows of three, in such a way that for seven consecutive days no girl would walk with any of her schoolmates more than once in the same triplet. He led me gently to a solution, but wisely refrained from examining more difficult cases of the problem. We discussed many other topics and he took the trouble to answer questions in a way that I could understand. 'What are logarithms,?' I asked one day, though I do not remember what prompted the question. He gave a sensible answer, beginning with a discussion of integral powers of a number, and then borrowed a slide-rule from one of the ship's officers to carry the discussion a stage deeper. On another occasion I asked him 'What is the calculus?' Again he gave a helpful answer, but what is more, he advised my father to get for me, when we arrived home, a copy of Silvanus Thompson's book, *Calculus Made Easy*.[6] This duly arrived on my next birthday, and the effect it had on me was similar to the effect that Chapman's translation of Homer had on John Keats.

I know now that the book lacks what mathematicians call rigour, but the fact remains that, apart from the Bible, it has had a greater influence on me than any other book I have ever read. I do not question the importance of rigour, and have deep respect for the great mathematicians of the nineteenth and early twentieth centuries, like Cauchy, Weierstrass and Dedekind, who established rigorous methods of analysis. But one must have something to be rigorous about, and it would be absurd to denigrate the work of their forebears, among them Newton himself, even if it 'did not quite attain modern standards of rigour'.[7] Few would dare to challenge so great a mathematician as J. E. Littlewood on questions of mathematical propriety, yet it was he who said that 'given ideas, any competent mathematician can supply the rigour'.[8] It is no less absurd to denigrate the work of great teachers like Silvanus Thompson. He admits, in the epilogue to what he calls his 'very simplest introduction to those beautiful methods of reckoning which are generally called by the terrifying names of the differential and the integral calculus,' that he has not demonstrated 'with rigid and satisfactory completeness the validity of sundry methods which he has presented in simple fashion, and even dared to use in solving problems'. But he goes on to point out that we do not forbid the use of a watch to every person who does not know how to make one, or object to a musician playing on a violin that he has not made himself; nor do we teach the rules of syntax to children before they have become fluent in the use of speech, and he concludes that it would be equally absurd to require general rigid demonstrations to be expounded to beginners in the calculus.

In Melbourne I did not return to Trinity Grammar School, but went as a day boy to Wesley College. This was a Methodist foundation, but a very ecumenical one, with boys from many Christian denominations including a few Roman Catholics, and quite a large number of Jews. R. G. Menzies, who became Prime Minister of Australia, was an Old Wesley Collegian. His successor, H. E. Holt, was two years my senior at school; A. S. Brown, who became Australian Ambassador to Japan and later Permanent Head of the Prime Minister's Department, was in my year. The Headmaster, L. A. Adamson, was a product of Rugby and Oxford. He was an Anglican, a lay canon at St Paul's Cathedral, Melbourne, and a great friend of the Cathedral Organist and Choirmaster, Dr A. E. Floyd, about whom I shall have more to say later.

The general standard of teaching was high, and two of my teachers, A. E. ('Fido') Gwillim and F. W. ('Jerry') Campbell were superb.

Mr Gwillim was the senior English master. He had the ability to communicate to boys his deep love of English poetry; as a result, I learned by heart a great deal of Milton, Keats and Tennyson without really trying to do so, and remember much of it to this day. An unusual feature of the school, for which he was,

I think, responsible, was the annual award of a prize for reading aloud some poetry or prose of the reader's choice to the assembled school. I would have liked very much to win this prize but never came close to doing so.

Mr Campbell taught senior mathematics. He encouraged us to venture beyond the prescribed texts, and I still possess a copy of E. W. Hobson's *Plane Trigonometry*[9] that I obtained during my last year at school, which discusses the analytical properties of the circular and related functions at quite an advanced level, including the difficult topic of uniform convergence, which I did not encounter again until my second year at university. Mr Campbell kept open house on Saturday evenings for members of his senior class, where we could discuss mathematics and enjoy the cake and coffee his wife provided. He was a qualified actuary, and soon after I left school he too left, and became actuary to a large insurance company — a sad loss to the school and to the cause of education.

Sport played an important part in the life of the school, but one did not have to be especially good at it to enjoy it. The sports that interested me particularly were cricket and rowing, but they overlapped, and one had to opt for one or the other. I chose rowing, but was never heavy enough to get beyond the third crew, in which I rowed No. 7. Admittedly, this was not very distinguished, but we trained quite seriously and managed to win in the inter-school regatta. I did some more rowing later on, and it taught me a very important lesson: when things are going wrong, start by assuming that it is you, and not someone else, who is at fault.

It was customary for the whole school to sing songs from the Wesley College Song Book for half an hour or so every Friday morning. This book had its origins in a pamphlet containing eight songs put together by L. A. Adamson soon after he joined the staff of the school in 1887; the custom of singing together as a school became established when he was appointed headmaster in 1902. When I was a new boy in 1924, the fifth edition of the Song Book had just been printed, and the contents provide an illuminating commentary on the times. Some songs, like Sir Henry Newbolt's *The Best School of All,* or the Headmaster's *Schola Carissima,* might have been sung by any school; others, not surprisingly, related more or less specifically to Wesley. But there were two kinds of song which, in retrospect, astonish me, though they did not do so at the time, and will, I suspect, seem even more astonishing to anyone unfamiliar with Australia in the 1920s.

First, there were poems and ballads about England, set to music composed by the headmaster and others connected with the school, including Richard Lovelace's *To Althea from Prison*; Austin Dobson's *Song of the Seasons* and *The Milkmaid*; a ballad, *Chalk and Flint*, first published in *Punch*;[10] and Dorothy Stuart's *Est Deo Gratia*,[11] which we sang on St George's Day.

Secondly, there were many songs about the First World War. Some of these were English in origin, like C. A. Alington's *The School at War* and Lawrence Binyon's *For the Fallen* sung to tunes by the Headmaster, the Music Master or the School Musician. Many others, though England-orientated, were written in Australia by Old Wesley Collegians and others, and these had such an impression on me that I feel impelled to give some examples.

My first is a poem by an Old Wesley Collegian, Alan Gross, which we sang to a tune composed by the headmaster, with an accompaniment by Dr A E Floyd.

> When from this Land's unbroken Peace
> 　　I see, with mind aglow
> A band of gallant gentlemen
> 　　As ever you may know,
> How shall I fail to tell their praise
> 　　Whose very deeds do sing
> That Honour is to Action spurred
> 　　To serve our gracious King?
>
> How shall I fail to praise their deeds
> 　　When standing by our shore,
> I see the guarded, southern main
> 　　A-rippling as of yore?
> Between the hills the bell birds call;
> 　　The river murmurs by;
> The sweet, grey piles of Melbourne reach
> 　　Towards a tranquil sky.
>
> Now greet you, greet you who account
> 　　Man's life a merry thing,
> Yet put the ways of Peace aside

> Till Peace again shall spring.
> Now march you gay or rest you loved
>   Astir with dream of home;
> My heart goes with you, friend o' mine,
>   Where'er your feet may roam.

My second example, which gives no indication of its Australian origin, consists of the first verse of another poem by Alan Gross, which inspired a stained glass window in the School Hall, and which we used to sing to a traditional English tune, *The Mill Wheel*:

> Young Galahad has gone to fight
>   In countries o'er the sea,
> For King and Empire, God and Right,
>   And Truth, and Liberty.

My last example is a poem entitled *For England* by an Old Scotch Collegian, Corporal J. D. Burns, who was killed in action at Gallipoli, which was published in his school magazine. Once again, we sang this to a tune written by our headmaster.

> The bugles of England were blowing o'er the sea,
> As they had called a thousand years — calling now to me;
> They woke me from dreaming in the dawning of the day,
> The bugles of England — and how could I stay?
>
> The banners of England, unfurled across the sea,
> Floating out upon the wind, were beckoning to me,
> Storm-rent and battle-torn, smoke stained and grey,
> The banners of England — and how could I stay?
>
> O England! I heard the cry of those that died for thee,
> Sounding like an organ voice across the winter sea;
> They lived and died for England, and gladly went their way,
> England! O England! How could I stay?

In the preface to the fourth edition of the Wesley College Song Book, Mr Adamson thanks Scotch College 'for leave to use the fine words of J. D. Burns *For England*, which so splendidly expresses the feelings of the Australian Public Schoolboy as regards the Great War'. I doubt if these feelings were quite as universal as Mr Adamson believed. In particular, Irish Australians, many of whom served with great distinction in World War I, and also in World War II, and, like all Australians who served overseas did so as volunteers, would, I think, have expressed their motivation differently. I do not know of any published expression of the views of boys from Catholic schools like Xavier College, many of whom were of Irish extraction, and it would be impertinent for one whose roots are in England, and who is moreover a protestant, to speculate on what they would have said, but in World War I the fighting, in France and at Gallipoli, was geographically so remote from Australia that the urge to protect family and friends at home cannot have been the only reason why they enlisted.

Though Burns may not have been speaking for all Australians of his generation, he was certainly speaking for many, and his feelings correspond closely to those expressed by Rupert Brooke and others of his generation in England. It must be very difficult for anyone brought up in the second half of this century to understand these feelings. I do not see how any sensible person could regard Brooke or Burns, and others in the same mould, as warmongers, but there are certainly people who today see them as naive victims of propaganda about 'a war to end wars'. I shall return to this subject later, and here confine myself to two comments: first, whatever could or should have been done to prevent the situation that led up to the outbreak of the first world war, I do not believe that, when Britain declared war on Germany in 1914, it had any acceptable alternative. Secondly, I believe that the consequences for the world would have been much worse if the allies had been defeated.

Why, it may be asked, should an alumnus of a school with a strong Scottish tradition, who bears the same name as Scotland's famous poet, speak of *England* rather than *Great Britain* or *The United Kingdom*? Admittedly, *England* is more euphonious and easier to build into a metrical form, but the real reason, I think, is that at the time, at any rate in Australia, *England* was often used to denote England, Scotland and Wales, or even the British Isles as a whole, and this was not just a convenient abbreviation but an indication of how people thought. With a Scottish stepmother (Fig 5), and a maternal grandmother of Scottish descent, I could not fail to be aware of the pride that Scots take in their history and culture, but the Scots I knew were proud also to be part of the nation that produced Shakespeare and Newton. Similarly, the English people I knew, or knew of, were proud to identify themselves with the nation that produced Robert Burns and Clerk Maxwell, and my edition (1924) of *The Oxford Book of English Verse* contains no less than fourteen of Burns' poems. It was not until I came to live in Scotland, many years later, that I encountered people who wanted to put the clock back to 1707 and undo the Act of Union.

I left school in December 1928. I had spent only one year in the upper sixth, studying mathematics and physics, and hoped to stay on for a second year, as many boys did. This was prompted by the hope that I would get a place in the crew, but, as I had managed to win a Government scholarship, which covered university fees, and a residential college scholarship, my father rightly decided that it would be ridiculous for me to spend another year at school.

4

Undergraduate Life

The Australian universities, with the exception of the Australian National University of Canberra, which is a Federal Government institution, were established by the various State Governments. All are secular institutions, but the Victorian University Act of 1853 granted land to the Anglican, Methodist, Presbyterian and Roman Catholic Churches (the order is alphabetical) on which to build colleges that would be affiliated with the university, and similar arrangements were made in other states. In Melbourne four residential colleges for men were established: Newman (Roman Catholic), Ormond (Presbyterian), Queen's (Methodist) and Trinity (Anglican). All accepted both men and women as non-resident students, entitled to attend college tutorials and participate in various activities. Later, residential colleges for women were established, initially Janet Clarke Hall (affiliated with Trinity) and St Mary's Hall (affiliated with Newman), and then the University Women's College and St Hilda's (affiliated with Queen's). Since the end of World War II all the men's colleges have come to accept women in residence, and the women's colleges, including the Women's College, which changed its name to University College, to accept men. Though all but one are church foundations, the colleges have considerable independence, and, in the case of Ormond and Queen's, this was maintained when the Methodist, Presbyterian and other non-Anglican, non-Catholic churches joined in 1977 to form the Uniting Church of Australia.

The Australian university colleges are a species *sui generis*. They are not dependent on public funds but are nevertheless much involved in the life and work of the university, and in

Melbourne two Heads of Colleges serve in rotation as *ex officio* members of the University Council. They are more like Oxbridge Colleges than Halls of Residence in other British universities, but differ significantly from both. Like Oxford and Cambridge colleges they have an important teaching function; the Heads of Colleges have always been people of academic distinction; and interesting people, including a satisfactory proportion of eccentrics, are to be found among the members, resident or non-resident, of their senior common rooms. They conduct their affairs with a certain formality, and though they are open to people of all religious persuasions, or of none, they reflect their ecclesiastical origins by their chapel services and in other ways. The system differs sharply from that obtaining in Oxford and Cambridge, however, in that only a small proportion of undergraduates ever reside in college, and many never have a college affiliation of any kind.

My college, Queen's, was founded in 1887.[1] It originally housed eighteen undergraduates; a century later this number had increased ten-fold.

The junior common room was a lively place. It elected a president — an office I held in 1933 — and a committee responsible for organizing various sporting and social events. Many people who were not competent to engage in competitive intervarsity sport were able to gain a place in a college team. I enjoyed rowing in the college eight (Fig 6) and would have liked to row for the university, but was not heavy enough to have any prospect of doing so and therefore transferred my sporting allegiance to hockey. I played occasionally as a substitute in the university eleven, but more regularly as captain of the second eleven at centre half.

The Queens' debating society, named the William Quick club after a founding father of the college, was a good nursery in which to learn the art of public speaking, and many who were active members in my day later occupied prominent positions in public affairs.

An important event in the social life of the college was the annual play, staged in the college hall. The most ambitious venture of this kind I remember was the production of James Elroy Flecker's *Hassan*. This was, of course, on a scale that appears miniscule when compared with descriptions of Basil

3.   My father in 1915.

4. My father entering one of the Hastings caves.

5. My stepmother, brother and myself, 1926.

Dean's sumptuous first production of the play at His Majesty's theatre in London in 1923, or even the later production by the Oxford University Dramatic Society. The college used back-cloths in place of elaborate scenery, but the tragic dilemma confronting Pervaneh and Raki came across starkly enough, and picturesque lines, like the Caliph's 'Hassan, thine impertinence hath a monstrous beauty, like the hind-quarters of an elephant', are still vividly engraved on my memory.

On weekdays during term there was a short chapel service immediately before dinner. Attendance was voluntary; many men never attended, but a surprising number did, though often rather sporadically. Gowns were worn in chapel and, except at weekends, at dinner. Members of the senior common room dined at a High Table, everyone else at small tables in the rest of the hall. The senior man at each table sat at the head and it was his duty to carve, and I am glad that I was obliged to acquire this skill in my undergraduate days. On entering hall we went to our tables and remained standing until everyone at the high table had arrived and grace had been said. College scholars were on duty for a week at a time in rotation to say the college grace, which ran as follows:

> Domine, qui aperis manum tuam et omnia implentur
> bonitati,
> Benedicere dignare cibum istum, et nos ex io gustantes;
> Inde corporis et animi recipiamus sanitatem,
> Per Jesum Christum, Dominum Nostrum

There was a crib on the lectern, but it was unwise to rely on this as it was liable to be removed by practical jokers and replaced by something less suitable. Occasionally some unhappy indi-vidual forgot his lines and had to be rescued by a peremptory *Amen* from the high table.

When I lived in Queen's I derived much pleasure from access to the organ in the chapel. I decided to learn the instrument properly, and if possible become, one day, College Organist. I achieved this ambition some years later. My first step was to find a teacher, and I became a pupil of Dr A. E. Floyd, who was organist and choirmaster at St Paul's Cathedral, Melbourne. He was a fine musician and organist, and had a splendid choir, though his biting tongue occasionally reduced a choirboy to tears. Before coming to Melbourne he had been deputy organist at Winchester Cathedral, where Samuel Wesley (son of the hymn writer, Charles Wesley), and his son, Samuel Sebastian Wesley, had both been organist, and when I had learned to play some of Bach's choral preludes and some of the eight short preludes and fugues, I was introduced to S. S. Wesley's music.

Soon after I became one of Floyd's pupils the cathedral organ was rebuilt and converted to electric action, and while this work was in progress a small pneumatic-action organ was used as a replacement. This made things difficult for me because there was an incredibly long delay between depressing a key and hearing the expected sound, whereas the college organ, on which I practised, had tracker action and responded immediately. There was, however, a price to pay for this quick response because the action was old-fashioned, rather rattly, and very heavy when the swell was coupled to the great. Successive college organists, myself included, complained about this, but the college council invariably responded by inviting Floyd to give a recital. He had opened dozens of church organs and knew what music to choose and how to play it in order to get the best out of an inferior instrument; the recital was therefore always a resounding success, and everyone except the unfortunate college organist concluded that the complaints were just another example of a poor workman blaming his tools.

Floyd was a low churchman, and sometimes said outrageous things — fortunately usually in private — about high churchmen. When, years after I had ceased to be his pupil, I introduced my wife to him and she told him that she was a member of the Society of Friends, he replied that he was, at heart, 'an Episcopalian Quaker'. This sounds puzzling, but I think he was saying two things: firstly, that he accepted the need for a hierarchical system of church government and the importance of historical apostolic continuity, but accepted also the concept of the priesthood of all believers. Secondly, that silence, as well as music, has a role in Christian worship.

There were other fine organists in Melbourne in my student days, the greatest being the Melbourne City Organist, Dr William McKie, who later became organist at Westminster Abbey. It was the custom in Queen's that the college organist should, from time to time, arrange for a series of recitals to be given in the chapel and, on the principle of keeping the best wine until last, should give the first in the series himself. A single programme was printed to cover the whole series, and I look back with a mixture of pride and astonishment at seeing my name alongside those of A. E. Floyd and William McKie.

It would have been an even more remarkable coup if I could have persuaded Marcel Dupré, who came to Melbourne about that time to give some recitals on William McKie's concert organ in the Town Hall, to contribute to my series. At the time I did not have the effrontery to ask him, but in retrospect it seems just conceivable that he would have accepted, for the very great can be astonishingly kind to those who are young and earnest, as I was at the time. I was greatly impressed by Dupré's recitals, which he always ended with an incredibly skilful improvisation on a theme handed in during the recital by a member of the audience, or in the form of a double fugue on two such themes.

During my time as college organist I had to play at the Memorial Service for the Master, Walwyn Kernick, who died in office after a long and painful illness. When he first became ill he was very unhappy, but this turned out to be because he was not told the diagnosis and felt that his doctors were making light of what he was sure was a serious illness. When the doctors realised this, and told him that he had an inoperable carcinoma of the oesophagus, he accepted the situation with dignity and courage, and colleagues and students, who had previously found it an ordeal to visit him, found it a source of inspiration. I learned a salutary lesson from this experience that has guided me ever since in dealing with patients with incurable diseases. Shortly before he died Mr Kernick discussed with the Acting Master and with me the Memorial Service that he knew would soon take place. He chose every hymn and every tune, among them Isaac Watts hymn:

> There is a land of pure delight,
> 　　Where saints immortal reign;
> Infinite day excludes the night,
> 　　And pleasures banish pain.
>
> There everlasting spring abides,
> 　　And never-withering flowers;
> Death, like a narrow sea, divides
> 　　This heavenly land from ours.[2]

This can be sung to various common metre tunes, but Mr Kernick insisted that it should be sung to a tune called *Prospect*, to which it was set, so he told me, in the *Primitive Methodist Hymnbook*. I was surprised, because Kernick was a Wesleyan — what might be termed a High Methodist; indeed, at heart, I suspect, an Anglican. I knew the hymn well enough but had never heard of the tune. When I looked it up I found that it was the tune to which we sing *Drink to me only with thine eyes*. I was horrified, and had the temerity to suggest to Mr Kernick that some other tune would be more suitable. He listened kindly and smiled. 'No,' he said. 'Please sing it to *Prospect*,' which, of course, we did. The tune actually suits the words very well. Should it be excluded from the hymnary on account of its association with Ben Jonson's love song? I thought so at the time, but today I am not so sure.

When I left school I was advised to read Electrical Engineering. It required four years to take an honours degree in Engineering, but it was possible in this time to cover also the work of the first two years of the three-year course for an Honours BA degree in Mathematics, and this I decided to do. College tutorials in Physics and Mathematics were given by H. S. N. (later Sir Harrie) Massey,[3] who became Professor of Physics at University College, London, and Physical Secretary of the Royal Society. He was a brilliant physicist and applied mathematician, and in 1929, consciously or unconsciously anticipating things to come, asked me to write an essay on the problems involved in making a projectile become a satellite of the earth; but he was not very interested in pure mathematics. The University Professor of Mathematics, Pure and Applied was T. M. (later Sir Thomas) Cherry.[4] His lectures were stimulating, but demanding. For analysis, our first year textbook was G. H. Hardy's *Pure Mathematics*,[5] which was within our compass, but in second year we were advised to read Goursat's immense three volume *Cours d'Analyse*,[6] and, needing additional help, I got into the habit of going to see D. K. Picken,[7,8] a friend of my parents, who was Master of Ormond College. He was a pure mathematician who had taken a degree in Mathematics and Natural Philosophy in Glasgow, and then gone to Cambridge, where he was sixth wrangler in the mathematical tripos in 1902. Before coming to Ormond he was Professor of Mathematics at Victoria College, Wellington, New Zealand. I shall have more to say about him later.

By the end of my third year I was worried about the prospects for young engineers in Australia, which was in deep economic depression. Having managed to get a first in the examination at the end of two years of the honours mathematics course, I considered aiming at a career as a mathematician, but although I greatly enjoyed mathematics I was by no means sure that this was what I wanted to be. After much heart searching I decided to make a complete change, and embark on medicine.

My younger brother, Philip, who later became Director of Public Health for South Australia, was already a medical student; my father was Professor of Bacteriology in Melbourne; my step-mother's father, John Glaister Snr., was Regius Professor of Medical Jurisprudence in Glasgow; and his son, John Glaister Jnr., was Professor of Forensic Medicine in Cairo, and shortly to succeed his father in the Glasgow chair. But what influenced me more than these family examples was my wish for the close contact with people, and the opportunity of helping those manifestly in need of help, that Medicine provides. It was a difficult decision, made easier by the understanding and wise counsel of my parents, and was contingent on their generous offer of financial support.

Having gone so far with Engineering, it seemed best to continue for another year and obtain my degree, especially as this would enable me, as a graduate in another science-based faculty, to start the second year of the six-year medical curriculum and catch up with first year zoology and botany as and when I could. I felt a strong urge to do as well as possible in my engineering finals, and was fortunate enough to end up with a first, and top place in the year.

I remained in Queen's for three more years, so was in college for a year more than I would have been had I started Medicine when I left school. There were only five days between my final examination in Engineering and beginning to study anatomy, physiology and biochemistry. As I knew nothing of biology, this was hard going, and at the end of the year I badly needed a holiday. My mother gave me a hundred pounds to let me visit England and Scotland in the long vacation. Such was the value of a pound in those days, this was enough to pay my fares and leave me a little money to spend. I had, of course, so many uncles, cousins and aunts that I did not have to pay anything for board and lodging.

About two thirds of the holiday was spent at sea. I returned on RMS *Orsova*, the same ship that had taken me to Australia as an infant, which I joined in Toulon. It was now one-class but still elegant and comfortable. The same can not be said of the train journey from London to Toulon, which I made in the company of a friend, John Wood, who was returning to Australia from Oxford to take up an appointment in the University of Sydney. To save money we travelled third class and from Paris onward shared a crowded compartment with French colonial troops. In Paris we were puzzled to find the streets almost deserted, and discovered that we had arrived on the day of the Stavisky riots (6th February 1934), precipitated by the suicide — some said murder — of Alexandre Stavisky,[9] a fraudulent financier. We could not find a taxi, and the Metro was not running, so we had to walk from the Gare du Nord to the Gare de Lyon. We were very glad that our heavy baggage was already on the ship. We reached Toulon before the *Orsova* docked, and spent the morning exploring the town and taking photographs. Once on board we found the ship plastered with notices forbidding anyone to take photographs near the harbour, and threatening dire penalties to those who did. *Ignorantium legis neminem excusat*, I imagine, applies in French, no less than in British, law, and I am glad we were not detected. In recent years, when my wife and I kept a boat in Toulon and there was no longer a ban on photography, I have taken dozens of photographs there, but always with an irrational feeling that big brother might be watching.

My fellow passengers on the *Orsova* included the violinist and cellist, Tossy Spivakowsky,[10] and his brother and sister-in-law, who were emigrating to Australia because of the growing anti-semitism in Germany. Someone — I suspect John Wood — had asked Tossy Spivakowsky to play his violin for the passengers, and had suggested that if he wanted an accompanist I might fulfil this role. Spivakowsky soon discovered my limitations, but I had played some of the Mozart violin sonatas with my father, who was a good amateur violinist, and Spivakowsky seemed to think that I might just manage before the end of the voyage if I practised hard every day. I never reached the point where he was prepared to play with me in public, but he took me off every day to a room in the bowels of the ship where there happened to be a piano, and drilled me unmercifully. At first he simply listened to, and criticised, my piano playing, but eventually he brought along his fiddle and we played together, albeit without an audience. It must have been a bit painful for a first-rate professional violinist, but for me it was an unforgettable, though exhausting, experience. When we were not making music he asked me to play chess, which fortunately was a more equal contest.

This was my fifth journey by ship between Britain and Australia, and I have made the journey by sea several times since; indeed, I have spent more than a year of my life as a passenger at sea, travelling between the United Kingdom and Australia or New Zealand, or crossing the Atlantic. I do not regard this as lost time. One can get a lot of reading and writing done on a ship if one's work programme is planned in advance, and at the same time enjoy oneself and recharge one's batteries. Today it would seem eccentric to try to go by sea when visiting Australia for professional or business reasons and the chance of finding a ship at the right time is very small; nor is the situation so very different when one just wants to cross the Atlantic. I am glad to have lived much of my life in a less hurried era. Air travel is quick and convenient, but I have never found it enjoyable for journeys lasting more than five or six hours. This is still true even when I have been given a first class ticket, though the physical discomfort is certainly reduced.

As a student I became interested in the Australian Student Christian Movement (ASCM), which was part of the World Student Christian Federation (WSCF). In those days the ASCM welcomed students of all religious beliefs, or of none, to take part in its conferences and discussion groups, and welcomed into its membership all who had resolved 'to seek God and the truth by which to live'. Its chairman for many years was D. K. Picken (Fig 7), whom I have already mentioned, and among its senior leaders there were many other people distinguished in science, mathematics, philosophy, history or theology. They were practising Christians, but it would, I think, be true to say that their primary commitment was to the search for truth; certainly they held no brief for the uncritical acceptance of dogma. E. H. Barnes,[11] one time Bishop of Birmingham and a distinguished mathematician, would surely have found their company congenial.

Many students, especially perhaps those reading science, dismiss religious belief as superstition; others — and their number appears to be increasing — seem content to oscillate between two different views of reality without trying to unify them. For me, and many of my generation, however, the question of whether religious belief, and in particular Christian belief, is compatible with scientific knowledge, was of great concern. I shall return to this question later, but I record here that it was through contact with the ASCM that I arrived at an affirmative answer.

Much of the work of the ASCM was done at its annual summer conferences, and these made an important contribution to my general education. I was introduced to books such as Streeter's *Reality* and Whitehead's *Science and the Modern World*, which I might not otherwise have read, and at one conference had my first lessons in Freudian psychoanalysis from the Rev. R. S. Lee, who later became vicar of St Mary's, Oxford. My recollection of his seminars has dimmed somewhat, but I remember the inspired doggerel in which one of his colleagues[12] encapsulated some of what he had to say:

When the Super-Ego goes into a skid,
And the Ego's at the mercy of the Id,
Man stands helpless mid his slums
And the rattle of war-drums,
And he gets half a quo for his quid.

The conference I remember most clearly was the one held in 1931, at which we used a booklet prepared by D. K. Picken entitled *Purpose*.[13] This had such a profound influence on me that it seems appropriate to end this chapter with a brief summary.

Purpose begins by examining the problem of the meaning and purpose of life. 'The Bible,' says Picken, 'is concerned with this problem from cover to cover; it calls the solution God.' He then traces the development of the idea of God in the Old Testament, and points out that the Hebrew prophets spelled out very clearly that man is like God but God is not like man: 'The distinctiveness of God from man ... is adequately expressible in terms of the infinitely greater, as used in comparison of things ... which are otherwise of the same kind: the qualification 'otherwise' being inserted because it is "characteristic" paradox of the infinite that *difference of degree*, when it is infinite difference, becomes assimilated to difference in kind.' This sentence is typical of Picken's careful, but hard-to-read, prose; to keep his readers on their toes he refers them to passages in the Bible that use terms like 'the Most High God' and invites them to consider such questions as 'How high is Most High?' He discusses next the Messianic element in Hebrew prophecy and its fulfilment in Jesus. The apparent paradox of the humanness of Jesus and his unique oneness with God is resolved, according to Picken, if we see Jesus as 'the supreme revelation of God and true manhood', provided that we give the word *supreme* its true value. Finally, Picken examines Jesus' gospel of the Kingdom of God and its implications for individuals and society. In discussing God's will and human freedom he reminds us that 'it is his freedom that makes man so immeasurably more wonderful than all the wonders of the natural world (he is the wonderer). But it is this, also, that accounts for all that is so wrong with the world'. To make the right choice between God and Mammon we need *faith* in the love and power of God, and to live the life of faith requires *prayer*, 'not prayer that is "much speaking" but prayer that is adequate to the Christian conception of God'. In discussing society Picken considers the role of the Church, and concludes that 'The true conception of the Church is the Christian conception of the community, operating in and through the lives of those who make that conception of the community their own. The "visible church", in all its divisions — that tragic Broken Body of Christ — must be won back to the unity of this conception, that is, to oneness with, and in, God through Christ.'

I have returned again and again to this little book, and it still rings true for me today.

On Mathematics

I am glad that I spent a fair amount of time studying mathematics before turning to biology. There are three main reasons for this: (1) Wrestling with mathematics has trained me to think and write more lucidly than I would otherwise have done. (2) Some of what I learned has proved directly applicable in my later research. (3) Mathematics has given me much pleasure over many years, comparable to the pleasure I have had from music.

These reasons prompt some reflections of a general kind.

Mathematics as a way of training the mind
The study of mathematics is an excellent way of training people to think logically. Such training is, in my view, much more important for a scientist than the acquisition of 'do it yourself' ability in statistics or other branches of applied mathematics. Mathematics illustrates how creative ideas develop, and demonstrates *inter alia* the importance of an appropriate notation in which to express new ideas, and the necessity of logical rigour if false conclusions are to be avoided.

J. E. Littlewood[1] has described four phases in creative work in mathematics, which he refers to as *preparation, incubation, illumination,* and *verification. Incubation* is performed in the subconscious and may take a long time, sometimes years. *Illumination,* on the other hand, which is the emergence of the creative idea into the conscious mind, can happen in a fraction of a second. This accords well with the experience of other mathematicians, for example Henri Poincaré,[2] and of scientists working in many different fields. If it is true, as Littlewood suggests, that the subconscious does all the real work and is on duty all the time, then the best thing to do, when we seem to be stuck in our efforts to solve a problem, may be to get on with something else and wait for illumination to occur.

The critical importance of choosing the right notation in which to express new ideas is well illustrated by comparing the Arabic and Roman ways of writing numbers, or Leibnitz' use of the symbol *dy/dx* in preference to Newton's symbol $\dot{y}$ to denote the first derivative of the function y with respect to x. Today, Leibnitz' notation is universally accepted, and its superiority to Newton's is apparent to everyone with any knowledge of the differential calculus, but old ideas, especially if associated with the names of famous people, may take a long time to die. I recently looked up a paper published in 1825 by Gompertz,[3] which is still cited (though, I suspect, seldom read) because the function Gompertz describes can sometimes be fitted to data concerning the growth of populations of people or cells when a simple exponential curve does not provide a good fit. I was amazed to find that almost a century after Newton's death, and more than a century after the death of Liebnitz, Gompertz used Newton's notation, and defended this in a later paper[4] on the grounds that 'the fluxional notation of our great Newton is more luminous', and that the use of what he calls the 'furtive differential notation' gives undue credit to Leibnitz and 'may obstruct the brilliant light of Newton's lamp from being perceived by the scientific eye'.

The arguments that developed between biologists about what notation to adopt for the antigens of the human Rh blood-grouping system are reminiscent of this ancient controversy. This system was discovered by Landsteiner and Wiener in 1940, and before its genetics had been elucidated, a cumbersome notation developed in a rather piecemeal fashion in which antigens were denoted by symbols such as R^1, r, R^2, R^0, R^{1w}, r^{11}, r', R^z, r'^w, and r^y. R. A. Fisher, after analysing a vast amount of genetic data, concluded that there were just three allelic pairs of Rh antigens, and proposed that these should be denoted by the letters C, c, D, d, E, e, since the letters A and B were already in use to denote antigens of the ABO blood group system. But the old notation persisted and was passionately defended, particularly in America, long after Fisher's conclusions had been shown to be correct, and this was the source of much confusion.[5]

In mathematics, and especially in the branch of mathematics known as the theory of numbers,[6] there are many propositions, customarily referred to as conjectures, whose truth or falsity has never been established. A famous example was 'Fermat's last theorem', which asserts that the equation $x^n + y^n = z^n$ has no solution in integers when n is an integer greater than 2, apart from the trivial case where one of the variables (x, y, z) is zero. This has been proved for a wide range of numbers, and no exceptions have been found. Attempts to find a proof that the theorem is universally true have led to important developments in mathematics, but only recently has a proof been found.

Sometimes propositions appear intuitively to be true but turn out, on rigorous examination, to be false. On the other hand, propositions that have been shown to be true may seem obvious to some people but not to others who are less endowed or less highly trained. It is recorded,[7] for example, that Lord Kelvin (as he became), when discussing with his students the hallmarks of a mathematician, wrote on the blackboard

$$\int_{-\infty}^{+\infty} e^{-x^2}\, dx = \sqrt{\pi}$$

and then said that 'a mathematician is someone to whom this is as obvious as the fact that $2 + 2 = 4$ is to you'; adding, by way of illustration, 'Liouville was a mathematician'. It is, in fact, not very difficult to show that the integral is convergent and to find its value by making appropriate use of polar coordinates,[8] but I wonder how many mathematicians would measure up to Kelvin's criterion if they were meeting the integral for the first time. I suspect not many.

In any investigation, mathematical or otherwise, the choice of the starting point and of the general direction to be followed, though of critical importance, are very much matters of taste.

Consider, for example, *number*, which plays a key role in many branches of mathematics. When I was an undergraduate I was content to take the positive integers as God-given,[9] and accepted that the first step in laying the foundations of mathematical analysis was to define other categories of number, real and complex. Some years later (see Chapter 8), I encountered

Bertrand Russell's *Principles of Mathematics*,[10] which takes an earlier starting point and sets out to formulate logical definitions of the integers. I found this quite intriguing, though I was not fully convinced that the gap between logicians' logic and mathematics had been successfully bridged. Had I gone on to tackle Russell and Whitehead's monumental *Principia Mathematica*,[11] I might perhaps have changed my mind, but this was not available to me at the time (see Chapter 8). Instead, I happened to come across Carnap's *Logical Syntax of Language*,[12] which discusses, among other things, the work of Kurt Godel, including his celebrated proof that, in any symbolic language rich enough to contain arithmetic, it is possible to construct sentences such that neither they, nor their negations, can be formally derived from the axioms of the system if these are consistent, nor can the consistency of a system be formally derived from its axioms. After reading Carnap and, at second hand, Godel, I no longer felt moved to tackle *Principia Mathematica*. In saying this I am, of course, simply recording my personal experience and inclinations.

I find it interesting to compare my experience with that of a distinguished biologist, and friend, P. B. Medawar. He encountered *Principles of Mathematics* more or less by chance and after reading it became determined to master *Principia Mathematica*. This 'lengthy and difficult exercise', he tells us, had a profound effect on his prose style and on his style of philosophic thinking.[13]

Science and Applied Mathematica

The physical sciences clearly depend heavily on applied mathematics. The same is true of biology (though this is perhaps not so immediately obvious), partly because biology depends so much on the physical sciences, and partly because of the direct application of mathematics in many areas of biology, for example in the study of populations, in genetics, in the statistical handling of experimental and clinical data, and in developing mathematical models of biological phenomena such as embryonic development and carcinogenesis.

How much mathematics does a biologist need to know? The answer depends on what field of biology he is engaged in. It may be *not a great deal*, but is surely, never, *none*.

By way of illustration, let us consider the problem of drawing valid inferences from data provided by biomedical experimental or clinical investigations.

It is, in my view, essential for anyone engaged in such investigations (1) to appreciate what is meant by *randomization*; (2) to have grasped the notion of regarding sets of observations made in a properly controlled experiment or randomized clinical trial as samples drawn from a hypothetical infinite, normally-distributed population of observations of the same kind; and (3) to be able, with the help of an appropriate 'instruction manual'[14] and a set of tables, to apply tests of statistical significance himself, or, at the very least, to appreciate the value and limitations of such tests when they are used by others. Is it *necessary* for a biologist to understand the theory underlying the statistical procedures he uses? R. A. Fisher, who has contributed enormously to the development of statistical procedures applicable to the assessment of small samples, that are widely used in biology, thinks not, and has maintained that 'modern statistics could not have developed without the elaboration of a system of ideas, logical and mathematical, which, however fascinating in themselves, cannot be regarded as a necessary part of the equipment of every research worker'.[15] I humbly concur, though I think Fisher overestimates the difficulty of mastering at least the rudiments of the mathematical theory.[16] I accept that for many biologists the time it would take to acquire this knowledge might well be spent more profitably in other ways, but I believe that those who take the trouble to do so will be less prone than those who do not to draw false conclusions or fail to draw conclusions that can validly be drawn, or to discover too late that their experiments are inconclusive because they have been badly designed.

Mathematics for pleasure

The number of people who derive aesthetic pleasure from mathematics is undoubtedly much smaller than the number of people who derive pleasure from the visual arts, music and writing. Why?

Most painters, sculptors, musicians (whether composers or performers) and poets would, I believe, agree that they aim to create beauty, though this may not be their only objective. For me, discussions of aesthetics can be extremely dreary, and it is not my intention to analyse in detail what is meant by beauty; I think, however, that the Oxford English Dictionary is on the right track when it says that beauty denotes, *inter alia*, 'that quality or combination of qualities which affords pleasure to the senses ... or which charms the intelligence or moral faculties'.

Mathematicians are seldom thought of by the general public as creative artists, and the creation of beauty may often not be part of their conscious purpose when they are engaged in research, but many mathematicians have written of the beauty of mathematics. Here are three examples:

Bertrand Russell (1892–1970)
Mathematics, rightly viewed, possesses not only truth, but supreme beauty — a beauty cold and austere, like that of sculpture, without appeal to any part of our weaker nature, without the gorgeous trappings of painting and music, yet sublimely pure, and capable of a stern perfection such as only the greatest art can show. The true spirit of delight, the exaltation, the sense of being more than Man, which is the touchstone of the highest excellence, is to be found in mathematics as surely as in poetry.... In the most beautiful work, a chain of argument is presented in which every link is important on its own account, in which there is an air of ease and lucidity throughout, and the premises achieve more than would have been thought possible, by means which appear natural and inevitable.[17]

J. J. Sylvester (1814–1897)
May not Music be described as the Mathematic of sense, Mathematic as Music of the Reason? Thus the musician *feels* Mathematic, the mathematician *thinks* Music — Music the dream, Mathematic the working life — each to receive its consummation from the other when the human intelligence, elevated to its perfect type, shall shine forth glorified in some future Mozart-Dirichlet or Beethoven-Gauss — a union already not indistinctly foreshadowed in the genius and the labours of a Helmholtz![10]

Karl Weierstrass (1815–1897)
... a mathematician who is not also something of a poet will never be a perfect mathematician.[19]

A characteristic feature of the visual arts, music and poetry is that many people not engaged in creative work in these fields can derive great pleasure from the work of those who are. I suspect, however, that non-mathematicians, while they may accept that mathematics can give aesthetic pleasure to mathematicians, doubt if they can share this experience, even in the smallest degree. I think this is unduly pessimistic, and reflects the way mathematics is often taught at school. So many become frightened of mathematics, so few find it fun. There is, I believe, a large inherited component in mathematical ability, and I am convinced that it is the duty of a teacher to give all possible help and encouragement to specially gifted pupils; but the less gifted can learn to appreciate mathematics just as people without much musical ability learn to appreciate music, and it is also the duty of the teacher to help them to do so.

Appreciation in all domains of art may be limited by lack of technical knowledge, and this seems to be of greater importance in mathematics than in music or the visual arts. One can not, for example, appreciate Lindenmann's beautiful proof of the transcendence of π, which ought to have put an end to futile attempts to 'square the circle', unless one knows what is meant by a transcendental number, and even if one possesses this knowledge and understands the strategy on which the proof is based, the proof is not easy to follow in detail.[20] But quite a lot of beautiful mathematics is accessible to people whose knowledge of mathematics is limited to what is commonly taught at school, and one may derive pleasure from a result even when one cannot follow the proof, still less discover a proof for oneself. A few examples will suffice.

Everyone who did elementary geometry will remember the theorem of Pythagoras. The result is not only important but beautiful, and the proof is easy to follow. The same is true of many theorems in the theory of numbers.[21] A good example is Fermat's Theorem (not to be confused with Fermat's Last Theorem), according to which p divides $(a^{p-1} - 1)$ if p is a prime number and a is an integer not divisible by p. Another beautiful result in the theory of numbers, which is however much more difficult to prove, is Lagrange's Theorem, which states that any positive integer can be expressed as the sum of four squares (counting 0 as a square). Projective geometry,[22] though nowa-

6. Queen's College Crew, 1933.

7.   D.K. Picken, for many years my guide,
philosopher and friend.

days regarded by most mathematicians as unlikely to yield anything new (a view similar to that of biologists concerning gross human anatomy), is another repository of beautiful things that are readily accessible, as is the study of finite groups in algebra. Concepts like continuity, limits, orders of infinity, and functions of a complex variable, are more difficult to grasp, but even here a good teacher can help the uninitiated to gain some idea of what it is all about.[23]

Besides deriving pleasure from contemplating the work of professional mathematicians, an amateur can enjoy trying to solve problems himself when their solution does not require great technical knowledge. Many problems of this kind are to be found in Rouse Ball's delightful *Mathematical Recreations and Essays*.[24] Littlewood's *Miscellany*[25] is more demanding, but some of it is accessible to those with only school mathematics, and a great deal to those with a little more background knowledge if they really try.

Another source from which I have derived much pleasure is the series of questions set for the International Mathematical Olympiads, which a mathematician friend has sent me from time to time. The Olympiads are open to boys and girls up to the age of twenty, and the papers are designed to test a candidate's ability to tackle questions of a kind he is unlikely to have met before. Here is an example that requires only elementary school mathematics, and no knowledge of calculus:

'Let a and b be positive integers such as $ab + 1$ divides $a^2 + b^2$. Show that $(a^2 + b^2) / (ab + 1)$ is the square of an integer.'

I thought about this intermittently for a few weeks, and did not discover a proof until I found a clue in a published solution[26] to a question (that looks quite different) that had originally appeared as a 'Brainteaser' in a Sunday newspaper. But 11 of the 268 candidates competing in the 1988 Olympiad solved the problem in the time allowed, which was only nine hours (sub-divided into two sessions) for a total of six questions.[27] Lest any readers are frustrated by not finding a proof, one is given in the notes.[28]

The enjoyment one can obtain from mathematics as a hobby depends on one's ability. This increases with study and practice. It is also age-related, as the example given above suggests, and after reaching a maximum may decline disturbingly rapidly. The same is true of all human activity, be it golf, or playing a musical instrument, or writing, or what you will. In mathematics, the maximum seems to be reached at a relatively early age, but the decline can be slowed by regular practice. Herrick's advice, *Gather ye rosebuds while ye may*,[29] is a sound maxim, not only for the restricted class of people to whom it was addressed, but for everyone, and especially perhaps for mathematicians.

6

Medical School and Hospital

When I was a student it normally took six years to qualify in Medicine in an Australian university. The first year was spent studying physics, chemistry and biology. Many students had done physics and chemistry at school to something approaching the level required, and some had done biology as well, and for them it was not very demanding. This was, I believe, a good thing, because it allowed time to grow up and adjust to a new pattern of life, and to become involved in a variety of extracurricular activities; and the risk that it would inculcate habits of idleness seems, in retrospect, to have been small. I had already enjoyed my salad days, however, and, as mentioned earlier, started in second year and caught up with first year biology *en passant*.

The second and third years were devoted to the study of human anatomy, physiology, biochemistry and histology.

The time devoted to anatomy was considerably greater than is the case today, and allowed us to dissect the human body completely twice. It has been fashionable for many years to denigrate the study of anatomy, but I enjoyed it enormously. It developed my visual memory, taught me how to arrive at a compact, methodical and memorable description of a mass of data, and brought me face to face with a situation in which ignorance cannot be concealed by waffle. Clearly, the curriculum has had to change in conformity with the explosive growth of experimental biology, and especially of molecular biology, but it is pertinent to ask whether the curtailment of anatomy has gone too far. Everyone would accept that surgeons, and people in various other specialties such as diagnostic radiology, need to know more anatomy than they learn as undergraduates, but, it is argued, they can, and indeed do, acquire this later. In my view, however, a strong case can be made for retaining more anatomy in the undergraduate curriculum, primarily for its general educational value, but also because the smattering of anatomy required of present day students is a poor foundation for later post-graduate study.

It was my good fortune to study anatomy in Melbourne when Frederick Wood Jones[1] was Professor and Head of the department. He was, as Wilfred Le Gros Clark aptly says in the biographical memoir[2] he wrote for the Royal Society, 'a man of restless curiosity and strong opinion'; he never stayed more than seven or eight years in the same place but, wherever he went, he made an enormous impact, especially on students, but also on his colleagues. Soon after qualifying in London, he had spent a short time in the Cocos Keeling Islands, where he met and later married Gertrude Clunies Ross. After various other jobs, including a period in Egypt as Anthropologist to the Egyptian Government, where he became involved in archaeological work with Elliot Smith, he was appointed to the Chair of Anatomy in Adelaide, and then to the Chair in Hawaii, before coming to Melbourne in 1930. Like his hero, John Hunter (1728–1793), Wood Jones was greatly interested in anthropology and comparative anatomy, and wrote several books on these topics, including *Arboreal Man*,[3] *The Problem of Man's Ancestry*,[4] and *Man's Place Among the Mammals*.[5] While in Australia he became interested in the Aboriginal people, and also in Australian marsupials. He never tired of reminding students and others that structure and function are facets of an indivisible whole, and that one cannot even begin to explain one without reference to the other. He developed this thesis in various books, notably *The Principles of Anatomy as Seen in the Hand*[6] and *Structure and Function as Seen in the Foot*.[7] He was fond of asking questions like 'Why does a giraffe have the same number of cervical vertebrae as a man?', and 'Why does a tiger not have a clavicle?', which some people regarded as trivial but which others, including the writer, found thought-provoking. He had an impish sense of humour, and delighted in challenging dogmas for which there seemed to be little evidence. This is illustrated by the following story about a distinguished visiting anatomist who claimed to be able to decide whether a dried human skull was male or female in origin. Wood Jones, who did not believe that this was possible, gave the visitor two aboriginal skulls which were known, from examination of the rest of the skeleton, to be male. They were returned to him a couple of weeks later with a statement that they were both female, but the only evidence that appeared to support this diagnosis was that on one skull was written *Charlotte Waters* and on the other *Alice Springs*.

Wood Jones was a superb lecturer. He never used notes, but his apparently effortless presentation concealed a vast amount of preparatory work. I recall, in particular, a series of lectures he gave on the structure and evolution of the central nervous system, based partly on a book he had written with S. D. Porteous called *The Matrix of the Mind*,[8] and two informal talks to student societies. One of these was a light-hearted account of the *History of Medicine in China*, which he gave after he returned from a period of leave spent as Temporary Director of Anatomy at The Peiping Union Medical College. As I recall, his account began in 3000 BC and continued up to the current year. It included a story about a Veterinary Surgeon who had the unnerving experience of being consulted one day by a dragon. His treatment was so successful that his fame spread far and wide, and within a short time his practice consisted exclusively of dragons. The other was a disturbing talk entitled *The Anatomy of Judicial Hanging*[9] in which Wood Jones recounted how, when he was in Egypt with Elliot Smith, they had found in a trench some skeletons with grossly deformed skulls, one of which had the remains of a piece of rope around the neck. They concluded that the deformities were the result of death by hanging, with the knot of the noose placed to one side, and after further investigation Wood Jones concluded that this deformity, and the protracted death associated with it, could be avoided if the hangman placed the knot of his noose in the midline below the victim's chin, when death was associated with fracture of the odontoid process of the axis vertebra. I was already opposed to capital punishment on moral grounds; this terrible story convinced me, and others who were not opposed to capital punishment in principle, that, if it was to be used, serious efforts had to be made to ensure that death occurred quickly and with as little pain as possible.

Wood Jones rejected the deterministic view of evolution that was fashionable in my student days, and was reiterated *ad nauseam* by many of our teachers. He regarded himself as a *vitalist*, a better lable might, perhaps, be a *neo-Lamarkian*, with something of the mystic in his makeup, as is apparent in some of his later books like *Design and Purpose*,[10] *Habit and Heritage*,[11] *Hallmarks of Humanity*[12] and *Trends of Life*.[13] Needless to say, his views attracted plenty of criticism, some of which I now accept as valid, but they profoundly influenced my own thinking.

W. A. Osborne, the Professor of Physiology and Dean of the Faculty of Medicine, had come to Melbourne in 1904 from University College, London, where he had been Assistant Professor of Physiology under E. H. Starling. He was a good physiologist and excellent lecturer, but neither he nor his colleagues in the department of physiology produced much original research, largely, I think, because the department was understaffed and had to operate on a ludicrously small budget. It was his custom to choose twelve students at the end of second year to form his third year honours class — his twelve apostles, as he called them — and I was fortunate enough to be one of the chosen. This gave me a chance to see a little beyond Osborne's rather severe facade; but, while I admired him, I never developed the warm affection I felt for Wood Jones.

Towards the end of second year (i.e. our first year of anatomy and physiology) we learned that the Royal College of Surgeons of England would be conducting a Primary Fellowship Examination in about a year's time. In those days students who had passed the university examinations in anatomy and physiology were eligible to sit this examination. Eight people in our year decided to do so and, somewhat surprisingly, four of us passed, myself included. Not surprisingly, perhaps, three of the four became surgeons. The big hurdle was anatomy, particularly in view of the fact that the examiner, Sir Gordon Gordon-Taylor, though a very distinguished surgeon, had a reputation for asking esoteric questions about matters that Wood Jones properly regarded as inappropriate, such as the ossification of the sphenoid bone, and we had to learn the answers to such questions and remember them at least until the end of the examination. Sir Gordon himself had an astonishing memory. I did not meet him again until twelve years later, when he visited the Royal Melbourne Hospital soon after the end of the war. When I was introduced to him he said at once that he had met me before, and added, after a few moments thought, 'Yes, you passed the primary FRCS here in Melbourne in 1934'.

In the following year we studied pathology and bacteriology, and began clinical work at one of Melbourne's general teaching hospitals — at that time (in alphabetical order) The Alfred Hospital, The Melbourne Hospital (later named the Royal Melbourne Hospital), and St Vincent's Hospital.

In pathology we encountered three remarkable men who encouraged us to examine pathological processes in the light of biological principles. The excitement they engendered is undimmed, and I cannot find words to express adequately my indebtedness to them.

Professor (later Sir Peter) MacCallum was a Scot, and a disciple of Sir Robert Muir, who liked to talk about general topics — inflammation, neoplasia, atrophy, hypertrophy, hyperplasia, pigmentation, and so on. He abhorred the sloppy use of terms; in particular the uncritical use of the term *degeneration*. In a lecture on carcinoma of the breast, I remember him referring to a phenomenon then (and, alas, sometimes still) referred to as *mucoid degeneration*, challenging the propriety of labelling as degeneration such a complex process as the synthesis of mucin, and asking how cells that do not normally make mucin can do so after they have undergone neoplastic transformation. In the 1930s few pathologists were asking questions such as this, and it was not until many years later that the outlines of an answer began to be discernible.

MacCallum encouraged me to do some experimental work while I was an undergraduate, and suggested that I should repeat an experiment in which fragments of auricle and ventricle from a 10-day chick embryo were cultured in the same plasma clot. It had been reported that they contracted initially at different rates but that when the gap between the fragments was completely bridged by cells they contracted synchronously at the original rate of the auricular fragment. This, indeed, proved to be the case. There were, of course, no antibiotics in those days, so I learned a lot about how to avoid bacterial infection, and I found the result interesting from the point of view of cardiac physiology.

Dr (later Professor) R. A. Willis was engaged in studying the spread of tumours in the human body. Little did any of his students realize that the notes we took down in his lectures would be expanded and refined during the next seventeen years to form a book that has now become a classic.[14]

Mr (later Professor) E. S. J. King was a member of the surgical staff of the Melbourne Hospital, serving as junior to Mr W. A. Hailes, and it was my great privilege, three years later, to be their house surgeon. King had a profound knowledge of surgical pathology, and like MacCallum thought in biological terms. He won the Jacksonian Prize of the Royal College of Surgeons of England on three occasions, a feat that, so far as I know, has never been equalled. This prize is awarded for an essay, based on original work, on a set subject. The subjects of King's winning essays, namely, *Ovarian Tumours*,[15] *Localized Rarifying Conditions of the Bone*,[16] and *Surgery of the Heart*,[17] could hardly have been more diverse. The essay has to be submitted under a *nom de plume*, with a separate sealed envelope containing the author's real name that is not opened until the winning essay has been chosen. When he submitted his last entry, King thought that the Council of the College might be reluctant to award the prize again to someone who had won it twice already, and that his literary style, plus the fact that the essay was posted in Australia, might give him away. He therefore changed his style, and posted his essay to a friend in England, asking him to forward it in a new envelope to the College. It was rumoured that when the envelope containing the name of the author of the winning essay was opened there was consternation in Lincoln's Inn Fields, but I do not know whether there is any truth in this.

During World War II, King contracted pulmonary tuberculosis while serving in the Middle East with the Australian Army Medical Corps (AAMC, later the RAAMC). He retired from surgery, but responded well to such treatment as was available in those pre-streptomycin days, and was subsequently appointed to the Chair of Pathology in succession to MacCallum.

The Chair of Bacteriology was occupied by my father, Professor H. A. Woodruff. He was an excellent teacher, both in the lecture theatre and the laboratory, and kindled in me an interest in immunology that I have never lost.

In my student days, the Australian teaching hospitals were staffed by honorary physicians and surgeons who had, perforce, to earn their living in private practice. In each medical or surgical firm there was a senior, called Physician or Surgeon to In-patients, and a junior, called Physician or Surgeon to Out-patients. The senior had most of the beds; the junior saw patients referred by general practitioners to the out-patient department, was responsible for patients admitted to the wards as emergencies, and had a few beds to which he could admit non-urgent cases. Both could admit patients from their private practice or from a common waiting list of patients seen in the out-patient department.

The members of the honorary staff were nearly all general physicians or surgeons, because subspecialties were only just beginning to develop. Although at the time the preparation of patients with toxic goitre for operation consisted simply in sedation and the administration of Lugol's iodine solution, Sir Alan Newton performed two thousand consecutive subtotal thyroidectomies without a death — a feat that continues to amaze me, as does the diagnostic skill of physicians like Dr Leslie Hurley despite the lack of so many of the laboratory investigations and radiological techniques that we take for granted today.

Below the honorary staff were part-time assistants, many of whom had completed their post-graduate training (usually in the United Kingdom) and were hoping to be appointed to the staff. Unlike present day registrars and senior registrars they were unpaid, and unless they had private means, had to live on what they made from assisting in private practice, demonstrating in subjects such as anatomy and pathology, and coaching students. In consequence the relationship between the house physician or surgeon and his 'chief' was closer than it usually is today.

Undergraduate teaching followed the English, as distinct from the Scottish, pattern. There were formal lectures, which we could attend or not as we wished, but what was far more important was the instruction we received when, in groups of eight to ten students, we were attached to a particular medical or surgical firm, where we functioned as supernumerary housemen. This could be demanding. In medicine, for example, Sir Sidney Sewell, whose house physician I later became, expected a student to be able to recount from memory the history of each patient allocated to him, together with the findings on clinical examination and the results of any special investigations. The ordeal of the house physician was worse still because he had to be able to supply this information — also from memory — about any patient in the wards if the student concerned faltered. A student attached to a surgical firm was expected to go to the operating theatre and scrub-up when a patient allocated to him was to be operated on. Often he simply became the animated end of a retractor, but he had to be ready to answer questions about the patient and what was happening during the operation. Occasionally the student managed to launch a successful counter-attack. A memorable example of this occurred when a colleague of mine, who was not particularly bright, was assisting at an operation, now obsolete, termed apical pneumolysis, which consisted in dividing adhesions at the apex of a tuberculous lung. The following remarkable dialogue occurred:

> *Student:* Sir, What is the structure you have just divided?
> *Surgeon:* Surely you can see for yourself; you tell me.
> *Student:* Sir, I think you have just divided all the roots of the brachial plexus.
> *Surgeon:* Good God, why ever would I do that?
> *Student:* That's what I want to know, Sir.

The surgeon, of course, had done nothing of the kind, but he was reduced to speechlessness and asked no more questions during the operation.

The system I have described resulted in a high standard of patient care and excellent clinical teaching, but did little to foster research. It was not until the creation of University departments of Medicine, Surgery and other clinical subjects that clinical research began to catch up with research in physiology, bacteriology, pathology and immunology.

Students who were members of a College benefited greatly from College tutorials in both pre-clinical and clinical subjects. In Queens we had particularly good tutorials, in Medicine from Dr Leslie Hurley and in Surgery from Mr K. H. Hadley, and for many years a Queen's man obtained top place in the final examination in Medicine. The fact that I obtained the Beaney Prize for top place in Surgery, and also won the Ryan Prize for Surgery awarded by the Royal Australasian College of Surgeons, was due very largely to Hadley. An aphorism he liked to quote was 'better a live mouse than a dead lion', and when, in the final examination in surgery, I was shown a woman with a disorganised ankle joint caused by tuberculosis with superadded pyogenic infection, and evidence of amyloid disease, and was asked what I would do, I said, as I felt sure Hadley would have said, that I thought a below knee amputation should be performed promptly before the patient died. 'Yes indeed,' said the examiner, 'that's precisely what I am going to do.'

I spent one holiday as a medical student in central Australia, having been offered a free ride to Alice Springs by a man if I would drive his old car. Some two hundred miles north of Adelaide the road ended, and we were in desert until we reached grassland (spinnifex) north of Oodnadatta. The river beds were dry, and we often had to dig the car out of the sand. From Alice Springs I climbed in the MacDonnell ranges, and visited the Hermansberg Mission to Aborigenes (Fig 8). I continued to Tennant Creek on a three-ton truck loaded with five tons of beer, but the driver was careful not to break a single bottle! I returned by truck to Alice Springs and then by train.

My first six months after qualifying were spent as house physician to Sir Sidney Sewell, Dr C. H. (later Sir Clive) Fitts and Dr E. Graeme Robertson; my second six months as house surgeon to Mr W. A. Hailes and Mr E. S. J. King. My annual salary was only £90, but we lived very well in the residents' mess. Thirty years on, when my wife and I were staying in the Visitors' Flat in the new Royal Melbourne Hospital, I was delighted to learn that Millie Parish, who had served in the mess when I was a resident, was still working in the hospital, and to meet her again.

Sewell was a very good general physician and clinical teacher. He expected much from his juniors, but took great interest in their welfare. He had a delightful home, and a small farm with a pedigree herd of Aberdeen Angus cattle, some 30 miles from Melbourne, and made a point of inviting his house physician to spend a weekend there during his term of office. Lady Sewell was such a charming hostess that even the very shy soon felt at home. The Sewells also entertained distinguished visitors from all over the world, many of whom planted a tree or shrub in the garden before they left, and I remember an oak in which they took great pride that had been planted by Harvey Cushing.

Sir Sidney did a formal ward round twice a week, which lasted the whole afternoon except for a brief interval for tea in the ward sister's room. After tea it was the custom for the house physician to offer Sir Sidney a cigarette of his favoured brand. He was a regular but not heavy smoker, and at that time no one suspected that cigarette smoking was likely to cause lung cancer. A few years later, however, while visiting the Mayo Clinic, primarily to see for himself the use of exfoliative cytology in the diagnosis of cancer of the lung, Sewell mentioned that he had developed a chronic cough, and was persuaded to provide a specimen of sputum for examination. He had just returned home when he received a letter telling him that the test was positive, and further examination revealed an inoperable carcinoma of the bronchus. He did not tell anyone about this apart from members of his family and a few close colleagues, and went on working until shortly before he died.

The transition from house physician to house surgeon was more of a shock than it is today, partly because we had to do much of the work now done by registrars, and partly because medicine was a more leisurely pursuit than it now is. When I was a house surgeon it was difficult to find time to sleep and eat, let alone to think. We admitted emergencies, including patients with all kinds of acute injuries, on one weekday, and every sixth Sunday, and on three days each week there was a long operating list. It was inconceivable that the house surgeon would leave hospital on any of these days. This left two days in the week, apart from Sundays, when, after work in the wards and out-patient department was finished, the houseman might get out for an hour or two, provided — and this was seldom the case — that there were no very sick patients in the wards. The first time I managed to get out I went to have a hair cut and fell asleep in the barber's chair! Fortunately, things have improved appreciably, though junior members of the profession find this hard to believe; even today, however, the hours worked by house surgeons are often much too long.

Mr Hailes was an eminently sound surgeon; decisive but prudent, and competent without being showy, who never wasted time when operating but saw no virtue in speed for speed's sake — a model I have tried to emulate throughout my surgical career. Mr King was also a skilful surgeon, but was more prepared to venture from the beaten path.

At the end of my first year as a houseman I was due for four weeks holiday, and spent this very happily as locum ship's surgeon on the SS *Katoomba*, one of several ships which carried passengers as well as freight between the Australian state capital cities. She was a ship of about 10,000 tons, with accommodation for first and second class passengers, and at that time was maintaining a shuttle service between Melbourne and Sydney. Each week we left Melbourne on Tuesday afternoon and docked in Sydney in Darling Harbour early on Thursday morning. In port, after doing a sick parade for the crew, for which there was little demand, I was free for the rest of the day, and spent this either surfing or walking round Sydney. We left at 2 pm on Saturday, and rarely got clear of Sydney harbour without having to put the engines astern on account of yachts which amused themselves, but certainly not our captain, by cutting across our bows. We arrived back in Melbourne on Monday morning, and as Melbourne was my home port I was able to stay at home overnight. I was paid quite a good salary, and supplemented this by charging fees to any passengers I was asked to see. A soft job, indeed, in which I earned more in a month than in a year as a house surgeon.

There was a little excitement one night when we were returning to Melbourne in company with another ship of the same line, the SS *Kanimbla*, which was on her way back from Brisbane to Perth. A member of my year, A. S. Ellis, was doing a locum on the *Kanimbla*, and about 4 am I was awakened by our radio operator with a message from Ellis about a junior engineer on his ship whom he thought might have appendicitis. The history and clinical findings did not appear to me to support this diagnosis, and, after we had exchanged several more messages, I signalled to Ellis: 'Your patient is constipated but I do not think he has appendicitis. Suggest you give him an enema.' I thought it unlikely that my colleague had ever administered an enema himself, and that it was time he learned how to do this, but he was too clever for me and found a qualified nurse among his passengers who did it for him. The patient, I should add, made an uneventful recovery.

I found internal medicine interesting from the point of view of diagnosis, but disappointing in that so often little could be done for the patient apart from trying to alleviate his symptoms.

This was certainly the case in neurology; and in cardiology, apart from regulating the patient's diet and exercise, treatment consisted largely in administering digitalis to patients with auricular fibrillation, and to some without; and treating those with congestive cardiac failure by performing venesection, administering diuretics and, if one was so minded, applying leeches. And when a surgeon at the London Hospital, Sir Henry Souttar,[18] made so bold as to perform a valvulotomy in a patient with mitral stenosis, this aroused violent opposition from cardiologists like Sir Thomas Lewis,[19] who believed mistakenly that the narrowing of the valve was of little or no importance in comparison with the associated weakness of the heart muscle. The situation was very different in surgery, where treatment, despite its limitations, was of the essence and diagnosis was seen as a means to an end, and by the end of my house-surgeon appointment I had made up my mind to seek a career as a surgeon. The situation has changed dramatically with the great advances that have occurred in recent years in so many fields of medicine, and if I were able to start again today my choice might well be different, but if one waits for what has not yet happened one ends up by not making up one's mind about anything.

When I told Sewell of my decision he agreed that this was the right choice for me, but advised me to spend a little more time in internal medicine as a senior house officer and try to obtain my MD by examination before embarking on higher surgical training. I accepted this wise advice with some hesitation because events in Europe suggested that war might break out within a year, as indeed it did.

The rise of Hitler forced me to reconsider my former pacifist position. For my 28th birthday my uncle, Leslie Burgin, who was then Minister of Supply in Neville Chamberlain's government, had given me a copy of Chamberlain's 1937–1938 speeches,[20] and, as mentioned in Chapter 3, had written on the flyleaf:

> To Michael from Leslie
> The author of these speeches is the world's most commanding figure.

Though I never quite accepted this estimate of Chamberlain, I greatly admired his courageous efforts to prevent the outbreak of a second world war, but by the time of the Munich agreement

(30 September 1938) I thought that war was inevitable. I came to the conclusion that one must draw a distinction between how one should respond to threats to one's individual life and liberty, and to threats to the life and liberty of millions of one's fellow men; and by the time war was declared (3 September 1939) I was convinced, like the majority of people in both the United Kingdom and Australia,[21] that to go to war was a lesser evil than to allow the Nazis to occupy more and more of Europe, and perhaps also of other parts of the world. I decided therefore that I would enlist in the Australian Army Medical Corps for service wherever and whenever required.

Fortune was kind to me. I obtained my MD in 1940 and enlisted as planned. I was again wisely advised that I would be of more use to the army if I had a higher surgical qualification, and since it was now out of the question to go to London to sit the final FRCS examination, I decided to resume surgical training in Melbourne for long enough to try for the degree of MS, unless the army decided otherwise. This degree could be obtained by passing a two-part examination, and I was exempt from the first part on account of my having already passed the primary FRCS examination. Again fortune favoured me and, although I was not really quite ready to sit the final, I did so early in 1941 and managed to pass. During this phase of my training I worked as a part time, unpaid surgical assistant at the Melbourne Hospital, and earned just enough to live on by working as a part-time junior assistant lecturer in the University Department of Pathology and assisting surgeons in private practice. Fortunately, I was able to live at home with my parents, and had their strong moral support; I also had their assurance that if I needed financial help they would provide it.

7

The Fall of Singapore

I was commissioned in the Australian Army Medical Corps (AAMC) in September 1940, with the rank of Captain (Fig 9), and placed on the reserve of officers, but was allowed to complete my MS degree before being called up. I continue to be astonished by, but very grateful for, this indulgence on the part of the army.

In April 1941, I was appointed to the 10th Australian General Hospital (2/10 AGH — the 2 being inserted to indicate that it related to the second world war, not the first!), which was established at Malacca in the Straits Settlements, though this was supposed to be an official secret. On 1 May, I was ordered to go to Sydney to attend a two-week course in Tropical Medicine before going overseas, and my father came to see me off on the night train. On the platform we saw an officer with the badges of rank of a major general, and to my amazement he and my father greeted each other as old friends. He turned out to be F. A. MacGuire, recently appointed Director General of Medical Services (DGMS) for the Australian Army, and he and my father had been together for a time on General Monash's staff in World War I, when my father was a major in the Australian Army Veterinary Crops. General MacGuire asked me to have dinner with him on the train, and in the course of the meal asked me what I was doing. He was delighted when I replied that I was going to Sydney to attend a course in tropical medicine before going to Malaya, and told me that one of the first things he had done when he became DGMS was to ensure that, whenever possible, any medical officer going overseas should attend such a course. When I duly reported in Sydney, however, I was told that there was no place for me on the course about to start, and

8.   Hermansberg Mission, Central Australia.

9. Myself when commissioned in the Australian Army Medical Corps (later the Royal Australian Army Medical Corps).

that I was being sent to Dubbo — some 300 miles from Sydney — where there was a large military camp that was very short of medical officers. Here I remained for the next two weeks, and was then ordered to return immediately to Melbourne, and two days later I embarked for Singapore in the SS *Zealandia*. Not only had I not done my course in tropical medicine, but I had no time to buy tropical kit or even to say goodbye to anyone except, very briefly, my parents. At the time I was annoyed, but in retrospect was glad to have been spared the distress inseparable from long-drawn-out farewells; moreover, tropical kit was much cheaper in Malay than in Australia, and, being in a large hospital, I soon learned about malaria and other tropical diseases by practical experience and instruction from colleagues.

The *Zealandia* was carrying mainly combatant troops, but there was a small AAMC party comprising three officers — Major Charles Osborn, Captain Frank Cahill and myself— and some twenty other ranks. We stopped in Fremantle and I took the opportunity of visiting friends in Perth, including Christopher and Joan Storrs and Kenneth Henderson. Storrs and Henderson, who were a good deal older than me, were both in Anglican Orders; Henderson, however earned his living as a journalist and was leader-writer for the *West Australian*. He gave me a copy of a little book of prayers and meditations that he had just written,[1] the flavour of which is suggested by the following brief quotations from the preface:

> I have tried to bring my awareness of the contemporary situation as realistically as I can into the light of the Eternal, and to present this experience as a help to the judgment and will of fellow-Christians and would-be Christians… . The tragedy of Christianity is not in the fact that it has lost contact with the general run of Sunday golfer, but that it has lost influence with so many of the men and women who are making the world.

I added Henderson's book to the New Testament, and four other books I was taking to Malaya: J. H. Oldham's *Devotional Diary*,[2] given to me by my father, and inscribed by him, *Semper Fidelis*: Matthew Arnold's *The Light of Asia*, an epic poem about Buddha given to me by a dear friend, Miss Jane Finlay, who was for many years Housekeeper at Queens College; E. B. Jamieson's *A Companion to Manuals of Practical Anatomy*;[3] and Whittaker's *Operative Surgery*[4] — a brief, but useful, summary of the subject, with good descriptions of the approach to major arteries, that I had annotated extensively when working for my Master of Surgery degree. Unlikely as it may seem, I still have this heterogeneous collection. I said goodbye to the books I could not carry with me when I had to abandon my officer's steel trunk soon after becoming a prisoner-of-war, and never expected to see them again, but six unopened officer's trunks were subsequently delivered to our camp, and mine happened to be one of them.

This trunk also contained a supply of pipe tobacco and two carbon copy books in which, at my father's suggestion, I had kept copies of my letters home written up to the time when Japan entered the war. I have drawn heavily on them in the account which follows.

After clearing Fremantle and Rottnest Island the first land we saw was Java Head at the entrance to the Sunda strait between Java and Sumatra. The journey was uneventful, and, apart from running a small daily sick parade and giving the other ranks lectures on first aid, our time was spent writing letters, and playing deck games and chess. We proceeded by a rather circuitous route, and eventually docked in Singapore on 13 June. The same day I caught the overnight train to Tampin and went on from there to Malacca by car with the other two medical officers and our men, and reported to the 10 AGH, which occupied about half of the Malacca civilian hospital (Fig 10).

The CO was Colonel E. R. White, a Melbourne gynaecologist. Lt. Col. A. E. Coates, also from Melbourne, was senior surgeon, and Lt. Col. Cotter Harvey, a chest physician from Sydney, was senior physician. The registrar, Major Marsden, was also from Sydney. There were two padres; Padre Smith (Roman Catholic) and Padre Benjamin (Methodist). Attached to the hospital were representatives of the Salvation Army and the YMCA. The Red Cross Commissioner for South East Asia, Basil Burdett, a most interesting man who had been music and drama critic for the Melbourne Herald, also lived in the mess until, sadly, he was killed in an air raid shortly before the surrender of Singapore to the Japanese in February 1942. We received frequent visits from Lt. Col. Glyn White, who assumed responsibility for base medical units soon after I had arrived in Malaya, and less frequent ones from the Assistant Director of Medical Services 8 Div., Col. A. P. Derham.

There were about seventy nursing sisters, headed by Matron Paschke, Royal Red Cross, and two female physiotherapists in the hospital. They ranked as officers, but had their own Mess and were not allowed in ours. Needless to say, they were in great demand socially. In the course of six months I did manage on two occasions to take a nurse out to dinner, but the competition from officers in combatant units in the vicinity was intense — as a senior colleague of mine has put it, 'army nurses were always attractive to fighting men'.[5]

Our Mess President, Lt. Col. Cotter Harvey, thought that the rule about our Mess being out-of-bounds to the nurses might be relaxed on Christmas Day, and invited Matron and her colleagues to our Christmas party. He did not consult the CO about this in advance, and mentioned it to him quite casually as they were about to arrive. The CO, in the words of P. G. Wodehouse, 'if not exactly disgruntled, was very far from being gruntled',[6] and met them at the door with the chilly greeting, 'I'm sorry, Matron, you are not expected'.

The hospital was modern and well equipped. Our mess occupied a single storey building in the hospital grounds. The mess servants, both Chinese and Malay, who were recruited locally, were efficiently supervised by Padre Benjamin, but could be slow to adapt to western methods. I saw an astonishing instance of this when one of the mess boys was sent to collect a new stove and provided with a wheelbarrow in which to transport it. He returned with the traditional Chinese carrying-pole across his shoulders, with the stove on one end and the wheelbarrow on the other. Food in the mess was excellent. For most of us breakfast began with papaya and pineapple, though a few people demanded more familiar fruits such as apples, which had to be imported, and were expensive and often of poor quality.

Malaya, when we went there, consisted of the Straits Settlements (including Singapore, Malacca and Penang), the Federated States, and the Unfederated States. The population consisted of Malays, Chinese, Indians and Europeans.

The Chinese, who were hard-working and well organized, covered a wide social spectrum, ranging from millionaires to coolies. Chinese cemeteries, typified by the local one known as Bukit China, were spread over huge areas, because the graves, shaped to represent the human uterus, were constructed in the

belief that the bigger the grave the better the occupant's prospects in the hereafter; once occupied, however, the grave was
often neglected. In Chinese funerals the body of the deceased was
typically conveyed by a circuitous route in a shabby-looking
vehicle, while an elaborately decorated, but empty, hearse followed a more direct route, the object being to outwit any
malevolent spirits. I stood to attention when one such funeral
passed and to my astonishment a small boy, who had concealed
himself in the hearse, suddenly jumped up and called out 'Hello,
Jo' — a cheeky formula with which local youngsters liked to
greet soldiers in uniform if they thought they could get away
without being caught.

The Malays were often people of remarkable dignity, but
many were lazy, and they were often ruthlessly exploited by the
Chinese. Their philosophy was well summarized by the Malay
expression *tid apa*, roughly equivalent to *what does it matter* in
English.

At the time, the White Australia Policy was entrenched in
Australia, and accepted uncritically by many Australians; despite
this, however, Australian soldiers often developed a more friendly
relationship with the indigenous population than did their
counterparts from the UK. When, for example, the Number
One Boy in our mess — a Malay who lived in a nearby kampong
— was about to be married, he let it be known that he would feel
greatly honoured if any members of the mess cared to attend his
wedding feast. We hesitated to accept this invitation because we
feared gastrointestinal complications; the problem was solved,
however, by arranging for food to be prepared in the mess
kitchen and transported, with appropriate cutlery and crockery,
to the kampong, and many members of the mess attended the
feast, to the astonishment of the Malay population.

The humid climate in which we found ourselves was, to say
the least, unpleasant. Indoors we had no air-conditioning, and
the clothes we wore were often unsuitable. By day, a shirt and
shorts were fine, especially if one did not engage in strenuous
exertion, or could follow this by a cold douche; for dinner,
however, we always put on khaki slacks, and on Mess Nights we
added a tie and a khaki drill jacket. Many people, including some
other ranks despite the fact that they did not have to wear so
much, developed heat rash, often with superadded fungal infec-

tion (*tinea*), and in some this covered virtually their whole body. The worst sufferers were sent back to Australia, but for this we were severely criticised because, by the time they arrived, after three weeks during which they wore almost no clothing, the condition had greatly improved, and in some cases had disappeared completely. When we became prisoners and, perforce, often went about shirtless, our skin rashes disappeared equally dramatically; moreover, to our surprise nobody got heat stroke, because they were cooler without a shirt, and nobody became sunburned, thanks to the high humidity which caused much of the solar ultraviolet radiation to be filtered out.

We were greatly bothered by mosquitoes, though fortunately there were very few flies. We also had to be on the *qui vive* to avoid scorpions and, worse still, centipedes, which grew to about ten inches in length and whose bite was more painful than that of a scorpion. Even the bees were extraordinarily aggressive, as my batman, a professional apiarist in civilian life, discovered when he tried to capture a swarm in the hope of getting some honey. As I said in a letter to a zoologist friend of my parents,[7] I developed a dislike for the whole phylum *arthropoda*. If one swam in the sea there was a considerable risk of being stung by another unpleasant creature, the so-called Portugese man of war (*Physalia*), whose sting resulted in extremely painful abdominal cramps requiring heavy sedation.

There were too many surgeons in 10 Australian General Hospital for the amount of surgery to be done when we were not involved in war, and during my first ten weeks in Malacca I was engaged mainly in treating skin diseases, and tropical diseases like malaria, dengue, dysentery, hookworm and typhus, contracted by troops exercising in the jungle. I was delighted when the CO asked me to organize a blood and plasma bank for the hospital, and the position improved further when Lt. Col. Coates arranged for me to assist him, and also our otorhinolaryngologist, Major Farmer, who taught me to do tonsillectomies — a skill I had not previously acquired and which I found useful when Farmer went on leave. Another duty, of a non-medical kind, that fell my way was to go once every two weeks to Seremban (about fifty miles away) to collect pay for our men. At first I sat in the front of the car with the driver, and occasionally drove — this being allowed because before leaving Australia I had learned to drive an ambulance and passed an army driving test — but this came to an end when an officer in a combatant unit drove an army car into a rubber tree after a party, and a divisional order was issued that forbade officers to drive except in an emergency. Thereafter I sat in solitary state in the back of the car and, as the road was narrow and winding, often felt car sick.

We had plenty of enjoyable leisure activities, many centred on the Malacca Club, which generously offered honorary membership to all officers. I played tennis there regularly on beautiful grass courts, and enjoyed the luxury of having Malay boys to pick up balls for us. I also played hockey with a combined UK-Australian team, and cricket for the hospital. Everyone in our hockey team had played top-grade hockey at home, but we had learned to play on grass whereas in Malacca we played on a baked mud pitch of the kind often used in India. This resulted in our being beaten quite often by the local Chinese High School team, who were used to this surface, on which they played in bare feet with astonishing speed and accuracy. Cricket, which we played on Sundays, was less serious. The only way to win was to bat first and pile on a good score before the inevitable curry tiffin followed by a siesta, after which the standard of play by those not used to this degenerated markedly.

We enjoyed generous hospitality from members of the local European and Chinese communities, and also enjoyed dining out in Chinese restaurants. The proprietor of the restaurant I liked best, the *Suan Kee*, was said, after the war, to have been a Japanese spy, but we had, of course, no inkling of this at the time. We also enjoyed the cinema, and went occasionally to Chinese opera, though I never acquired a real taste for it. The main lack was good music, but I went some way to solving this problem by buying a radio that picked up quite good programmes from a Dutch station in Sumatra.

Another enjoyable activity can best be described as tourism. Armed with a Leica camera that I had bought in Malacca, I visited rubber plantations, the seventeenth-century Portugese church, in which the body of St Francis Xavier had rested for a time before being translated to Goa, a Buddhist temple slightly older than the church, and so on. So, despite the infernal arthropods, I wrote in a letter to a friend[8] in Melbourne, 'If this is war, it's not too bad'.

Of course it was not war, as we were soon to discover, but in the meantime the entry of Russia into the war in Europe on 22 June 1941; the Roosevelt–Churchill meeting; and the broadcasts of Churchill's resounding speeches that we listened to avidly, engendered a feeling of optimism that Hitler would soon be defeated, and the threat of war with Japan would disappear. The one item of news that seriously disturbed me was the resignation of R. G. Menzies as Australian Prime Minister. In my student days I had thought him pompous and reactionary, and did not vote for him when I lived in his constituency, but my opinion about him had changed, as the following comment in a letter to my mother shows: 'I have thought much more of him as a result of the last two years, but apparently he can't work with other people. His main fault, if it is a fault, seems to be a complete inability to suffer fools gladly.'[9]

In October I had a week's leave at Fraser's Hill, in company with a fellow officer and friend of long standing, Captain P. N. (Pat) O'Donnell. As we were at an altitude of over 4,000 feet, it was much cooler than in Malacca; indeed, after dinner each evening we sat in a room with a log fire, which was very pleasant, but perhaps not strictly necessary. By day, Pat tried hard, but not very successfully, to teach me to play golf on a picturesque nine-hole course, and when we got tired of this we went walking on jungle paths. It was said to be too cold for tigers, and, although there were supposed to be plenty of panthers about, we never saw any.

Soon after I returned from leave I was sent on a brief errand to Singapore, and while there met Australia's Chief Justice, Sir John Latham, and Lady Latham. Sir John became ill while visiting Singapore, and was accompanied back to Australia by Lt. Col. Coates. The general feeling in Singapore seemed to be that war with Japan was still unlikely, but by the beginning of December the situation had become so tense that all leave was cancelled, and only urgent cases were being admitted to hospital. It was, nevertheless, a great surprise to us — as it seems to have been to people in high places in Washington and London — when the Japanese attacked Pearl Harbor without warning, and we found ourselves at war. Fortunately, Lt. Col. Coates arrived back in the hospital the very day this happened.

After Christmas, to my delight, I was seconded to the 2/4 Casualty Clearing Station (CCS), commanded by Lt. Col. Thomas Hamilton, a surgeon from Newcastle, NSW. It was installed under canvas on the Menkibol Estate, a large rubber plantation situated between Kluang and Ayer Hitam on the edge of Kluang military aerodrome. It was not a very good situation, but it was a very happy unit,[10] which I found far more congenial than the 10 AGH. This was, no doubt, partly because we soon were very busy, and partly because the average age of the officers was considerably less, but most of all because Lt. Col. Hamilton was such a fine person and splendid CO, who was greatly liked and respected by his officers and men, and inspired them to give of their best, and then a bit more. He was completely unflappable, and although our subsequent frequent moves kept him very busy with administrative duties he was ready to lend a hand in the operating theatre or elsewhere whenever possible. He had the respect of the ADMS and the DADMS, and on several occasions managed to persuade them — so quietly that they thought they had persuaded themselves — to revise their decision about where and when we should move when their original decision seemed to him to be, and indeed was, flawed.

Hamilton's team included two surgeons, Majors Alan Hobbs and Sidney Krantz, both from Adelaide; Major Ted. Fisher, a physician from Sydney, who was primarily responsible for resuscitation and blood transfusion; Major John Chalmers, a radiologist from Hobart, who besides being responsible for his own professional work functioned as adjutant to the unit; several Captains like myself who were prepared to turn their hands to anything; and eight nursing sisters. I spent most of my time giving anaesthetics or assisting at operations until Major Fisher went down with dengue fever, when I took over his resuscitation work.

Our first battle casualties arrived on 14 January. Twelve days later, as the relentless Japanese advance continued, we had to move to a large rubber estate some twenty-two miles north of Johore Bahru, and then to a rather derelict mental hospital in Johore Bahru itself. This had been occupied until shortly before we arrived by the No. 1 Malayan General Hospital, and a recent copy of their routine orders was still stuck on the wall which, to our amazement, contained the following paragraph:

The attention of other ranks is drawn to slackness in saluting. Henceforth officers, when recognized as such, will be saluted at all times.

In relating this in his book[10] Tom Hamilton comments: 'Good old British Empire! *Morituri te salutamus!*'. Not to be outdone by his Latin, I would add (although it was, I think, originally said in Greek: *Quos Deus vult perdere prius dementat.*[11]

Our next move was to Singapore Island, and as we crossed on the causeway over the Strait of Johore my eyes were caught by the huge water pipe carrying Singapore's main water supply from a reservoir in Johore. When, a few days later (on the night of 30/31 January), the last of our forces had retreated to Singapore Island, it seemed, even to a non-combatant medical officer, that Singapore, with its large civilian population, could not hold out for very long, and so, of course, it proved. Presumably even Malaya Command, which seemed to have been living in cloud cuckoo land, must have realised this when it decided to evacuate the naval base and destroy its huge floating dock, yet when General Wavell paid a brief visit to Singapore in its agonal moments, he issued an order of the day which included the following words:

> There must be no thought of sparing the troops or civil population and no mercy must be shown to weakness in any shape or form. Commanders and senior officers must lead their troops and if necessary die with them. There must be no question or thought of surrender... .

The GOC Malaya, Lt. General Percival, tried to reinforce this with comments critical of some of the men under his command, but just three days later had to sign a document of unconditional surrender.

When we moved to Singapore Island our intended destination was the Singapore Dairy Farm. The risk of clostridal infection (gas gangrene and tetanus) made this a very unsuitable environment for a casualty clearing station, but there seemed nowhere else to go. Our CO, however, with his usual initiative, found a school at Bukit Panjang occupied by some thirty RAF personnel who were due to fly out of Singapore next day, and persuaded both them and our ADMS that we should move in. Unfortunately, an artillery regiment installed itself only two hundred yards away, and their guns attracted return fire from Japanese heavy artillery in Johore, which blew up some nearby large oil tanks, so we soon had to move again, this time to the Swiss Rifle Club. Soon after this the CCS was split up between the 10th and the 13th Australian General Hospitals, and I was sent to the Singapore Civil General Hospital to join Lt. Col. Coates, who was already there with a small team from the 10th AGH.

The operating theatres were located in a tile-roofed single-storey building, and the day after I arrived a shell hit the roof while I was assisting Coates in an operation on a patient with a nasty head wound. Mercifully, the shell exploded on impact, neatly removing the roof but not causing serious injury to anyone in the theatre. A day or two after this unnerving experience I was again assisting Coates when an urgent order was delivered to him in the theatre, ordering him to report immediately at the docks. He learned later that he was one of a small number of Australian officers, the only medical officer in fact, chosen by the Australian command to take home important information about the fighting in Malaya. He had, of course, no option but to obey the order. After reading it he said to me: 'Michael, I have to go; you must finish the operation.' The patient was bleeding from a facial wound, probably from the maxillary artery, and Coates added: 'You know your anatomy as well as I do' [an exaggeration, because although I did have quite a good knowledge of anatomy Coates' knowledge was encylopaedic]. 'Find the maxillary artery and tie it at its origin or, if necessary, tie the external carotid.' In the event it sufficed to tie the maxillary artery, which had been partially divided.

That night I went up to the roof of the hospital and looked at the pall of smoke extending in every direction as far as the eye could see. When, next day, we found that our water supply was cut off — as I had predicted would happen — I felt that even General Wavell would agree that the battle was lost.

At the Singapore General Hospital we were, at least, spared the horrible ordeal of the patients and staff at the Alexandra Hospital, where Japanese troops with fixed bayonets rampaged through the hospital killing 270 people, including an anaesthetized patient in the operating theatre. The surgeon, Captain Thomas Smiley, RAMC, who was subsequently awarded the

MC, was himself bayoneted several times while trying to protect his patient, but fortunately survived.

For me, the saddest part of the sad story of the battle for Singapore was the loss of so many of our nurses. The day before the surrender the SS *Vyner Brook*, carrying sixty-five Australian nurses, was bombed and sunk near Banka Island. Many, including Matron Paschke (10 AGH), Matron Drummond (13 AGH), and Matron Kinsella (2/4 CCS), were drowned. Fifteen, including three nurses from the CCS, managed to get ashore, but were marched to the edge of the water and machine gunned in cold blood by the Japanese. Of the fifteen, there was only one survivor, Sister Bulwinkle (10 AGH), who feigned death and subsequently managed to escape. Other nurses perished in Sumatra. Of the eight nurses we had known and worked with in the CCS, only one, Sister Hannah, survived the war. After the war, when Miss Sage, RRC, Principal Matron of the Australian Army Nursing Service, told Lt. Col. Hamilton this terrible news, she said, 'It is rather an ordeal speaking of it. You must have known these nurses very well. What fine women they were'. He could not find words to answer her, but wrote later that, if speech had been possible, his reply would have been, 'Australia had none better'.

The day of the surrender, with our patients and the rest of our officers and men, I rejoined the 10th AGH, which was located in the Cathay building, near the centre of the city. Two days later we moved to Changi. Before we left, the Japanese commander, General Yamashita, visited the hospital and seemed not unfriendly, though he was well aware that there were combatant troops in the building despite the fact that we were still displaying the red cross. After this visit the Japanese agreed to give us enough fuel to transport our most seriously wounded to Changi by ambulance, but the only way to get any equipment there was to load it on whatever trucks we could find and, by pulling on two ropes and pushing, manhandle these all the way to Changi.

Wisely, we loaded everything we had, plus as many books as we could lay our hands on from the University library, and gramophone records from the headquarters of the Malayan Broadcasting Authority, which had been located in the Cathay building. I suggested that we should collect guinea pigs from hospital laboratories in Singapore, with the idea that we might breed them as a source of food, but this eminently sensible suggestion was laughed to scorn by my colleagues, either because they believed that the allies would recapture Singapore within a few weeks, or because they were convinced that we were all going to be killed by the Japanese. The first of the beliefs was manifestly absurd; the second, I thought, might well turn out to be true, but, if it did not, then shortage of food, and not least of animal protein, was almost certainly going to be a major problem.

Looking back, I think that the fall of Singapore was inevitable, given the lack of air cover, the fact that the heavy guns on the island were intended to repel an attack from the sea and could point only southward, and the large civilian population for whom there was little protection. It cannot be attributed to lack of determination on the part of the troops, though it was, I believe, hastened by Malaya Command's decision to withdraw completely from the mainland, leaving Singapore's water supply in enemy hands.

Adapting to Captivity

After the surrender, more than 50,000 British and Australian troops were interned in the Changi area at the eastern extremity of Singapore Island. The Australians, numbering about 12,000, including 4,500 sick and wounded, were located in Selaring barracks; the British in nearby Roberts barracks.[1] Most of the Indian troops were in another camp at Buddi Barri. There were at first separate British and Australian hospitals, but these were later merged to form a combined hospital. To keep us in place the Japanese initially simply drew a line on the map, and told us that any prisoner of war (POW) caught west of the line would be beheaded or shot; at the same time they offered a reward of five Japanese dollars to the locals for every prisoner they captured. This proved remarkably effective.

Before the move to Changi, but, it has been claimed,[2] immediately after the formal surrender, the Australian commander, Lt. Gen. Gordon Bennet, and two other officers he had invited to accompany him, escaped in a small boat and eventually reached Australia. This aroused much criticism from his officers and men, who had been ordered not to attempt to escape. Two members of Gordon Bennett's staff, Capt. Harry Jessup and Capt. Adrian Curlewis (later Sir Adrian), declined invitations to join the party, and Curlewis wrote later: 'I didn't think it was ethical for a general to leave his troops. But the general made up his own mind. I wasn't asked my opinion and didn't give it at the time. I didn't quite know whether it was an order or a request that I should join his party to do some swimming through mangrove swamps to get a boat ... I started to think it over: would the men feel that they had been let down by the officers? I made up my mind that I wouldn't go, and two or three others joined me.'[2]

I think Curlewis was right. Bennett's escape must have been planned before the surrender, and arrangements had already been made for a group of officers to be evacuated to take home information about the tactics used by the Japanese. This was, in essence, the view of the Royal Commission appointed to look into the matter.[3]

After the surrender it was surely proper for — and many would say the duty of — a combatant officer to try to escape if he could do so without hazarding the lives of others in an attempt that was unlikely to succeed. I met recently one of the very few who did succeed, an Englishman, Rollo Edwards-Kerr,[4] who got away with a small party of English and Dutch troops; for the most part, however, those who tried were caught, and in most cases shot or beheaded by the Japanese.

For a medical officer there was no question of attempting to escape at this stage; our duty was to stay with, and do all that we could to help, our sick and wounded, and for some weeks we were extremely busy. There was a short time later, however, when this work had greatly diminished and deficiency disease had not yet become a problem, when it no longer seemed unethical for a medical officer to try to escape, and I was invited by Major John Wyatt — who had been GSO II on Gordon Bennett's staff — to take part in two such attempts, both of which were abortive. The first involved fitting out a Malay fishing boat that Wyatt had found in a creek. We had a good compass and reliable watches, and made a rather primitive sextant from bits and pieces we obtained from one of the big guns of the Changi battery, and we took lessons on navigation from a naval officer in the camp. To our bitter disappointment, though I think in retrospect most fortunately, when the work on the boat was nearly finished, the Malay owner appeared and took possession of it himself. The second plan was devised by Wyatt and an RAAF officer, Fl. Lt. Jack MacAllister, who planned to seize a Japanese transport plane and fly it to Cocos Keeling Island. They had located what seemed to be a suitable plane, and were engaged in further reconnaissance to find out when it was normally refuelled. They invited me to help in this task, and go along for the ride, but John Wyatt was caught by the Japanese and sentenced to death. This was commuted to imprisonment in solitary confinement. Wyatt suffered appalling torture at the hands of the Kempi Tai (Japanese Secret Police) in Outram Road gaol, but never breathed a word about McAllister or me. Towards the end of our captivity he successfully feigned appendicitis and was brought to Changi, where a normal appendix was removed. The Japanese seemed to forget about him for a time, but eventually took him back to Outram Road. A brave and gallant man to whom I owe my life, for I am sure I would not have survived the kind of hardships he endured.

I soon became quite busy again clinically, mainly in dealing with deficiency disease that began to appear as a consequence of our miserable diet, but also assisting Lt. Col. Osborn in the operating theatre. Much time was spent in treating patients with peptic ulcer, which was common in the camp and, if untreated, often resulted in bleeding or acute perforation. Severe bleeding called for blood transfusion. There were many courageous and generous people willing to act as blood donors, but by this time their health had deteriorated to such an extent that we felt obliged to limit donations to 100ml instead of the customary pint (600ml), and the small amount of blood available for our patients had to be supplemented by intravenous infusion of saline and glucose solutions. Our stocks of these had been largely used up in dealing with our battle casualties, but we managed to prepare solutions using local water which were surprisingly well tolerated. Acute perforation of an ulcer was dealt with by simple closure of the perforation.

To prevent these complications in patients with chronic ulcers, Lt. Col. Osborn performed a relatively simple procedure termed *gastrojejunostomy* (in which an artificial opening is made between the stomach and the upper part of the small intestine), on the grounds that this would suffice in most cases for months or possibly years, by which time the war might be over. The senior British surgeon, Col. Julian Taylor, on the other hand, preferred to do a larger operation termed *Polya gastrectomy* (in which much of the stomach is removed); he carried out this procedure in over thirty patients, all of whom survived except one with severe bleeding before operation. This is an astonishing feat when one remembers that the members of the surgical team, like their patients, were suffering from severe malnutrition, and in consequence took three to four hours to perform these operations. The only general anaesthetic we had was chloroform, and as it was in very short supply the anaesthetist, Lt. Col. David Middleton, RAMC, administered it in a closed system so that the patient rebreathed the same chloroform throughout the operation. Surely, only a Scottish anaesthetist reared in the tradition of Sir James Young Simpson could have done this. When, years later, I came to the Chair of Surgery in Edinburgh, I met David Middleton again; and his son, Michael, became my Senior Registrar. David was qualified in Dentistry as well as in Medicine, and in Edinburgh he practised as an oral surgeon. He told me that he learned to give anaesthetics because the solution of many of the problems referred to him by his dental colleagues depended simply on better anaesthetic technique. At the outbreak of war he had offered to serve as either an oral surgeon or an anaesthetist, and was sent to the Far East as Consultant Anaesthetist.

About the beginning of May 1942 the Japanese decided to send a working party, known to us as A Force, to Burma to work on the Burmese end of what became the notorious Thailand — Burma railway, and assured us that those who went would find the diet and working conditions much better than in Changi. I was delighted when I was chosen to go as a medical officer, and mortified when an attack of dysentery prevented me from doing so, but looking back I clearly had a lucky escape.

As there were still many surgeons in Changi, but less and less surgery to be done, it seemed that the right thing for me to do was to develop a serious interest in deficiency disease, about which I knew very little. My teacher was Major R. C. ('Jim') Burgess, Nutrition Officer, Malaya Command, who had been on the staff of the Institute for Medical Research in Kuala Lumpur and after the war joined the staff of the World Health Organization, and under his guidance I learned quickly. I also managed to convince Lt. Col. White that it would be a good idea to appoint a medical research officer to coordinate efforts to deal with the new problems confronting us, and that I was the man for the job.

I met Burgess again recently in Scotland when he was celebrating his ninetieth birthday.

Before describing the work in which I quickly became involved, however, I must first recount the bizarre incident of the

10. The 10 AGH, June, 1941.
    A. The Malacca Hospital in which we were
       accommodated.
    B. Officers. I am third from the right, in the back row.

C. The C.O. with the C. in C., Malaya, Air
  Vice-Marshall Brooke-Poppham. April, 1941.

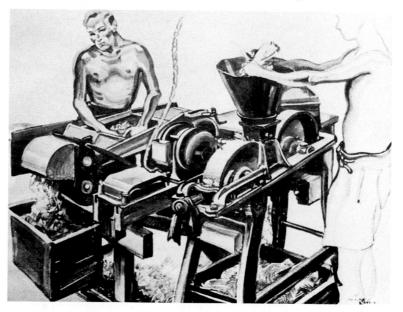

11. Machine for making grass extract in Changi.

Selarang Barrack Square,[5] when all the British and Australian prisoners in the Changi area, including the sick and wounded, were crammed into an area that normally housed a single battalion, and told that we would remain there until everyone had signed a pledge not to attempt to escape. There were few water points, almost the only sanitary facilities were those we created by making holes in the ground, and shelter had to be improvised with tents and derelict vehicles. The conditions were insanitary in the extreme, and the risk of mosquito-borne and fly-borne infection was very high. To put further pressure on us to sign, three men who had been caught previously while trying to escape were shot in the presence of some of our senior officers, who had been ordered to attend. The firing party was composed of Sikhs who had deserted to the Japanese, and they took several shots to kill each prisoner. After this the British and Australian commanders decided that they had no option but to order everyone to sign the pledge demanded by the Japanese, and told us that we need not regard this as binding because it was being signed under duress. So sign we did, after being incarcerated for three days under conditions that were bad enough for those who were relatively fit and intolerable for those who were not.

The diet provided by the Japanese was grossly deficient in quantity and quality, and consisted mainly of polished rice, i.e. rice from which the pericarp and germ had been removed by milling to make it keep better in storage.

Polished rice contains a surprisingly large proportion (seven per cent) of high class protein, but is very deficient in thiamine (vitamin B_1), riboflavin, pantothenic acid, nicotinic acid, and other vitamins of the B-complex. In addition to rice we received red palm oil or coconut oil, dried fish (*ikan belas*), occasional very small amounts of fresh fish or meat, and, from January 1944, occasional supplies of soya beans. We supplemented this thin diet with (1) salt in the form of sea water used for cooking; (2) items from Red Cross Parcels, which began to arrive in October 1942, but had not infrequently been rifled by our captors; (3) items bought with pooled funds derived from the meagre pay allowed by the Japanese to officers and to men in working parties; (4) produce from the vegetable gardens we established as quickly as we could; and (5) extracts made, as described below, from rice polishings, grass and other green leaves.

Soya beans are rich in protein and fat, and in many of the vitamins we so badly needed, but if they are simply boiled they are extremely indigestible. Some Dutch POWs suggested that this problem could be overcome by converting the beans into a product known in the Netherlands East Indies as *tempe*, by subjecting them to the action of a fungus (or a mixture of fungi) that can be harvested from withered petals of the hibiscus plant. This alters the protein, and perhaps also hydrolyses some of the cellulose, and the resulting product, after it has been fried in oil, though certainly not before, looks and tastes quite appetizing. Once we had learned how to make *tempe* we would have gone far towards solving the problem of deficiency disease in Changi if we had been able to obtain adequate amounts of soya bean to supplement the things we already had, but, while we purchased all we could, we never had enough.

The rice polishings issued to us contained a lot of husk, which caused diarrhoea, and innumerable weevils, alive and dead; in consequence, many of our men refused to eat them. By making an extract with water acidified with a small quantity of sulphuric acid from the battery of a derelict truck, we conserved most of the thiamin and pantothenic acid, and eliminated the husk and weevils. This extract was far from palatable, but we managed to persuade many men to take it, and so greatly reduce their risk of developing beri-beri and the burning feet syndrome.

Grass, and green leaves generally, are rich sources of riboflavin, which is readily soluble in water, and it was suggested independently by two colleagues that aqueous extracts of grasses and leaves could be used to prevent or treat riboflavin deficiency, which we thought played a major role in several disorders that became common in Changi, including ulceration of the lips and tongue, dermatitis of the scrotum, ulceration of the cornea, and possibly also a form of blindness known as deficiency amblyopia. Nebuchadnezzar, we are told, ate grass, but man, unlike common herbivorous animals, does not possess digestive enzymes that break down cellulose, and cannot possibly obtain anywhere near the amount of riboflavin he needs simply by following this example.

After many experiments, performed in collaboration with Jim Burgess, it was decided to set up a combined British-Australian 'factory' to make a 'green' extract on a scale commensurate with the anticipated demand. We had plenty of skilled engineers capable of building the plant; and plenty of electric power because our engineers operated the local power station for the Japanese, and when demand exceeded supply they simply screwed down the circuit breakers (designed to cut off the power supply in the event of overload) a little tighter. Of course, the system broke down from time to time, but our engineers did not mind because this gave them an opportunity to go into Singapore to try to find what they needed to put things right.

Our preferred raw materials were the leaves of wild passion fruit (*Passiflora orientalis*), Serangoon grass, and another grass, *Paspalum conjugatum*, but there was not enough of these and we had to rely mainly on a coarse native grass known as *lalang*. The machinery we used has been described elsewhere;[6] it consisted essentially of a stationary power-driven lawnmower which cut up grass (Fig 11) harvested by men with sickles, and large conical-ended cylinders made by welding sheet steel obtained by cutting up army steel lockers. The cylinders were packed tightly with grass cuttings, and water was added at the top and collected at the bottom. In the course of a year (May 1943–May 1944), we processed 300 tons of grass, which yielded about 20,000 gallons of extract. The extract tasted horrible and many men would not drink it; in consequence, all the time the factory was in production there was enough for the sensible minority who were prepared to drink it. The effect in preventing or treating the conditions I have listed was dramatic.

I thought at the time that refusal to take extracts that were potentially life-saving or sight-saving simply because of their taste was a manifestation of mental weakness resulting from the dismal conditions of our incarceration, but it now seems on a par with the refusal of many people today to give up smoking despite the vastly increased risk of developing cancer of the lung that smoking entails.

Another important task that our engineers undertook was the manufacture of artificial limbs, under the guidance, initially, of Col. Julian Taylor.

The attitude of POWs in Changi to captivity took three main forms: blank despair, irrational optimism, and supra-rational faith.[7]

Prolonged despair was rare, though temporary fits of depression were quite common. The majority of men overcame these by adopting a kind of optimistic fatalism, an attitude that is common also among fighting soldiers, who feel that if their number is on a particular bomb or shell it will kill them, whereas if it is not it won't. I have called this *irrational hope* because, in my view, fatalism is never rational, and optimistic fatalism is a contradiction in terms. A minority of men, but a large and important one, faced the reality of the situation, and, having accepted the fact that they might well never get back to their homes, set themselves the task of living a purposeful and creative life in spite of hunger and disease, and the humiliations imposed on us by the Japanese.[8] These men, though many of them might not accept the description, had *faith*; faith that there is purpose in the universe, and that the human spirit can endure all things. Hope helped men to avoid going mad, faith made them free. I have described faith as supra-rational because it could not be arrived at by any purely logical process. It found expression in those fruits of the spirit that are traditionally classified as Beauty, Truth and Goodness (see Chapter 16).

To be able to come to terms with the situation it was necessary to arrange one's time, and especially such leisure time as one had, creatively. Different people found different ways of doing this. Activities that particularly helped me included (1) reading, (2) participating in organized educational activities, (3) listening to recorded music, (4) attending organized entertainments, (5) playing chess and bridge and, (6) gardening.

As mentioned in the previous chapter, we had collected many books and gramophone records from the headquarters of the Malayan Broadcasting Service in the Cathay Building, and books from Raffles College and the King Edward VII School of Medicine had been collected by others. All these were pooled in a lending library established in Changi.

Among the medical books was Rodney Maingot's *Postgraduate Surgery*.[9] While looking through this one day I happened on the statement that skin grafts transplanted from one individual to another (now called *allografts*) often took for a time but did not survive permanently. Hitherto the only grafts I had learned about, apart from blood transfusion, were grafts of a person's own skin, bone and fascia (called autografts) and allografts of cornea and bone. I was ignorant of the many attempts by surgeons to use allografts of skin, and of the long controversy

12. Myself when I became engaged to Hazel.

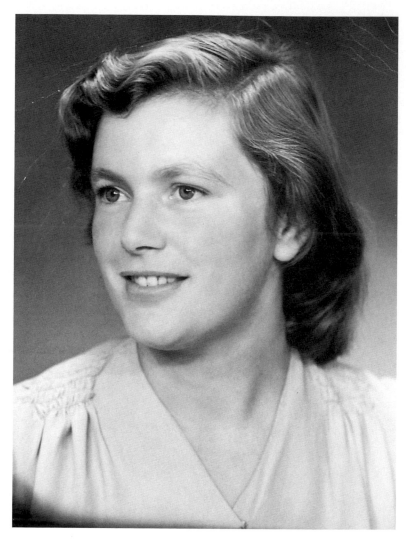

13. Hazel when we became engaged.

about whether these could survive permanently, and had assumed, if I thought about the matter at all, that autografts were used simply as a matter of convenience, except where this was manifestly impossible, as in the case of cornea. If Maingot's statement was true it followed that an individual could distinguish between his own and someone else's skin. This seemed much more subtle than our well known ability to distinguish between different kinds of bacteria, or between hen egg albumen and duck egg albumen but, if we could do this, why did we not distinguish between our own and someone else's cornea and reject corneal grafts too? I resolved then and there that, if I survived the war, I would investigate the matter. When the war did end I learned of the work of Medawar and others on this problem, and in 1947, as soon as possible after we had settled in Sheffield, I went to see Medawar in Birmingham, where he was then working.

Among other books I read in Changi were Sir James Frazer's single volume version of *The Golden Bough*;[10] various mathematical texts, including Whittaker and Watsons' *Modern Analysis*;[11] Carnap's *Logical Syntax of Language*,[12] a book on symbolic logic,[13] and a textbook on the history of philosophy.[14] I made notes on these on odd pieces of paper, or, when no one else seemed to want it, in the book itself, and some of these I still possess.

I was fortunate to be able to keep in touch with surgery during the early days of our captivity by going twice a week with a colleague, Capt. Tom Smiley, RAMC, to what amounted to private tutorials from Col. Julian Taylor. JT, as we called him, taught me a great deal of surgery, and he inspired me with the picture he conveyed of his own surgical hero, Wilfred Trotter. Unfortunately, there was not a copy of Trotter's essay, *The Herd Instinct in Peace and War*,[15] in Changi, but I hastened to obtain a copy and read it when I got home. It seems scarcely credible that, when I sat the final FRCS examination in London in 1947, JT should be my examiner in the clinical part of the examination, but he was. I knew no one else in the examination hall, and contrary to long-established custom, he got up from his chair, shook hands with me, and said, 'How good to see you, Woodruff'. After this, I would not have dared to fail!

There were many educational activities in Changi that were open to anyone. I particularly enjoyed lectures on physiology by

'Joe' Markowitz,[16] and on early British and Roman history by Richard de Gray, and took the opportunity to brush up my German, which I had studied for only one year at school. When the war began Markowitz was part-time Associate Professor of Physiology in the University of Toronto and spent the rest of his time as a general practitioner; before that he had worked with F. C. Mann at the Mayo Foundation. He was by birth a Roumanian Jew, but was a naturalized British subject and intensely anglophile. In addition to English, he spoke various Balkan languages, and on the outbreak of war he came to London to offer his services as an undercover agent in the Balkans but, when it became known that he was medically qualified, he was posted as Regimental Medical Officer to an infantry battalion in the ill-fated British 18 Division, and arrived in Singapore a few days before the surrender.

We had amassed a very good collection of gramophone records but at first had only a very poor portable gramophone on which to play them; after much persuasion, however, the Japanese — who rightly suspected that we were also interested in making clandestine radio sets — allowed our engineers to build an electric gramophone, on which outdoor recitals were given regularly. I listened again and again to Mozart's piano concerto in Bb major, K 595, with Arthur Schnabel at the piano, until the records wore out, and found that the extraordinary way in which this music expresses both deep melancholy and unconquerable hope exactly matched my feelings. Another favourite, though easier to appreciate when one was in less sombre mood, was, as might be expected, Beethoven's ninth symphony.

Theatrical performances were popular, though the female parts had, perforce, to be played by men, which gave them something of the flavour of school plays when I was a boy, but the most fascinating shows were those put on by a British NCO, Sergeant Piddington, in which he transmitted to a colleague messages submitted by people in the audience. It looked like telepathy, though Piddington carefully refrained from either asserting, or denying, that it was, but it now seems that the message was encoded in remarks he addressed to the audience. Piddington refined his act after the war, and gave many broadcast performances in collaboration with his wife.

Playing chess and bridge were other popular diversions. Some people played poker, but, while I share Somerset Maugham's high opinion of poker[17] under ordinary circumstances, it became absurd when, instead of playing with real money, one chalked up huge debts to be settled after the war, if ever; and it seemed improper to play for stakes that could be converted into food.

My main outdoor diversion was working in our vegetable garden. Although I love gardens, I have never cared much for gardening, but in Changi it provided the sort of exercise we needed and contributed significantly to our diet. Initially, people were allocated small plots on which they could grow vegetables for their own consumption, but this was hopelessly inefficient, and did nothing to meet the needs of the sick. The next plan was to try to develop a combined garden in which people were asked to work voluntarily, the produce of which would be shared equally by all. There were some saintly people who were prepared to work hard under these arrangements, but the great majority of men would not. A compromise plan was therefore devised in which work in the garden was voluntary but, instead of distributing all the produce evenly throughout the camp, a quarter of the produce was set aside to be distributed among the workers, in shares proportional to the number of hours they worked; a further amount was set aside for patients in hospital, and only what remained was added to the general rations. This rough and ready scheme worked remarkably well, and left me in no doubt that to get the best out of most people one must be prepared to use both the stick and the carrot.

When we first moved to Changi some regular British officers brought their dogs with them, and shared their meagre rations with their pets. Surprisingly, perhaps, the dogs accepted a diet of rice and very little else, but as the amount of food available was inadequate for the human population it was decided that all dogs must be destroyed, and an order to this effect was issued by the British and Australian commands. One day, before this happened, I passed a rather elderly officer who was strolling through the camp with a small dog walking smartly to heel. He was engrossed in a book, and as I passed him I saw that it was about dogs. I was unable to resist looking more closely at the title and saw, to my amazement and delight that it was not just *Dogs*, or *Dogs in the Tropics*, but *The Englishman's Dog in the Tropics*.

The dog owners whose pets had to be destroyed liked to give them a decent burial, but there were others who saw the dogs as a source of food. This is perhaps not quite as repulsive as it sounds, because in Changi the dogs, like the people, were living on a largely vegetarian diet, but the dog owners took no chances, and mounted a guard over the graves of their pets for at least twenty-four hours, after which even the keenest dog eaters seemed to lose their appetite.

In May 1994 I was sent to a combined British-Australian camp at Kranji, not far from the old British naval base at Selita. There were also a few Dutch troops in the camp, and one day I met the Dutch Warrant Officer who was responsible for distributing their rice ration, and was using some of this to fatten a cat he had mysteriously acquired, which he and his friends planned to eat in due course for Christmas. He invited me to inspect 'ze great big cat'. It looked revolting — an enormous fat black cat in a wooden cage from which the animals head and tail projected — and was being stuffed like a goose, only with rice. When Christmas arrived the cat was killed and eaten, and I was invited to the feast; hungry as I was, however, I couldn't face it.

After I had been at Kranji for about a year I was sent with three other Medical Officers, including my friend Victor Brand, who had been in my year in Melbourne, and some Australian and Dutch troops, to a mainly Australian working party that had recently been set up at River Valley Road. The senior Medical officer was Major K. B. Burnside, another friend who had been in my year in Melbourne. We remained at River Valley Road until shortly after the Japanese surrender, and during this time Burnside kept a diary that was printed for private circulation after the war. I have found this of great help in preparing the following account of the final phase of my captivity.

Among the Dutchmen who had come from Kranji to River Valley Road was my cat-eating friend, W. O. Kukup. Six days after we arrived he developed a perforated duodenal ulcer. The Japanese refused to evacuate him to Changi, but were persuaded to fetch from there whatever I needed to operate on him in our camp. It took several hours to fetch instruments and some chloroform, but when these did arrive I proceeded to operate, and found and closed the perforation. Conditions were primitive. We had, as would have been the case in Changi, no gowns or gloves; where things differed were that the only light available was a 60-watt bulb with a simple shade, and there was no one with Lt. Col. Middleton's experience in administering chloroform, though it is of interest that Victor Brand, who gave the anaesthetic, later took up anaesthetics as a specialty and was appointed to the staff of the Alfred Hospital. The operation lasted about an hour, and during this time I had a sizeable audience of Japanese soldiers, apparently overcome by curiosity. To my great relief the patient made a rapid recovery.

A week later a patient was admitted from a nearby camp with signs of acute intestinal obstruction, but fortunately settled down without operation. I did have to operate on the next patient, who had acute appendicitis. Fortunately, he too made a good recovery, but my next patient, who had acute cholecystitis that obstinately refused to settle down in the course of a week, died shortly after I had performed a drainage operation.

By this time we had no chloroform left, and only a little local anaesthetic. As the Japanese refused to fetch any more, or to evacuate patients to Changi, a Dutch colleague, Rudi Sampimon, who was a qualified dentist and also a skilled hypnotist, suggested that in suitable cases I should try to operate without conventional anaesthesia after he had hypnotised the patient.[18] We tried this first in a patient with a painful onychogryphosis (deformed ingrowing toenail). At a preliminary trial Sampimon put the patient to sleep without difficulty, but next day, when I was about to operate, he became no more than slightly drowsy. Every doctor in the camp, and many other people as well, seemed to have heard about the operation, despite our attempts to keep it secret, and it seemed clear that if the procedure was a fiasco all hope of using hypnosis as a substitute for conventional anaesthesia would be lost irretrievably. Inspired, no doubt, by Sergeant Piddington's impressive demonstrations in Changi of what passed for telepathy (p. 78), I decided to try my own hand at a little deception in a good cause, and managed to inject enough local anaesthetic to produce an effective regional anaesthesia of the big toe without the patient, or anyone else apart from my assistant and Sampimon, realizing what I had done. I went on to perform the standard operation of removing the nail and nail bed, and shortening the distal phalanx of the toe, and even the sceptics went away convinced that hypnotism was a great success. Thereafter it was used in several cases, especially by Sampimon for extraction of painful carious teeth.

One day a dental patient asked Sampimon whether 'local hypnotism' was possible, so that he could have his tooth painlessly removed without being put to sleep. This was an opportunity that Sampimon had been waiting for, and, without a moment's hesitation, he replied: 'But of course'. He proceeded by pure suggestion to convince the patient that he had lost all feeling in the affected jaw, and extracted a carious tooth without the patient experiencing any pain. When one has been held prisoner for three years under the kind of conditions we experienced one is apt to become abnormally subject to suggestion, and the number of patients who could be treated in this way under normal circumstances might well be smaller, but I feel sure there would still be some.

About this time we began to hear rumours from some of our guards that Germany was finished, and their attitude towards us softened somewhat. Our diet, which had yielded only about 1900 calories, also improved slightly, as did the supply of Red Cross parcels, which had hitherto averaged 0.4 of a parcel per man per year, of which many had been rifled before they reached us.

On 18th August (1945) a bomber, which did not look like any of the Japanese planes we had seen, flew low over the camp, and some of the guards said that the war was over and that we would be going back to Changi tomorrow. Both these rumours turned out to be true. On our way back to Changi we saw groups of Japanese soldiers without rifles carting baggage on handcarts, and we received rapturous greetings from the civilian population. We also noticed the mouths of many tunnels, in which the Japanese had apparently planned to make a last ditch stand before they were ordered to surrender by their emperor, Hirohito.

In Changi we found that our status had changed from contemptible prisoners to honoured guests, and there was plenty of good food. Nine days later, a Liberator bomber dropped leaflets telling us that the Japanese had surrendered unconditionally; this was followed by another Liberator which dropped by parachute two combatant officers, two medical officers and two other ranks, and yet another which dropped copies of a special number of the South East Asia Command (SEAC) newspaper addressed to liberated prisoners of war. The type of bomber chosen for these missions seemed particularly appropriate. The first British officer to land, Lt. Wishart, apparently found some of our senior officers inclined to tell him what to do. It is said that he sent a signal to SEAC: 'Having trouble with Lieutenant Colonels', and received a reply signed by Mountbatten himself: 'Promoted temporary Colonel'.

On 3rd September we heard that the Union Jack was to be hoisted on Changi gaol in place of the Japanese flag, and I went to watch the ceremony. From where I was I could see not only the flagpole, but also the Cross on the gaol chapel, and in the magical moment when the Union flag was broken out I was moved to reflect on this conjunction of symbols. I do not pretend that the Flag has always followed the Cross, but I believe now, as I believed then, that Christianity has often played a decisive role in British history, and not least in the decision of Britain and the self-governing countries of the British Commonwealth to resist aggression, first by the Nazis and then by Japan, in the second world war.

Two days after the flag-ceremony British troops landed in force on Singapore Island without encountering any resistance from the Japanese. We were now able to send letters home, and plans for our repatriation began to move ahead, though it seemed a long time before we embarked on a ship to take us home. One of the highlights of our remaining time in Changi was the hospitality we received from the officers and men of HMS *Sussex*, anchored in Keppel Harbour. I visited the ship several times, and it was heaven to be entertained in her wardroom, wearing borrowed clothing while one's own tatty clothes were washed and ironed.

I had written to my friend Professor R. D. (later Sir Douglas) Wright, who was Medical Adviser to the Australian Commander-in-Chief, Field Marshall Blamey, telling him of the information I had amassed about deficiency disease in Changi. He felt that this was sufficiently important to justify flying me home, but the signal he sent to Singapore arrived just after I had left by sea. It caught up with me when we got to Brisbane, where I was whisked off the ship and flown direct to Melbourne. I landed at Melbourne's Essendon Airport with just one other repatriated POW, and was thus spared much of the emotional stress I would have experienced when the ship docked in Port

Melbourne. My father was at the airport to meet me. I had already received a letter from him in which he quoted the words of the father in the parable of the Prodigal Son: 'This my son was dead and is alive again; he was lost and is found.' I tried to say to him, 'The prodigal's come home', but I couldn't utter a single word, and for a time neither could he. As we drove home, and I recognized familiar landmarks, I became less tongue tied. My mother had wisely decided that it would be less of a strain for me if only one of them came to the airport, so she stayed at home, supervising the preparation of the fatted calf, and greeted me there.

14. Professor W.C. Wilson.

15. My first clinic in Edinburgh.
Dr Clunie and Dr Langlands are in the second row.
In the front row (L to R) are Dr Taylor, Mr Meikle,
Sr. Smith, Mr Ross, Sr. Muir, myself, Sr. Darling,
Mr Macpherson, Dr Burt, Dr Robertson and

9

Return to Freedom
Marriage

After returning home I remained in the army for six months, and was provided with a secretary, so that I could prepare a detailed report for the Director General of Medical Services on the subject of deficiency diseases among Australian prisoners of war in Singapore. The DGMS kindly let me send a copy of this report to the Medical Research Council in London, and I gladly accepted the suggestion of Sir Edward Mellanby, then Secretary of the Council, that it should be combined with a report about deficiency diseases in civilian internees in Hong Kong that had been submitted at about the same time by Dr A. Dean Smith, and published as an MRC Special Report.[1]

I needed to get back to surgery as soon as possible. I hoped to go to England to sit my final FRCS examination and complete my surgical training, but this would depend on my being able to obtain a berth on a ship to England and a suitable training post there, and it looked as if this might take months to arrange. The first problem was solved when I was appointed Surgical Associate to Mr A. E. Coates, who had just rejoined the staff of the Royal Melbourne Hospital. In those days posts of this kind were similar in status to Senior Registrar posts today, but were unpaid. It was possible to earn a little by assisting in private practice, but not enough to live on, so, as was the custom, I accepted a salaried University appointment as well — in my case a lectureship in the Department of Pathology.

While still in the army, I was invited to participate in the annual conference of the Australian Student Christian Movement, to be held in January 1946 at Frensham School, Mittagong,

NSW. I accepted with pleasure, and looked forward to renewing old friendships and becoming involved again in the life of the SCM, which had meant so much to me in my student days. All this happened as planned, and would have sufficed to make the week a memorable one, but these events were completely overshadowed by my meeting, falling in love with, and six months later marrying, a young science graduate from Adelaide, Hazel Gwenyth Ashby, who was also at the conference. She was a systematic botanist, and was working in the herbarium of the Adelaide University Department of Botany. Hazel's parents, and forbears on both sides of the family for many generations, were Quakers; she was a former pupil of The Friends' School, Hobart, and we were introduced by a mutual friend, W. N. (Bill) Oates, who had recently become headmaster of the school in succession to Ernest Unwin, who had been head when Hazel was at school.

After the Mittagong conference I joined my parents, who were holidaying on Philip Island in Western Port Bay, and Hazel came to stay with us there. Later, I went to stay at her parents' home, Wittunga, at Blackwood, in the Adelaide hills, set in a lovely garden that had been planted with Australian and South African native shrubs by her grandfather, Edwin Ashby, and which was surrounded by farmland and orchard. Hazel returned the visit and came to stay for a short time at my parents' home in Melbourne, where I was living (Fig 12), but, inevitably, much of our courtship, and our planning, had to be done by correspondence. At the time we found this extremely frustrating, but it had one compensation: I still have Hazel's letters, and in re-reading them can recapture something of those magical days.

Hazel's father was a farmer. He had two properties: the larger, Mount Alma, near Victor Harbor, devoted mainly to sheep, but with some cattle; and Wittunga, where, in addition to running sheep and cattle in conjunction with Mount Alma, he grew apples and pears. Although there was a resident manager at Mount Alma, the two properties kept him very busy, but he found time to play cricket and tennis, at both of which he was very good, and easily demonstrated the inferior quality of my tennis on the grass court at Wittunga. Hazel's mother, Edith Ashby (née Walker), was a quiet lady of great charm, who also came from a farming family. To my sorrow, I did not come to know her really well because she died suddenly less than a year after we were married. The Ashby household included also Hazel's sisters, Enid and Beth, her brother Eric, and Keith Ashby's unmarried sister Alison. Auntie Alison was a skilled botanical artist. Many of her watercolours of Australian native flowers have been reproduced and published as postcards by the Adelaide Museum and the Adelaide Botanic Gardens; she bequeathed the originals to the Botanic Gardens, and they are now housed there.

We were married in Adelaide on 12th June 1946 at the Pirie Street Methodist Church by the Rev. Frank Hambly. He was a friend of long standing, who had been a contemporary of mine in Queens, and he and Hazel had known each other for several years through the Student Christian Movement. He enthusiastically accepted our suggestion of incorporating a period of Quaker silence in the marriage service, but we gained the best of both worlds by including also two hymns, Bach's *Jesu Joy of Man's Desiring*, and an organ voluntary based on the tune to which Schiller's *Ode to Joy* is set in the last movement of Beethoven's ninth symphony. To our delight, despite the strict rationing of clothes and materials that had been introduced during the war and was still in force, Hazel managed to have a white wedding dress made, thanks to gifts of clothing coupons by relatives and friends.

We spent our honeymoon in the Victorian Grampian Mountains — a familiar haunt of the Ashby family. Nearly forty years later, we went back there and again climbed Mount Rosea, though this time more slowly, but went by car to the summit of Mount William — the highest mountain in the group — on a recently-built road. Two years after this we went back again with our elder son, Keith, his wife Sue, and their two boys.

I had been offered a Travelling Fellowship by the Australian Red Cross Society that would enable me to spend two years at the Radcliffe Infirmary in Oxford, but decided not to accept it when we were told that the award would be conditional on my promising to return to Australia at the end of this time. We thought it likely that we would make our permanent home in Australia, but did not want to commit ourselves, and in any case the time limit of two years seemed too short. I therefore applied, early in May, for the post of Tutor in Surgery in the University of Sheffield, which I had seen advertised in the British Medical Journal. The chances of getting this seemed slim and, even if I did, it looked as if we might have to wait months before we could obtain passages on one of the few ships at that time carrying passengers to England, so we arranged to rent a flat in Melbourne as our first home. A fortnight before our wedding, however, we heard that some passages might be available on the SS *Stirling Castle*, which was expected to sail for Southampton in July, and decided to apply. While still on our honeymoon, we received a telegram saying that two berths were available, but that we must decide immediately if we wanted them. As we had still not heard from Sheffield, this put us in rather a quandary, but, with the optimism of youth, and in blissful ignorance of the intense competition for training posts in all branches of medicine among recently demobilised young doctors in Britain at the end of the war, we decided to accept. I resigned from the Royal Melbourne Hospital and the University, and we cancelled the lease on the flat we had arranged to rent. It was not until our ship arrived in Fremantle, however, that we heard that we had got the job in Sheffield — thanks largely, I am sure, to my two referees, Mr (formerly Colonel) Julian Taylor, and Dr Charles Kellaway, who had moved from Melbourne to become Director of the Wellcome Laboratories in London. Fortunate? Yes, indeed. Foolhardy? Probably. But *nothing venture, nothing win*, and I am glad that we decided as we did.

Most of the passengers on the ship were accommodated in large dormitories, some for men and others for women and small children. We were given a cabin to ourselves, presumably because the shipping agent or the purser knew that we had just been married, but two friends on board, Charles and Elizabeth Price, who were going to take up an appointment in Oxford and had been married considerably longer, were not so fortunate. Our lotus-eating existence was rudely shattered, however, when we entered the Red Sea. I happened to be on the boat deck talking to the Chief Engineer when we heard a series of loud explosions, apparently in the engine room, and the whole ship began to judder in an alarming way. The Chief disappeared in the twinkling of an eye, and soon afterwards the noise and juddering abated, but our speed dropped to a few knots. The ship was propelled by two diesel engines, and routine overhaul of these

16. Examiners in Cambridge, 1958.
I am in the middle of the back row.

17. At the R C S (Edinburgh) when I presented Sir
    Michael Swann for the Honorary Fellowship in 1967.
    From L to R myself, Mr Norman Dott, Lord Florey,
    Mr J.R. Cameron (President), Sir Michael (later
    Lord) Swann.

had been delayed because of the war. What had happened, as we heard later, was that the chain driving the valve control mechanism on the starboard engine had parted, and in consequence the timing mechanism was completely awry. This engine was stopped, and we proceeded for several days at a speed of five knots, but fortunately the engineers managed to get the engine back into service before we reached Suez and the trouble did not recur, so we were only a few days late in arriving at Southampton.

We went by train to London in a Pullman coach, which seemed extraordinarily luxurious in comparison with what we had expected to find. We stayed in London for a few days with my Uncle and Aunt, Frank and Steph Woodruff, and then went on to Sheffield, where the University had found temporary accommodation for us in a hotel. Here we soon became aware of the austerity of life in post-war England.

10

Sheffield. A foothold on the ladder of academic surgery

Before we left Melbourne I had decided that I wanted to
combine the practice of surgery with teaching and research, in
other words, to make a career in what, nowadays, is called
Academic Surgery. I hoped, indeed expected, that the post I was
going to in Sheffield would be a good starting point, but when
we got there, despite our warm welcome, I began to have serious
doubts about this. In the Royal Infirmary, which was the main
teaching hospital, there were only three general surgeons on the
Honorary Staff, including the newly-appointed part-time Professor of Surgery, Ralph St L. Brockman, one orthopaedic
surgeon, one plastic surgeon and one neurosurgeon. Each of
them had a fully trained and very experienced first assistant, but
these were not permanent members of the staff. At the Royal
Hospital there were only two general surgeons, and one urologist, on the permanent staff, and in both these hospitals staffing
on the medical side was on a similar scale. The University
Department of Surgery had no laboratory accommodation;
indeed it possessed but one room — the Professor's office.
Fortunately, however, the situation was soon changed by the
cooperation of colleagues in other departments.

Ten days after we arrived in Sheffield, Hazel became ill one
evening when we were dining with friends, and was found to
have acute cholecystitis — something of a rarity in a person of her
age. This did not subside with conservative treatment, so Professor Brockman removed her gall bladder. She made a good
recovery and after convalescing in Guildford with her great aunt
and great uncle, Eve and Sterry Ashby, returned to Sheffield to
find me installed in one half of an unfurnished house in

Wilkinson Street, just off Glossop Road. The other half was occupied by a medical colleague, Dr Edward (Eddie) Blackburn, and his wife, and this arrangement, which proved to be a very happy one, continued for the rest of our time in Sheffield.

In January, 1947 we went to London for me to sit the final FRCS examination. I was well prepared for it and, as mentioned earlier, was fortunate enough to encounter Julian Taylor as one of my examiners. It was customary at the time to gather at the College of Surgeons late in the afternoon of the day of one's last *viva* to be told whether one had passed or failed. Hazel joined me for a cup of tea in a Lyons cafe in Lincoln's Inn Fields and I told her that I was confident that I had passed, but she felt far from reassured as we made our way back to the college. Here the candidates lined up and were called forward one by one to hear the fateful words: 'I am pleased to inform you that you have passed', or 'I am sorry to inform you that you have been referred' — a polite way of saying that you have failed. If you had passed, you went up the stairs to meet the examiners and sign the fellows' book; if you had failed you disappeared as unobtrusively as possible. The first candidate was called forward and a moment later slunk away; likewise the next, and the next. Then one walked up the stairs to decorous applause from the people who had gathered to witness this strange ritual. And so it continued. When my turn came I noticed that my pulse rate had quickened appreciably, despite the confident way in which I had assured Hazel that I felt sure that I had passed. 'Your name, Sir?' asked the official. I told him. 'Your examination number?' I told him. 'I am pleased to ...' Pure joy flooded through me, and I heard no more, and a few seconds later I walked up the stairs. Julian Taylor was the first to shake me by the hand. I think that he was almost as pleased as I was, and asked if Hazel and I would have dinner with Mrs Taylor and himself the following day.

That evening we went to the theatre to see *The Wizard of Oz*, which accorded well with our state of euphoria, and next day, at the appropriate time, we made our way to the Taylors' house in Portland Place. There was an old-fashioned bell with a large, highly polished brass knob, and I gave it a rather tentative pull. Nothing happened. I pulled it a little harder, but again nothing happened and, as we did not hear a bell ring in the house, I gave it a vigorous tug. The effect was startling. The bell wire broke and

I found myself clutching the knob with about six feet of wire attached to it when a maid opened the door. To add to my embarrassment, Julian Taylor himself appeared before I had time to disengage myself from this unwanted object, but he kindly pretended not to notice and it was removed by the maid, who showed such admirable presence of mind that I wondered later whether a similar accident might have occurred before. After imbibing enough alcohol to restore my morale we were taken to the Ladies Annexe of the Athenaeum, which at that time was located not in the club itself but in another building in St James' Square. This was our first contact with the Athenaeum, of which I became a member some ten years later, and in which I have spent many pleasant hours.

The winter of 1946/47 was particularly cold, and when we got back to Sheffield we found that water pipes in our house had frozen and burst. The hot water pipes ran in wooden conduits about six inches square, in which they were surrounded by sawdust. After they burst the sawdust became thoroughly wet and the wet sawdust then froze, so that the pipes now ran in six inch square blocks of sawdust-reinforced ice. Our plumber sent a youth, armed with a candle to thaw the pipes, but, needless to say, he made no impression whatever on the situation, and we were without hot water until the spring. For about a fortnight we were also without cold water, except for what we fetched in buckets from the house next door.

Once I had obtained my FRCS my clinical responsibilities increased considerably. Each of the three surgical firms at the Infirmary took in all general surgical emergencies, including nearly all fractures requiring admission, for one week in three, and I dealt with many of the emergencies admitted to Professor Brockman's wards. For some weeks I had neither a telephone nor a car, so for emergencies admitted during the night a porter had to come and fetch me. We could both have taken a taxi if one had been available, but in practice this was almost never the case and both of us had to walk a mile and a half in each direction. The porters got tired of this as quickly as I did, and their protests were more effective; it was, therefore, thanks to them that my telephone was installed. Fortunately, about the same time, the new car we had ordered — a Ford Anglia — became available, and a month or two later the weather began to improve.

I got some major non-emergency surgery to do at the Infirmary, where I was much helped by a colleague, E. P. Hall Drake, and also worked as First Assistant to Mr Lytle at the Children's Hospital, which I particularly enjoyed. Here I acquired the gentleness needed in operating on infants with congenital pyloric stenosis (which I learned to do under local anaesthesia), intussusception and inguinal hernia. In addition, I gained experience of surgery of the neck in older children in dissecting out tuberculous cervical lymph nodes, which were very common in Sheffield at that time, when tuberculin testing of cattle had not yet come into vogue and milk was often unpasteurised.

Besides teaching medical students, I was asked to give a course of lectures on surgery to dental students. The students resented having to attend this course, which they regarded as of little relevance for their future practice, and at first I was inclined to agree with them. But when I began to think seriously about the matter, I realised that it could be important, and set out to convince my students of this. Although it was somewhat easier then to get accepted as a dental student than as a medical student. I found my dental students were often more mature than the medical students I taught, almost certainly, I think, because they were given responsibility for treating patients at an earlier stage. As a result, what I had thought would be a rather boring chore turned out to be an interesting and profitable exercise, and led me to write a textbook, *Surgery for Dental Students*,[1] that is still in use today.

Since the Department of Surgery had no space in either the university or the hospital apart from the professor's room, the only way I could do research was by finding accommodation elsewhere. The head of the department of pathology, Professor H. N. Green, came to the rescue and allowed me to use the excellent facilities in the Field Laboratories at Lodgemoor, some five miles from the University, of which he was director. Two other senior colleagues from whom I received help and encouragement were the professor of therapeutics, Professor (later Sir Edward) Wayne, and Dr (Later Sir Hans) Krebs, whose autobiography[2] contains much interesting information about the University of Sheffield at this time.

Helped by a letter of introduction from her professor in Adelaide to Professor Clapham, the head of the Department of

Botany in Sheffield, Hazel now had a part-time position in the botany department, but she became, in addition, my unpaid assistant at Lodgemoor. The only time we could find to work there was in the evening and at weekends, but we embarked on an extensive study of the behaviour of transplants of thyroid tissue in guinea pigs, and of why the anterior chamber of the eye is an immunologically privileged site for allografts. This work was continued in Aberdeen, and reported in a paper that was communicated to the Royal Society by Dr C. H. Kellaway and published in *Philosophical Transactions*.[3] It seemed a good beginning.

Hazel and I had many relations and family friends in England. Hazel's mother's cousins, Catherine Rowntree and Elsie Burt, lived in York, where Catherine's husband, Theodore, was for many years a director of Rowntrees, the well-known Quaker firm of chocolate manufacturers. Family friends in Sheffield included Ashley Ward, a former Master Cutler, who had been at school with my father, and Sir Irvine Masson, Vice Chancellor of the University. Ashley Ward's father, T. W. Ward, had started out by pushing a wheelbarrow from which he sold scrap metal round Sheffield, and this modest business eventually grew into the huge steel firm known as T. W. Ward and Sons.

We also soon made new friends, among them Jean and Bill Eastwood, whom we got to know when Jean and Hazel were working in the Botany Department and Bill was Lecturer in Engineering in Manchester. They moved to Aberdeen in 1947, but we caught up with them there a year later.

Soon after we arrived in Sheffield Professor Brockman gave his inaugural lecture as Professor of Surgery. His father was an Anglican cleric, but his wife was Roman Catholic and he had recently been received into the Roman Catholic church. His inaugural lecture was devoted to trying to reconcile current biology and orthodox Catholic teaching. It struck me as courageous, though far from convincing, but absolutely infuriated the Vice Chancellor, who was a rather militant agnostic, and wrote to Brockman, pointing out that Sheffield was a secular university in which the teaching of theology had no place. Brockman, unaware of the fact that I had come with a personal introduction to the Vice Chancellor, showed me the letter, which had clearly hurt him very much; Masson, who of course had no idea that

Brockman had shown me his letter, told me how much he disapproved of Brockman's lecture when, a few days later, Hazel and I were invited to his house. I felt that my position was fraught with danger, but fortunately neither of the people concerned ever suspected that the other had given me his view of the matter.

Living conditions in Sheffield were even grimmer than we had expected. Many buildings had been destroyed in air raids, and, except on the Derbyshire side, the city was smoky and dirty. Food rationing was strict — we were each allowed, for example, only two eggs and one shilling and twopence worth of meat per week — as was clothes rationing, and how Hazel managed to cope with the situation I do not know. There were, however, many compensations. The glorious Derbyshire countryside was unspoiled, there was a good repertory theatre company, some friends lent us a piano, and we had season tickets for concerts given by the Hallé orchestra, under Sir John Barbirolli, which came over from Manchester for two days every fortnight. Despite the near arctic conditions that often prevailed on the Snake Pass during the severe winter of 1946/47, I do not think the bus which brought the orchestra ever failed to get through, and they never missed a concert. They did have to change their programme once when Benno Moseivitch was billed to play one of the Beethoven piano concertos and his train from London was delayed, but instead of simply shortening the programme they accepted the offer of a well-known, albeit retired, Sheffield piano teacher to play with them, virtually unrehearsed, Tchaikowsky's first piano concerto. It must have taken a lot of courage, even if, as I suppose must have been the case, she had played it with the Hallé on some previous occasion. Once or twice during the performance it seemed as if things might come unstuck, but they didn't, and at the end there was the most whole-hearted and, I think, the most deserved, applause I have ever heard in a concert hall.

Hazel renewed contact with the Society of Friends, and combined attendance at Yearly Meeting in 1947 with a visit to the Chelsea Flower Show. In Australia, Quakers are somewhat rare, and I was surprised to find how many there were in England, and what a closely knit community they formed.

We spent our summer holiday in 1947 with my aunt, Brenda Cooper (later Brenda Lawrence), in Freshford, near Bath. During the war the Abbey Road Building Society, for whom she worked, moved from London to Somerset and, after the war ended, Brenda continued to live in Freshford in a cottage, ekeing out her pension by providing morning coffee and afternoon teas in a converted chapel, and also doing some outside catering for dinners and other functions. Just before going on holiday we heard the sad news of the death of Hazel's mother.

We had been in Sheffield about eighteen months when I heard that there was a vacancy on the surgical staff of the Royal Melbourne Hospital, and submitted an application, but this was unsuccessful. A few months later, however, with the support of Professor Brockman, I applied for the post of Senior Lecturer in the University of Aberdeen, which carried with it an appointment as Honorary Consultant in surgery to the Aberdeen Royal Infirmary, and the possibility also of a similar appointment to the Royal Aberdeen Hospital for Sick Children. We knew nothing of Aberdeen; indeed we had to look at a map to find out exactly where it was, and after we had located it we were far from sure that we wanted to move so far north. When I went to be interviewed, however, my doubts were quickly resolved. As the interview was to take place in the afternoon, and I had gone up by train the previous day, I had plenty of time to look around. I began with a quick tour of the fish market and the harbour, then spent a couple of hours wandering round King's College and the Old Town, and ended up with a visit to the hospital and medical school at Forresterhill, where I met the Head of the Department of Surgery, Professor W. C. Wilson. It was a glorious June day and the granite houses were sparkling in the sunshine; I attributed this to lack of atmospheric pollution, but realised that this was not the only explanation when I watched with amazement one proud owner washing his house with a hose as one might wash a car. I walked from Forresterhill to Marischal College for my interview, and stopped on the way for a few minutes to watch people playing open air chess in Union Terrace Gardens on huge boards marked on the ground, using long-handled tools like gigantic croupiers' rakes to move the pieces.

I was enchanted by what I had seen of Aberdeen, and went in to the interview feeling quite certain that I wanted the job. I was therefore delighted when I heard that I had got it.

For our summer holiday in 1948 we chartered a six berth sailing boat on the Norfolk Broads with two other couples. One member of the party had been in Air-Sea Rescue during the war and also had some experience of sailing, but the rest of us were novices. As the boat did not have an engine, indeed there was not even an outboard for the dinghy, we spent a lot of time 'quanting' — what anywhere else would be called punting — but we managed to get from our starting point, Potter Heigham, to Great Yarmouth without much trouble. To go to Norwich, as we hoped to do, it was necessary to lower sails and drift down towards Great Yarmouth on the last of the ebb tide, lower the mast — which was stepped in a tabernacle designed to allow this — before reaching the bridge, drift under the bridge and on into Bredon Water on the flood, raise the mast and hoist the sails. It sounds easy and, now that I have learned the hard way quite a lot about sailing, I would have few qualms about trying it again, but we badly mistimed things, and had still not got the mast up when the tide began to ebb. Fortunately we managed to tie up to a structure known in those parts as a 'dolphin', but there we had to stay until the tide changed again. An instructive, but humbling, experience.

When the time came to move to Aberdeen we arranged for our furniture to be transported by a removal firm, and Hazel and I drove our car by a circuitous route which allowed us to spend a few days with John Glaister (my stepmother's youngest brother) and his wife, Muff, in their country house at Gartocharn, near Drymen. John had succeeded his father in the Regius Chair of Medical Jurisprudence in Glasgow. He had qualified in both medicine and law and was a most erudite man and a formidable expert witness. He became well known to the general public when he gave evidence in a celebrated case that resulted in the conviction of Dr Ruxton for murder. I discussed the post I was going to in Aberdeen with him, and he gave me much good advice and some useful introductions to people he knew in the university.

Aberdeen — The next steps

The job I went to in Aberdeen fulfilled my highest expectations. The salary of £750 per annum at which I was appointed was, within a few weeks, suddenly multiplied by 2.4, when the National Health Service was inaugurated. I also became eligible for a distinction award, which was granted two and a half years later. More important was the job satisfaction I experienced, and the unfailing support and kindness of Professor W. C. ('Bill') Wilson (Fig 14), who not only provided me with a splendid environment in which to work but also encouraged me to visit the United States of America and opened many doors for me there.

Though a competent surgeon, Wilson was at heart an applied physiologist; in consequence, with patients at both the Infirmary and the Children's Hospital, I had as heavy a clinical load as I could manage.

My teaching responsibilities, though greater than they had been in Sheffield because there were more students, were not unduly heavy. I became a member of the Faculty of Medicine, and gained useful experience of the political manoevring that occurs in universities. I also gained experience as an examiner, first in Aberdeen and later as an Associate Examiner in Surgery in the University of London. In those days the clinical part of the examination for the qualifying degrees of MBBS (Lond.), like the clinical part of the FRCS examination, was held in the Examination Hall in Queen Square. Some of the patients brought there were veritable museum pieces, and I had the bizarre experience of examining several candidates on the very patient that I had been given as my 'long case' when I sat for my

FRCS. But despite the feeling of unreality one experienced at times in Queen Square, I learned a great deal about the art of examining, and about surgery in general, from my senior colleagues, among them Ralph Marnham, Charles Donald, Eric Crook, David Patey and S. H. Wass.

I see no point in accepting a university post in a clinical subject, as distinct from a purely hospital appointment, unless it offers an opportunity to undertake research, and so far as I was concerned this meant research in the general field of tissue and organ transplantation. Wilson, who was himself an able investigator, encouraged me to develop this interest. There was adequate laboratory space in his department, and a good animal house attached to the medical school available to people in all departments.

With Wilson's support, I obtained a grant from the Medical Research Council, which covered the cost of animals and materials plus the salary of a graduate Research Assistant — a position occupied by Hazel for a year, until the impending arrival of our first-born made her give it up. Our first task was to complete the experiments begun in Sheffield on the behaviour of transplants in the anterior chamber of the eye. We then turned our attention to the possible use of antilymphocytic serum as an immunosuppressive agent to prevent allograft rejection.[1] This topic was to interest me for many years and will be discussed more fully later, but it seems appropriate to mention here how my interest in it arose. I had been reading J. B. Murphy's remarkable monograph,[2] *The Lymphocyte in Relation to Tissue Grafting, Malignant Disease and Tuberculous Infection*, published as long ago as 1926, and I referred to this in a paper I gave in Aberdeen on allograft rejection. In the discussion that followed, Professor John Cruickshank, Head of the Department of Bacteriology, drew my attention to a more recent paper by Chew and Lawrence[3] in which it was reported that an antiserum raised by injecting rabbits with rat lymphocytes caused a marked fall in the blood lymphocyte count when injected into rats, and suggested that this material might therefore promote allograft survival. This proved to be the case and antilymphocyte globulin now has an established place in preventing rejection of clinical allografts, though as yet its potential has not, in my view, been fully realized.

In May 1950 Sir Macfarlane Burnet, a friend and colleague of my father in Melbourne, and Lady Burnet, stayed in our home for several days, and Burnet and I discussed his prediction[4] that an animal would become immunologically tolerant of antigens it encountered during early embryonic life. Hazel and I set out to see if this held good for the antigens concerned in allograft rejection by grafting a minute piece of skin from a rat of a different strain to rat foetuses *in utero* and challenging the survivors with a donor-strain skin graft when they were a few weeks old. None of our rats showed any evidence of tolerance, doubtless because our initial graft did not provide an adequate tolerogenic stimulus. This was disappointing, and it was chastening to learn later from Medawar and his colleagues[5] how the experiment should have been performed.

Soon after the Burnets' visit I was awarded a Travelling Fellowship by the World Health Organization that enabled me to spend four months in the United States and Canada, visiting medical schools, hospitals and research institutions.

I crossed the Atlantic on a French ship, the *De Grasse*. After clearing customs in New York a porter carried my bags to a taxi and, since the arrivals hall was plastered with notices saying that porterage was free and tipping was not necessary, I simply thanked him politely. He complained so loudly that a policeman appeared — the first real American policeman I had ever seen, and very formidable he looked. I tried to explain the situation, but the policeman simply said, 'Give him a dollar', and this I hastened to do.

The medical schools and hospitals I had arranged to visit had been carefully chosen. I soon became aware in talking to colleagues, however, that American Medicine had its weak points. In particular, by no means all medical schools were of the quality of those on my list, and, outside the university hospitals and well-known clinics, a considerable amount of surgery was being undertaken by people who were not adequately trained. But, as I wrote on my return in an article for the Aberdeen Medical Students' Magazine,[6] 'there are many medical schools in the United States that are good by any standards and the best are excellent'.

Among the many interesting people I met I have singled out a few for special mention, either because of the impression they made on me at the time or because of the way in which they have influenced me since.

At the Mayo Clinic I presented letters of introduction from Wilson to Dr Donald Balfour, who had recently retired, and Dr Waltman Walters, who was then the senior surgeon. I was most warmly received, and had the unexpected privilege of being invited by Mrs Will Mayo, the widow of one of the two brothers who founded the Mayo Clinic,[7] to her next 'family dinner'. I was the only guest who was not a Mayo or Mayo-in-law, and it became apparent that the Mayo Clinic was then still very much a family affair.

I was enormously impressed by the high standard of patient care in the Clinic, and the generous way in which a patient's bill was adjusted to take account of his financial means. Doctors, and Ministers of Religion (a term interpreted in a very liberal way), were not charged at all for medical care, but were presented with a receipted bill. I was also greatly impressed by seeing at first hand something of the scientific work of the Mayo Foundation, about which I had heard so much from Dr Markowitz when we were fellow prisoners of war in Singapore.[8]

It is only about eighty miles from the Mayo Clinic to the twin cities of Minneapolis and St Paul but they made Rochester seem like a village, as indeed it would be if the Mayo Clinic were not there. My first visit to the University Hospital in Minneapolis confirmed the feeling that I had moved into another world. The standard of medicine and surgery was high, and there was a great emphasis on clinical research, led, on the surgical side, by Dr Owen Wangesteen, one of the very few surgeons to be elected a member of the US National Academy of Sciences, but there was, I felt, a difference in ethos. As I pointed out many years later in my Edwin Stevens lectures,[9] *The One and the Many*, the one-to-one relationship of patient and doctor is fundamental to medical practice, but it is not the whole story, for the illness of one person may affect many other people, including *inter alia* people who may one day benefit from clinical research in which the patient is involved. It is not easy to strike the right balance between the needs of the One and those of the Many, and different people will have different views about this. I simply record that the emphasis on the One that I encountered in my visit to the Mayo Clinic was very much in accord with my own position.

At the University of Chicago I went first to see Dr Lester Dragstedt, who had developed a new way of treating chronic duodenal ulcer by dividing the vagus nerves to prevent acid secretion in the stomach. I then met another remarkable surgeon-scientist, Dr Charles Huggins, who established that some cancers are *hormone dependent*,[10] and can be held in check to some extent by hormonal manipulations, and was awarded the Nobel Prize for this work in 1963. He has remained a firm friend.

While in Chicago I also visited the Medical School of the University of Illinois to meet Dr Warren Cole, the Chairman of the Department of Surgery. I was driven there by car but returned on the Elevated Railway. There was nowhere on the station to buy a ticket but someone told me that I could pay on the train, so when it arrived I got in and sat down, expecting that the attendant would come round to collect the fares. Nothing happened for a few minutes; then, suddenly, there was a bellow like that of an enraged bull. It was incomprehensible to me, but my neighbour explained that the man was complaining that someone had got on without paying his fare. The someone was clearly me, and I had to walk the whole length of the carriage to where the attendant was stationed, submit to a public dressing down, and pay up before he would allow the train to start. It was rather embarrassing, but nothing compared to what Wilson told me happened to him on the same station in the days when the gangster, Al Capone, was a power in the land. Wilson was waiting with a doctor from Toronto, Laurie Chute (pronounced Shoot), and they became separated when the train, which was very crowded, arrived. Wilson saw a carriage with two empty seats and called out *Chute, Chute*, whereupon the people on the platform put up their hands. When they realised that it was a false alarm they tried to lynch him.

I had letters of introduction to two professors in Harvard Medical School: E. D. Churchill, who was about to retire from the Chairmanship of the Department of Surgery at the Massachusetts General Hospital, and Francis D. Moore, Surgeon-in-Chief at the Peter Brent Brigham Hospital. Both were distinguished surgeons, and both were very research-minded.

Churchill rejected the view that *all* young surgeons should have to spend some time on research, and held that no research was better than research of a perfunctory kind, but gave his full backing to those who really wanted to do research, were prepared to make sacrifices to this end, and had some original ideas, even if these seemed a bit naïve. I have tried to follow this example ever since.

Before I was able to present my letter of introduction to Francis Moore — affectionately known as Frannie — I unexpectedly met a group of surgeons and gynaecologists from the Brigham Hospital at the American College of Surgeons meeting. At one of the Surgical Forum sessions a resident from the Brigham presented a paper on the behaviour of tissue allografts in the anterior chamber of the eye. Hazel and I had done all that he described and a good deal more, though our paper[11] was still in press, so when he sat down I gave a very brief account of our work. At the end of the session about a dozen people from the Brigham were waiting for me, including David Hume, Gustav Dammin and Joseph Murray, all of whom I later came to know well. All three became widely known for their work on transplantation. David Hume's work was tragically ended by his death in a flying accident, but Murray went on to win the Nobel Prize. Next day, when I presented my letter to Francis Moore, I found that they had already told him about my comments. As we talked I formed the opinion, which later events confirmed, that Moore was destined to become one of the major figures in American, indeed in world, surgery; what I did not dream of at the time was that on one of my subsequent visits to Boston I would return to the Peter Bent Brigham Hospital as his 'Surgeon-in-Chief pro tempore'.

I went from Boston to Montreal, where I planned to spend most of my time at McGill University Medical School, but early in my visit I met Dr Hans Selye, Director of the Institut de Médicine et Chirurgie Expérimentales at the Université de Montreal, and was so fascinated by him that I cancelled my other visits and spent my week in his department. We discussed at length his work on stress and he generously gave me a copy of his monograph on the subject. What fascinated me even more was listening to his seminars to a postgraduate audience drawn from many countries. The accepted medium of communication in the university was French, but Selye — a Hungarian by birth who had studied medicine in Czechoslovakia — would change from French to English to Spanish to Italian to German as necessary.

Hazel was able to join me in New York because the Professor of Zoology in Aberdeen and his wife (Vero and Jenny Wynne-Edwards), with whom we had become friendly, offered to look after Keith, who was now almost a year old, for a month.

We went first, appropriately enough, to the Quaker city of Philadelphia, where I presented Wilson's letter of introduction to Dr Isidore Ravdin, Chairman of the Department of Surgery of the University of Pennsylvania; and he introduced me to Dr Jonathan Rhoads, who happened to be a member of the Society of Friends. I also had a letter of introduction to Dr John Gibbon, Chairman of the Department of Surgery at Jefferson University. Gibbon, like Wilson, was a surgeon who was very physiologically orientated. He was the first person to develop an effective pump-oxygenator — the machine that makes open heart surgery possible — and steadily improved this by careful research in animals extending over many years. Although he and his colleagues used the machine in only a few patients, John Gibbon must be reckoned the founding father of open heart surgery, and it is astonishing and deplorable that he was never awarded a Nobel Prize. To add to his other distinctions, Gibbon was for many years editor of Annals of Surgery, and was an accomplished amateur painter.[12]

In Baltimore my first priority was to meet Dr Alfred Blalock, who first became widely known for the operation he devised for treating 'blue babies'. After looking at the map, Hazel and I decided to walk from downtown Baltimore to Johns Hopkins Medical School. We soon found ourselves in a ghetto-like region, which seemed even more menacing than I had imagined Harlem could be. We kept on, hoping that things would get better, as they eventually did, but when we got to Johns Hopkins and told people what we had done, they said that we were lucky to have survived. Someone directed me to the Department of Surgery, where I encountered a man I thought was a technician, and asked him to direct me to Dr Blalock's office. 'I'm Blalock,' he said, 'what can I do for you?' Alas, I was repeating a mistake I made years before when I went to King's College, London, to look for Dr R. C. Johnson, the Master-Elect of Queen's College, Melbourne.

I next went to see Dr George Gey, a biologist well known for his work in the field of tissue culture. It was Christmas time, and

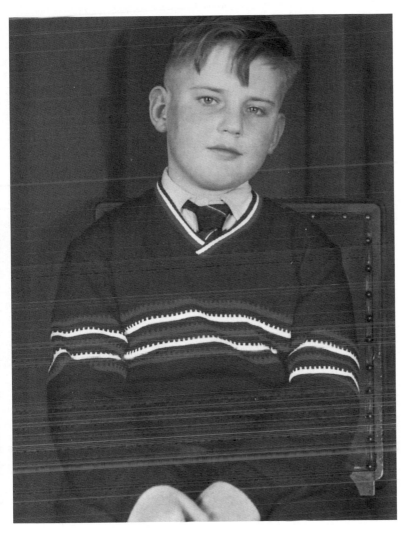

18. Bobby Kerr, who received a kidney graft from his
father in 1962, and is still alive (1996).

19. Kidney graft recipients, 1977.
Many of the early patients show evidence of
administration of steroids in high dosage, which

he invited me to come, with Hazel, to a party in his laboratory. In those days Gey's balanced saline solution was widely used in tissue culture media; the egg nog Dr Gey created for the party was equally famous, at least in Baltimore, and undoubtedly much more palatable.

Another person I had to meet in Baltimore was Mr Charles Thomas, the publisher. I had sent an outline of a book on *The Transplantation of Tissues and Organs*, that I planned to write, to his office in Springfield, Illinois, saying that I was in the United States for a few months and asking whether I could come to discuss this with someone in the firm. To my amazement I received a personal reply from Mr Thomas himself, with a list of places he would be visiting in the near future and the times when he would be there, saying that if we were going to be in the same place at the same time he would be delighted to see me there. It so happened that our paths would meet in Baltimore, and Mr Thomas invited Hazel and me to dine with him at the Maryland Club. We talked about the book and, after an excellent dinner, signed a contract that very evening for it to be published by Charles C. Thomas, Inc. The manuscript was to be submitted within two years, which seemed to me to be much longer than it would take to write. In the event, I was still writing nine years later, and the subject was growing so fast that I could not keep pace with it. The only thing to do was to stop and send in the manuscript without further delay, which I did. By this time Charles Thomas had retired and his son had become president of the firm, but despite the long delay the book was accepted and appeared in 1960.[13]

We went from Baltimore to Washington DC, mainly as tourists though I did manage to squeeze in a visit to the National Cancer Institute.

On the way back to New York we stopped at Rahweh, New Jersey to visit the pharmaceutical manufacturers, Merck, who had very kindly agreed to give me a supply of cortisone for use in our studies on ways of preventing the rejection of allografts. They gave me seven grams of cortisone acetate in suspension, in glass ampoules, but because the suspension was so dilute the ampoules, plus the protective packing, occupied two cases, each measuring about 2 x 2 x 3 feet. When the time came to embark on the *Queen Mary* for our journey home I was most reluctant to allow this precious cargo — the first cortisone to come to the United Kingdom apart from a small consignment given by Mercks to the Medical Research Council — to be stowed in the hold, so Hazel and I decided to allow it to share our cabin, and staggered up the gangway of the ship, each carrying one case. This was not the only problem which complicated our departure because we could not find our steamer tickets and came to the conclusion — which turned out to be quite correct — that they must have been included in one of the many bundles of reprints we had been in the habit of posting home each week. The purser accepted this true, but improbable-sounding, explanation and allowed us on board, subject only to the condition that if someone else turned up with our tickets he would have to reconsider the matter.

At that time the *Queen Mary* had not been fitted with stabilizers, and we had a very rough trip. When we disembarked at Southampton, clutching our precious cortisone, I tried to explain to the Customs Officer that cortisone was not a dangerous narcotic drug, but he was far from convinced and consulted a senior colleague, who in turn telephoned London. After some hours it was decided that the cortisone must be left in bond in Southampton until a decision was made as to whether it would be allowed into the country. While this discussion was going on the customs shed emptied completely except for us and a man who had been caught trying to smuggle in a considerable quantity of cigarettes and liqueurs of various kinds. The man in question had begun by saying that he had nothing to declare and, when his first suitcase to be opened was found to be full of cartons of cigarettes, he pleaded that the trip had been very rough — as indeed it had — and that this had caused him to forget them. The Customs Officer said very politely that every piece of luggage would now be opened, and that it would be very much in the man's interest, if he had any other goods that might attract duty, to say so at once. The man replied that he had nothing else, but when the next case was opened it too was full of cigarettes. With a slight edge to his voice, but still very politely, the officer again invited the man to make a declaration, but again he said that he had nothing else to declare. His next suitcase, however, turned out to be full of bottles of liqueurs, and this time he was taken away and we saw him no more. My parents, who were staying in London before coming to join us in Aberdeen, and had driven to Southampton to meet us, thought that it was Hazel and I who were in trouble, and were very relieved when we explained what had been happening. Some two months later I received a letter from the Customs Authorities telling me that the cortisone would be allowed in, and that there would be no duty to pay, but that we would have to pay quite a substantial sum to cover the cost of storage in bond while the matter was being considered. They refused to move from this decision, which I thought was unreasonable, but the University of Aberdeen, when told that the cortisone was to be used purely for research in the Department of Surgery, generously agreed to foot the bill.

When we got back to Aberdeen I resumed work on antilymphocyte serum and the induction of tolerance to allografts, and began to study the effect of cortisone on allograft survival as soon as the cortisone we had brought from America was released by HM Customs.

At this time it was known that in mice the antigens concerned in the rejection of allografts were represented on erythrocytes (red blood cells), but it was not known whether this was true also in humans. An opportunity to investigate this came when a colleague in the Blood Transfusion Service, Dr T. M. Allen, identified for me two unrelated volunteer blood donors whose blood had been typed in respect of all the human red cell antigens that were known at the time, and who were indistinguishable in respect of all of these. The donors concerned, one of whom happened to be a doctor, generously allowed me to interchange small skin grafts between them, and these were promptly rejected while control autografts survived permanently. We concluded, therefore, that identity in respect of all these antigens — which, *in toto*, were sufficient to divide people into some 30,000 different types — was not sufficient to ensure the survival of skin allografts. The obvious next step, as we pointed out in our paper,[14] was to look for other antigens represented on leucocytes, which, unlike erythrocytes, are nucleated cells, but it was not until 1958 that the first of these was identified in Paris by Jean Dausset. Although Dausset, in reporting this, made no reference to our paper, it is amusing to note that he gave his antigen the Scottish-sounding name of Mac.

In May 1951, I was one of ten people to be elected a Hunterian Professor by the Council of the Royal College of Surgeons of England, and this entitled me to give one lecture at the College on my chosen topic, *The Transplantation of Homologous Tissue and its Surgical Applications*.[15] Looking back it is interesting to see that the name just above mine on the list of people appointed was that of John Borrie, a New Zealand surgeon whom we came to know well when we moved to Dunedin some two years later.

Our domestic life in Aberdeen was complicated by the fact that the new University house that we had been promised was not ready for occupation until almost two years after we arrived, and in the meantime we occupied several different lots of furnished accommodation. In one of these, where we were living soon after our elder son, Keith, was born, Hazel was not allowed to hang nappies out to dry on the Sabbath! Food rationing, on the other hand, posed less of a problem than in Sheffield because we had registered with a butcher who also supplied the hospital, and he sent us each week a splendid joint of Aberdeen Angus beef. As this greatly exceeded our ration it did not appear on our bill; instead we were charged for non-rationed items such as haggis and mealy puddings that we had neither ordered nor received. Hazel at first wanted to correct these 'mistakes', but was easily persuaded to lie low.

In May 1950 we moved into the new terraced house in Old Aberdeen allocated to us by the university. We had congenial and mutually helpful neighbours, including the Dentons, who lived next door, and near to them Olivier and Renée Abrioux, who both worked in the French department. Eric Denton — a brilliant physiologist but an indifferent pianist — was apt to embark on *The Merry Peasant* when we were in bed, but stopped when we banged on the wall. Not far away lived our old friends, Jean and Bill Eastwood. Other neighbours included the Principal and Vice-Chancellor, Professor (later Sir Thomas) Taylor, whose wife had known my stepmother in Glasgow long before she was married; the Secretary of the University, H. J. (Harry) Butchart, who invited us to play tennis on his beautifully kept grass court; Ernest Wright, Professor of Mathematics, whose book on Number Theory[16] has been referred to in Chapter 5; and R. V. Jones, Professor of Physics, whose wartime exploits are

20. Myself and Hazel at Holyrood Palace when I was Knighted in 1969.

21. At the Carlo Erba Foundation, Milan, in 1969 to receive La Madonina Prize.

recounted in his enthralling book, *Most Secret War.*[17] Among his many other claims to fame, Reg. Jones was a crack pistol shot. The story goes that one day at the Bridge of Feuch, a famous spot on Deeside where salmon can be seen leaping, he pulled out his pistol and killed a salmon in mid air with his first shot. Subsequently, opinion was divided as to whether this was a brilliant feat, or a despicable act, such as one might expect from a Sassenach.

Hazel and I enjoyed exploring the beautiful country round Aberdeen, often in company with the Eastwoods. We climbed Lochnagar several times, and marvelled at the *table d'orientation*, which Harry Butchart had personally carried to the summit and installed there. But we were mountain walkers, not ice or rock climbers, and I will never forget the experience of being taken on a climb with the Cairngorm club by my neurosurgical colleague, Martin Nicholls. We left Aberdeen at about 5 am in a bus which took us to Glen Clova. Even to my untutored eye there seemed to be several tolerably easy routes by which we could have climbed out of the glen, but the members of the club, who, unlike me, possessed ice axes, ropes, and special footwear and other clothing, regarded these with disdain. They wanted something more adventurous, and soon found this. As a result I was pushed and pulled upwards on what turned out to be the most frightening journey I have ever undertaken. For most of the descent we glissaded down snow slopes, and I quite enjoyed this until I wore a hole in my trousers. My wind jacket was not long enough to cover this, and the term *bum freezer*, used in the Navy to denote the short jacket worn by officers on formal occasions, took on a new significance as I skidded back to Glen Clova. Only after several stiff doses of rum and green ginger — the club's favourite tipple after returning from a climb — did I begin to recover.

In summer we enjoyed swimming at Balmedie beach, just north of Aberdeen. I would certainly not want to try this now, but the sea was warmer than one might have expected, and certainly warmer than it is on the Yorkshire coast, thanks to the gulf stream.

In January 1949, Hazel and I attended a conference at Swanwick in Derbyshire ('Dons' Swanwick'), organized by the British Student Christian Movement and the Christian Frontier

Council, where we studied a book entitled *The Crisis in the University*,[18] led by the author, Sir Walter Moberly, who was then Chairman of the University Grants Committee. There were about a hundred delegates, and they included not only professors, lecturers and tutors but also vice-chancellors, registrars and others concerned with university administration; and every university in Britain was represented. Moberly argued that the new British universities, while claiming to adopt a neutral attitude towards religion in general and Christianity in particular, were in fact hostile. It was generally agreed by members of the conference that simply to ignore the claims of Jesus was contrary to the purpose of a university, whose essential commitment must be to seek truth. Opinions differed, however, as to whether, as I hold, Christian beliefs should be subjected to the same rigorous scrutiny as any other propositions or whether, as some delegates claimed, there are no external criteria of truth that can be applied to Christianity because the Christian faith is fundamental and provides the criterion by which all other propositions must be judged.[19]

In the summer of the same year Hazel and I went with two Adelaide friends, Ren Potts and Barbara Kidman (later Barbara Potts), who were then at Oxford, to the south of France in our little Ford Anglia car. We had decided, on the advice of the Abrioux, to go to Antibes, and, when the first hotel we wrote to did not reply, chose another (l'Hotel Josse) more or less at random. We could not have been more fortunate. The hotel was set in a large garden between Antibes and Juan les Pins, and had an excellent restaurant that seemed unbelievably luxurious after the austerity that still prevailed in Britain. On our journey home we followed a scenic route to Briançon via Col d'Allos and Col de Galibier, which was breathtaking. We returned to the Hotel Josse in 1951 with Hazel's father and sister (Beth), and our firstborn, Keith, now some twenty months old, for whom we paid only a quarter of the adult *en pension* rate. As he ate almost as much as his parents this must have meant an appreciable loss to the hotel.

Geoffrey, our second son, was born in December 1951. The following year we spent our summer holiday in Cornwall, at a farmhouse near Helston. Keith, who had loved bathing in the warm water of the Mediterranean, rushed into the sea on the first day but was dismayed to find the water so cold. He beat a hasty retreat exclaiming, 'Daddy, it's wet!' Geoffrey, meanwhile, remained well wrapped up in his carry-cot.

When I had been in Professor Wilson's department for a little over a year, the Chair of Surgery at St Mary's Hospital in London became vacant, and he encouraged me to apply. I was delighted, and rather surprised, to be short-listed, and had a very friendly interview with Sir Arthur (later Lord) Porrit and his colleagues, but was not surprised when a St Mary's man, Charles Rob, was appointed. A few months later I applied for the Chair of Surgery at St Andrews University and was again short-listed, but I was beaten by Donald Douglas (later Sir Donald), a St Andrews graduate who was then Senior Lecturer with Sir James Learmonth in Edinburgh. My next application was for the Chair of Surgery in the University of Otago, Dunedin, New Zealand. The interview was held in London, with Sir Charles Hercus, the Dean of the Faculty of Medicine in Dunedin, in the chair, and this time, although there was a strong local candidate, I was appointed. Within a few days it was announced that my friend Hugh Robson, Senior Lecturer in the Department of Medicine, had been appointed to the Chair of Medicine in Adelaide, and another colleague, who was Senior Lecturer in Obstetrics and Gynaecology, had been appointed to the corresponding chair in the West Indies. This 'hat trick' caused something of a furore in medical circles in Aberdeen, and the British Medical Association gave a dinner in our honour.

The University of Otago generously offered to pay our first class fares by sea to Dunedin, and our removal expenses, so we booked passages on the *Dominion Monarch*, a very comfortable ship that carried only 500 passengers, all in first class, to Wellington via Capetown and Australia; and we bought a piano, and a new car, to take with us. I was examining in London when I bought the car; it was handed over to me at the Examination Hall in Queen Square — the only time, so far as I know, that a car has ever been delivered to this address — and I drove it back to Aberdeen.

We spent our last few days in Aberdeen with the Eastwoods, and then drove to London, where we stayed with two other friends, Derrick and Zoe Randall. I was able to go on using the car because the shipping line had agreed to load it the day before we left so that it would be unloaded as soon as we arrived in Wellington. Two days before our departure I was stopped in London by a policeman for passing a traffic light at the moment it turned red. I explained that we were on the point of leaving for New Zealand, but he did not believe this unlikely-sounding story, and once a week for the next six months a constable came to the Randalls' house to try to serve a summons on me. Finally, Zoe invited the officer to come in and have a cup of tea, and convinced him that we really were in New Zealand. Solemnly he took a stub of pencil out of his pocket, licked it, and crossed my name off his list.

Return to the Antipodes
Otago Chair of Surgery

The *Dominion Monarch*, which carried us to New Zealand, offered an abundance of excellent food, though some people were so habituated to queueing in post-war Britain that they started to queue outside the dining saloon half an hour before dinner was served, and continued to do this until we reached Las Palmas! This was our first port of call and we had an interesting time ashore, which included a visit to the Cathedral. Here Keith began to fidget and I wondered what to do, but a verger interpreted the signs correctly and conducted him to a well-appointed lavatory which we guessed belonged to the Dean, if not the Archbishop.

After leaving Las Palmas the weather remained fine and warm all the way to Capetown. Here we were met by the brother-in-law of my future colleague, John Borrie, who held the post of Harbour Engineer. He took us to many interesting places, including the Constantia Vineyard, the setting for the novel, *Wine of Good Hope*.[1]

Shortly before we reached Fremantle, Geoffrey developed quite severe gastroenteritis. He had improved a little by the time we reached Wellington, but was still rather dehydrated because he feared that drinking would cause him to start vomiting again.

In Wellington our luggage, and the car, were unloaded so promptly that we were able to embark on the ferry for Christchurch on the evening of the day we arrived. It was a very rough crossing, and both the boys were seasick though neither had been sick on the *Dominion Monarch*. Hazel and I escaped a similar fate only by taking to our bunks. Next morning we drove to Dunedin. We were nonplussed when the road came to an abrupt end at the Rangitata river but, after watching three cars drive on to the single track railway bridge to get across, we decided, with considerable trepidation, to do the same. The bridge appeared to be about half a mile long, and I wondered what we would do if we encountered a train; fortunately, however, the bridge was not quite as long as it looked, and, as we discovered later, carried only two or three trains daily in each direction.

In Dunedin we went straight to the house in London Street that we had arranged to rent from the University, and were delighted that the Hospital loaned us beds and other necessary furniture until our own furniture, which was somewhere on the high seas, arrived.

Although I had not been to New Zealand before, I had tried to make up for this by reading about the country and the University. Otago University, as I knew, was a Constituent College of the university of New Zealand. There were other Constituent Colleges in Auckland, Christchurch and Wellington, and two Agricultural Colleges, but none of these had a medical school. Otago University produced about 100 doctors a year, and each year approximately the same number of doctors who had qualified elsewhere migrated to New Zealand.

I had wondered how a city of just under 100,000 inhabitants could provide enough patients for such a large medical school, and had been told that this was partly because many patients from outside Dunedin were referred to the Dunedin Hospital, and partly because about three quarters of the students spent their last year in either Auckland, Christchurch or Wellington. When I arrived in Dunedin, however, I found that, while the system of distributing final year students between four centres seemed to be working well, there were still not enough patients in the Dunedin Hospital to give adequate clinical instruction to the fourth and fifth year students and the final year students who remained. This was not due to a lack of beds — indeed, when a new hospital, Waikari, was opened as an addition to the Dunedin Hospital, there were more beds than we could fill — but to a shortage of patients. For this there appeared to be two main reasons:

Firstly, because of the way in which the Social Security system operated, the cost to a patient of treatment in a private hospital was remarkably small, and many patients preferred this to treatment in the teaching hospital.

Secondly, far fewer patients than I would have expected were referred to Dunedin from elsewhere. As I found to my amazement, hospital boards all over the country, like fire-brigade boards and harbour boards, were elected on the same franchise as town councils, and the boards of peripheral hospitals tried to make their hospital as self-sufficient as possible. If a patient needed neurosurgery, cardiac surgery or supervoltage X-ray therapy, referral was unavoidable, but many other patients were treated locally when it would have been in their interest to have been referred to Dunedin.

All that could be done in the short term was to try to attract patients by providing a good service, and to spread the teaching load as widely as possible. My part-time colleagues in general surgery, of whom the two senior were Stanley Wilson and Norman Speight, already did their fair share of undergraduate clinical teaching; my colleagues in the surgical specialties did much less, but, with perseverance, I managed to persuade them to give some clinical instruction of a general kind to junior students in addition to instructing senior students in their particular specialty.

It seemed clear to me, however, that the only long-term solution to the problem was to establish a medical school in Auckland — a city with a population some five times that of Dunedin — and greatly reduce the number of medical students doing their clinical work in Dunedin, or possibly have only pre-clinical students there. Soon after I arrived in New Zealand I had the opportunity of putting this suggestion to a Royal Commission headed by Mr Justice Barraclough that had been appointed to look into the matter. It was opposed by various powerful voices in Dunedin, but three years later commonsense prevailed and the Auckland Medical School was established.

Another feature of the New Zealand medical scene that worried me was the unambitious attitude of many students. Of course, no one wanted to fail, but only a few wanted to distinguish themselves; the majority preferred a position of decent obscurity in the middle of the class. Moreover, when it came to postgraduate work, the high-flyers went to Britain, the United States or Australia, and many of them did not return. One reason, undoubtedly, was that the income of specialists in New Zealand was often less than that of general practitioners of the same age. It is significant that, while the development of plastic surgery in the United Kingdom was due in considerable measure to New Zealanders like Harold Gillies, Archibald McIndoe and Rainsford Mowlem, there was no specialist plastic surgery service in Dunedin when I was there, and it fell to me — a general surgeon — to establish a unit for the treatment of burns.

It was important for me to become integrated as quickly as possible with the hospital, the medical school, the university as a whole, and the community in which we were going to live. Two events helped to speed this process: my inaugural lecture in the university, and an address I was invited to give in the Dunedin town hall as part of the annual Empire Day celebrations.

In many universities in the United Kingdom it is customary for a newly appointed professor, soon after his arrival, to give a public lecture on any subject he chooses, subject only to the proviso that it should be comprehensible to colleagues in different fields, and to students. This gives the newcomer an opportunity to engage, if he wishes, in the salutary exercise of examining his own particular discipline in relation to the purpose of the university as a whole. The possibility that the University of Otago, with its origins so firmly in Scotland, would not observe this excellent custom, did not enter my mind, and I spent quite a long time on the voyage to New Zealand preparing what I would say, but when we arrived the Vice-Chancellor said that no one had ever given such a lecture in Dunedin. It seemed high time to inaugurate Inaugural Lectures, so I decided to give mine and see whether anyone turned up to hear it. It proved much more successful than I had dared to hope. The Vice-Chancellor graciously took the chair; there was a large audience; and the lecture was subsequently published.[2]

I began by discussing three different views of the purpose of a university: *intellectual culture*, as defined by Newman in *The Idea of a University*,[3] *vocational training*, and *research*, and argued that these were not mutually exclusive. Newman himself held that study of the classics alone was sufficient to train the mind and enable it to 'bring a power and a grace to every occupation which it undertakes', but he accepted that study in other fields, including law and medicine, could achieve the same end. Today,

22. Myself leaving The Bield, about 1960.

23. Walking on the Pentland Hills with all the family
except Geoffrey.

24. Officers of the Transplantation Society received by
    Queen Juliana at the Hague in 1978.
    Front row (L to R) Dr Merrill, Prof. Hamburger,
    H.M. The Queen, Dr Russell, myself and
    Dr Congdon. Second row (L to R) Dr van Bekkum,
    Dr Ostrowsky, Dr van Rood, Dr Balner, Dr Greep,

with the virtual disappearance of the leisured class, the demand for vocational training is greater than ever; the problem is how to combine such training with education in the more general sense, and I tried to show how this could be achieved through the study of medicine in general and surgery in particular. The search for truth is complementary to the other functions of a university. It must be unfettered by considerations of expediency. This claim is often defended on the ground that a discovery which does not appear to have any immediate application often proves later to be of great practical importance, but this is begging the question. Truth is worth pursuing for its own sake, and a university that does not recognize this is not worthy of the name. Of course, this does not mean that there is no place for applied research in universities. Applied research contributes enormously to human prosperity, and indeed to our prospects of survival, and to denigrate it is, to say the least, an absurd academic affectation; but it is not the be all and end all of a university.

The invitation from the Mayor of Dunedin to give an address in the Town Hall came as a complete surprise. I did not know that Empire Day was observed with such ceremony in New Zealand, and was amazed to be asked to play such a leading role in the celebrations. I chose as my topic *The Meaning of Commonwealth*, and discussed the conditions under which the British Commonwealth might continue to exist, and to play a significant role, in the post-war world. After the ceremony the Mayor took me to his room and, after giving me a stiff drink that I badly needed, said, 'That was quite a good address, but in New Zealand we prefer the term British Empire to Commonwealth.' I was dumbfounded. Can 'time run back', I mused, 'and fetch the age of gold',[4] or are these people living in a fool's paradise? Maybe they were, but how heartwarming.

When I arrived in Dunedin construction of the new building promised for my department had not begun, and the building was not ready for occupation until some three years later. Meanwhile, the professor of pathology, Eric D'Ath, very kindly lent me office and laboratory accommodation in his department, and I had access to the Faculty of Medicine animal house, where we established inbred strains of mice and rats, and where there was also good accommodation for large animals.

Several of my colleagues in the Department of Surgery were involved in clinical research, including Anthony James and Richard Robinson in neurosurgery, and Norman Nisbet in orthopaedics; and one, John Borrie, was also actively engaged in experimental surgery in sheep. There was also distinguished work in progress in other departments in the medical school, notably Professor Horace Smirk's work on hypertension in the Department of Medicine; Professor Archie MacIntyre's work on neurophysiology, which continued the distinguished tradition established by Sir John Eccles, who subsequently won the Nobel Prize for Medicine in 1963; work on thyroid disease and antithyroid drugs by Drs Purvis, Griesbach and Kennedy in a New Zealand Medical Research Council Unit that had been established by Sir Charles Hercus: and work on experimental carcinogenesis by Drs Franz and Marianne Bielschowsky. There was an active Medical Research Society, and its Proceedings, edited by Professor Norman Edson, were indexed in the *Index Medicus.*

I had appointed Victor Pearce, who was already on the staff of the hospital, as my part-time senior lecturer in clinical surgery. I was able to appoint also a senior lecturer in experimental surgery and a graduate research assistant, and the first of these posts was filled by Dr Garcia Llaurado, a Spanish doctor — he preferred to call himself a Catalan — who came to us from the Postgraduate Medical School in London, where he had been working with Dr C. L. Cope on an adrenocortical hormone now called aldosterone.

It takes time to establish a new clinical department but within a few months I was able to resume research in the field of tissue and organ transplantation. This included five main topics:

(1) The behaviour of allografts in 'privileged' sites.
(2) Induction of tolerance to allografts after birth.
(3) The effect of cortisone and other hormones on the behaviour of allografts of skin and endocrine tissue.
(4) The use of cooling before and during transplantation to promote graft survival.
(5) The use of stored human skin in treating severe burns.

The following brief account of this work is intended for the general reader. The numbers relate to the bibliography I have deposited with the Royal Society.[5]

Our study of the behaviour of allografts in the anterior chamber of the eye (see Chapter 11) had shown that such grafts become less vulnerable to immunological attack as time goes on, apparently as the result of changes in the graft rather than in the host. Work in my own laboratory and elsewhere suggested that a similar phenomenon, which we called *graft adaptation*, might also occur with grafts in other privileged sites, and with grafts in hosts made partially tolerant of donor tissue. The term was used in a purely descriptive sense, and we envisaged — as now seems to be the case — that adaptation could occur in a variety of ways.[6]

The fact that allografts are rejected except under special circumstances raises the question of how the mammalian foetus, which possesses transplantation antigens inherited from the father as well as from the mother, manages to survive and develop. We investigated this in rats, and showed first that pregnancy proceeded normally even when the mother, before mating, had been immunized by a skin graft from the prospective father. In later experiments we removed just one of several foetuses from the uterus of either a normal or a pre-immunized mother, and transplanted pieces of foetal tissue intramuscularly to the mother. The results led us to conclude that the placental barrier, which normally prevents mingling of maternal and foetal blood, is sufficient, and also necessary, to protect the foetus from the immunological hazards of pregnancy,[7] though other factors may also contribute.

The fact that we had been able to induce tolerance to skin allografts in rats up to two weeks after birth, made me wonder whether the same could be done in human infants. Clearly, if tolerance could be induced to the tissues of one or other parent, for example, the problem of treating burns in children in whom there was extensive loss of skin — a problem we encountered surprisingly frequently in the burns unit in Dunedin — would be greatly simplified. I discussed the matter in a lecture I gave in the Medical School, and privately with various colleagues, and at the time it was generally agreed that this would not involve any danger if the recipient were male, though the possibility of causing Rhesus sensitization would have to be excluded first if the baby was female.

I was still pondering the question of whether the procedure would be ethically justifiable when a technician who had heard my lecture asked me if I would attempt to induce tolerance to his tissues in his newborn son. After full discussion with both parents I agreed, and proceeded to inject blood leucocytes from the father intramuscularly to the baby. This had no discernable deleterious effect so, six months later, I transplanted a very small piece of the father's skin to the baby under local anaesthesia. I repeated the procedure in another newborn boy, again after very full discussion with the parents. In each case the graft took, but was subsequently slowly rejected. We were disappointed at the time, though very relieved later when it was discovered that foreign leucocytes injected to newborn mice and rats can react against the recipient and cause a serious disorder known as graft-versus-host disease. There would seem to be two reasons, either of which is sufficient, to account for the fact that our infants came to no harm: we had injected the father's leucocytes intramuscularly rather than intravenously, and the newborn human infant is immunologically more mature than the newborn rat.[8]

While I was in Dunedin the first edition of my textbook, *Surgery for Dental Students*, was published. I also made considerable progress with *The Transplantation of Tissues and Organs*, but this was proving to be a Herculean task.

Soon after we arrived in Dunedin the Queen and the Duke of Edinburgh came to New Zealand on a royal visit. Their visit to Dunedin was something of a non-event so far as we were concerned because, like many others who were not native-born New Zealanders, we were not invited to any of the official functions, including Her Majesty's visit to the University, so Hazel and I decided to take our summer holiday near Auckland while the Queen was in Dunedin.

Not surprisingly, New Zealand attracts many less exalted visitors, who often seek to combine business with pleasure, for it is a beautiful country, with wonderful opportunities for climbing, mountain walking, skiing, trout fishing, and other outdoor delights, and New Zealanders are very friendly people. We were fortunate, during my time in Dunedin, in being able to welcome many distinguished visitors to the Medical School, among them three retired Edinburgh Professors, J. C. Brash, Murray Drennan and Sir Sidney Smith; Sir Stanford Cade; Robert Milnes Walker; Francis Stock; Sir James Learmonth; Leonard Colebrook, FRS; and Peter (later Sir Peter) Medawar, FRS.

25. At the Hotel de Ville, Paris, in 1957. Dr Kourilsky is signing the visitors' book; on his left are Prof. Medawar and Dr May.

26. Myself with Mrs Kazir and the President of Israel (Dr Kazir), when I presided over the meeting of the Transplantation Society in Jerusalem in 1974.

Robert Milnes Walker, from Bristol, and Francis Stock, who at the time was Professor of Surgery in Hong Kong, both had wide experience in treating patients with bleeding into the oesophagus as a result of cirrhosis of the liver, by a procedure known as *porto-caval anastomosis*, in which the excessive pressure in the portal venous system is reduced by establishing a connection between the portal vein and the inferior vena cava. From time to time I was asked to see patients with bleeding of this kind, and learned much about how to manage them from these two visitors. Milnes Walker's hobby was bird-watching, and he was delighted when, as a way of expressing my thanks to him, I got permission to take him to see the closely guarded colony of albatrosses that had become established on the Otago Peninsula.

Sir Stanford Cade told us about the remarkable results he was obtaining in some patients with disseminated breast cancer in whom a temporary remission had been obtained by removal of the ovaries, by going on to remove the adrenal glands as well. Again, the procedure was palliative, not curative, but the improvement in quality of life in some patients was dramatic and long-lasting. Sir Stanford had been one of my examiners when I sat the FRCS examination, and I had heard how, after the First World War, he had come to London as a refugee; had managed to qualify in Medicine while working in the evenings as a waiter at the Ritz Hotel; had, in due course, been appointed to the Staff of Westminster Hospital; and, during World War II, had headed the Medical Service of the Royal Air Force. I was delighted to have this opportunity of getting to know a man who was one of my heroes.

The Faculty of Medicine gave a dinner in Cade's honour at the Dunedin (Fernhill) Club, in the course of which I listened open-mouthed when I heard our Dean, who knew nothing of Cade's background, say, 'Sir Stanford, what did you do during the war?', without specifying which war. 'Oh,' replied Cade, 'I have held only two military ranks. In the first world war I was a private in the Belgian Army; in the second I was an Air Vice-Marshall in the Royal Air Force.'

Leonard Colebrook gave us an entrancing first hand account of how, during the war, he had contrived to bring together Thomas Gibson and Peter Medawar to investigate the possibility of using allografts of skin in treating air force personnel and others who sustained severe burns during the Battle of Britain.

Every three years the Faculty of Medicine had the opportunity of inviting someone from outside New Zealand to come to Dunedin for a month as Visiting Professor, and the time had come to fill this post. It was easy, after Colebrook's visit, to convince most of my colleagues that Medawar would be the best possible choice if he could be persuaded to come, but I found to my dismay that the Dean, without consulting the Faculty, had already invited someone else. He had, of course, no right to do this, but Deans are sometimes a law unto themselves, and, as a newcomer, I was disposed to accept this *fait accompli*. Fortunately, some of my colleagues were made of sterner stuff and, in the end, the Dean had to withdraw his unauthorised invitation. He was far from pleased, but the invitation to Medawar was sent off and, to my great delight, accepted.

The visit was a resounding success. Medawar's lectures aroused great interest that extended beyond the confines of the medical school. For my orthopaedic colleague, Norman Nisbet, meeting Medawar was like seeing a great light, such as St Paul saw on the road to Damascus, and he became so hooked on the idea of research that soon afterwards he gave up his position in Dunedin to become Director of Research at the Robert Jones and Agnes Hunt Orthopaedic Hospital in Oswestry. For me, the visit was an opportunity to engage in joint research with a great experimental biologist and, as the result of detailed planning before Medawar arrived, we managed to complete a study of the extent to which skin allografts to newborn rats induce specific immunological tolerance of donor-strain tissue.[9] I had long been aware of Medawar's intellectual brilliance, but it was a revelation to see how much he enjoyed working in the laboratory, and what a skilful pair of hands he possessed.

In January 1956 I flew to the United States to give two papers — one entitled *Postpartum induction of tolerance to homologous skin in rats*, the other *Cellular and humoral factors in the immunity to skin homografts: Experiments with a porous membrane* — at the Second Homotransplantation Conference organized by the New York Academy of Sciences. I stopped on the way at Honolulu, where I had a lesson on surfing on Waikiki beach and, after a few attempts, managed to ride in on the board in a standing position. I fell off a few times and sustained some painful abrasions from the coral, but this did not lessen my sense of achievement. One had to watch out for surf canoes that came in very fast; on the other hand, it seemed to be generally accepted that there was very little risk of being attacked by a shark, though no one seemed to know why this should be so.

I flew from Honolulu to San Francisco, and from there to Minneapolis, primarily to meet Irvine McQuarrie's successor, Robert Good, who was making a name for himself in cellular immunology. It was quite a shock to get off the plane in Minneapolis in a blinding snowstorm, with a temperature of -20 degrees F, two days after surfing in Honolulu.

I was the only person to read two papers at the New York meeting, and both were well received. It was a great pleasure to meet old friends and make new ones, among them John Converse, Gustav Dammin, Ernst Eichwald, David Hume, Nathan Kaliss, Hilary Koprowski, H. S. (Jerry) Lawrence, Joseph Murray, R. D. Owen, Richmond Prehn, Felix Rapaport, Richard Varco, and Guy Voisin. I came home via Chicago, San Francisco and Honolulu. In San Francisco I stayed with Frank Gerbode, a distinguished heart surgeon, and his wife Martha. They took me one evening to one of San Francisco's excellent Chinese restaurants, where we were received like royalty because Frank had recently performed a very successful operation on the son of the proprietor.

On the trip home one engine failed not long after we left Honolulu, and the pilot decided to make an unscheduled stop at Canton Island. As we had taken on enough fuel in Honolulu to fly to Fiji much of this had to be jettisoned, and it made me feel uneasy to see fuel streaming out close to where, during the night, I had seen the red glow of the engine exhausts, but nothing untoward occurred and we landed safely on this strange atoll. At that time it was a condominium, governed jointly by Britain and the United States. They each had a post office, which issued its own stamps, but shared the airport.

Dunedin was a pleasant place in which to live. We rented a comfortable house with an adequate garden from the University and, as mentioned previously, the Hospital lent us necessary furniture until our own arrived. This came by cargo ship and arrived in due course at Port Chalmers, some seven miles from Dunedin. I tried to arrange for the furniture to be collected from there by truck, but the New Zealand Government Railways, who controlled the port, insisted that it should go by rail to Dunedin and be collected by truck from there. As a result, our furniture spent a week in an open railway wagon, during which time it rained heavily every day. The damage was considerable. Two lovely bow fronted chests of drawers and other pieces had to be repolished, and some soft furnishings were a total loss. The railway authorities tried to maintain that the damage had occurred at sea, but our insurance assessor established that the water that poured out of the huge packing case in which the furniture was stowed was salt free, and the railways eventually had to pay up in full. We were to discover that bureaucratic behaviour by public authorities was, alas, even more common in New Zealand than it had been in Britain.

Fortunately we were well installed in our new home when the time came for Hazel to go into hospital for the birth of our third child. We were delighted when we found that we had a daughter, and named her *Margaret* after my own mother, and *Isabel* after my stepmother. Hazel's sister, Beth, had come over from Australia to help when mother and daughter came home, and when Beth left we found a mothercraft nurse — in New Zealand terminology, a Karitani nurse — who was excellent.

The Hospital was only five minutes walk from our house, the University about ten minutes away, and the city centre only slightly more in the opposite direction to the University.

We found a good kindergarten for Keith, and later a good primary school. There was some excellent music to be heard, especially chamber music and recitals by visiting soloists, among them a young American pianist, Julius Katchen, who impressed us greatly. As mentioned earlier, there were also excellent facilities for outdoor recreation, including tennis, swimming, sailing, mountain walking (plus, of course, ice and rock climbing for those who liked such hazardous pursuits), duck shooting, and trout fishing in both lakes and rivers. I had always preferred river fishing to lake fishing, and found that landing a four pound rainbow trout hooked on wet fly with light tackle in a fast flowing, snow fed, mountain stream was most exhilarating. A purist might claim that to catch small trout on dry fly in rivers like the Deben is more skilful, but it is probably truer to say that the skills required are different. Rugby football in New Zealand was more in the nature of a religion than a recreation;[10] cricket was not quite so serious, but was beginning to catch up.

Our first summer holiday was spent north of Auckland in a cottage loaned to us by a colleague; others were spent near Nelson. In the winter of 1954 we spent a week at *The Hermitage*, at the foot of Mount Cook, and learned what a glacier really looks like. Towards the end of the year it became apparent that I was suffering from thyrotoxicosis. The colleagues I consulted decided to treat this medically, and the condition was brought under control more quickly than I expected; sufficiently quickly, indeed, for Hazel and me to walk the famous Milford Track[10] two or three months later with a party of middle-aged doctors and their wives. This experience was memorable for the incredibly beautiful scenery, and also for the voracious sandflies we encountered, which seemed to be completely insensitive to any of the insect repellants we had been advised to bring with us. When we returned to the United Kingdom I was advised to stop taking antithyroid drugs, and despite this the thyrotoxicosis did not recur. It seems clear, in retrospect, that it was due to an excessive intake of iodine while I was in New Zealand. This occurred because, to combat endemic goitre, which is common in New Zealand, iodide is added in quite large amounts to table salt and flour, and I was in the habit of eating a lot of salt. This experience raises questions about the extent to which well-meaning public health authorities should be allowed to add substances of various kinds, including, for example, fluoride to combat dental caries, to drinking water or food. It certainly lends support to the view that it is better to encourage people to take such substances themselves rather than make it almost impossible to avoid them.

Later in 1954 I again became a patient when my colleague, Victor Pearse, repaired an inguinal hernia that had developed on the opposite side to the one dealt with by Bill Wilson in Aberdeen. This time I thought it might be salutary for a surgeon to see what it was like to have this operation done under local anaesthesia. The experience was by no means unpleasant, but I concluded that a general anaesthetic makes things easier for both patient and surgeon, and is to be preferred unless there is some special reason for using local.

Relations between the white ('Pakeha') and Maori populations seemed at first sight extraordinarily good, though we found later that they were not quite as good as we had thought. The general outlook in New Zealand was remarkably egalitarian except in two domains: in sport, which was fiercely competitive, and in the gentlemen's clubs in the main cities — the only places I found where one could put one's shoes outside the bedroom door at night and know that they would come back immaculately polished. The white population was very homogeneous, reflecting the fact that New Zealand, unlike Australia, was never used as a dumping ground for convicts. A friend of ours, Mary Nisbet, told us when we first arrived that the social spectrum ranged from lower-middle to middle-middle class. Apart from the fact that this left out of account wealthy sheep farmers, who at that time constituted a class of landed gentry, it seemed to sum up the situation quite well.

A feature of my job that I much appreciated was that I was expected to make annual visits to Auckland, Wellington and Christchurch, to see how those of our students who were doing their final year there were getting on. I usually managed to take an extra day or two as holiday, and enjoyed getting to know these cities. I have particularly happy memories of a weekend cruise to Kawau Island, near Auckland, in company with Sir Douglas Robb, then doyen of New Zealand surgery, and Sir Heneage Ogilvie, who had recently retired from the staff of Guy's Hospital and was visiting New Zealand. Sir Heneage was an experienced sailor, and like me would have preferred to be on board a sailing boat rather than a motor cruiser, but it was, nevertheless, an enjoyable and interesting experience.

To the great delight of the whole family my father came to visit us towards the end of 1955, and again a year later. He was still remarkably active, and mentally as bright as ever. We discussed almost everything under the sun, including the possibility of our moving one day to another job.

Why should we consider leaving this beautiful country? As pointed out earlier, the population of Dunedin was too small to support its large medical school, but one could envisage ways in which this might change. What was more intractable was the fact that so many of our best students left New Zealand soon after graduating, and never came back, except perhaps for a holiday. Those who stayed at home, and the one hundred or so doctors who immigrated to New Zealand every year from the United

Kingdom, were often content to rusticate, so far as their profession was concerned, and directed their competitive instincts into other channels. They were eager enough to attack the 'steep and rugged pathways' if this was interpreted in a literal geographic sense, but not otherwise. This lack of ambition extended into other fields. One of my students — by a remarkable coincidence his mother had been my music teacher in Melbourne when I was a boy — had remarkable talent as a composer, possibly amounting to genius. On three occasions, while a medical student, he entered for, and won, a prize for composition in the Faculty of Music. He ended up as a general practitioner in a small country town; a worthwhile job, certainly, but I am still haunted by the feeling that, had he chosen differently, the world might have gained another Leonard Bernstein or Percy Grainger; perhaps even another Mozart. Of course, if he had chosen that path, he would have had to leave New Zealand, just as Ernest Rutherford, a genius in another field, had to leave New Zealand; but why not?

In 1954 I applied for no less than four Chairs of Surgery that were vacant in London, Sheffield, Oxford and Melbourne respectively. So far as the chairs in the United Kingdom were concerned, I was given to understand that I should not be considering leaving New Zealand until I had been there for at least five years. A year before this time had elapsed, however, applications were invited for two surgical chairs in Edinburgh, the Regius Chair of Clinical Surgery, and the Chair of Surgical Science, that was intended to replace the University Chair of Surgery. The particulars relating to the latter chair stated that the person appointed would have charge of two wards in the Edinburgh Royal Infirmary, in which he would be expected to undertake clinical teaching of undergraduates, and be responsible for the training of postgraduates including, of course, his own house surgeons and registrars. He would not be responsible for arranging courses of formal lectures for undergraduates, though he might be invited by the Regius Professor of Clinical Surgery to give a limited number of lectures himself. He would be provided with adequate facilities and staff to develop both clinical and laboratory research. The new name for the chair seemed to me ill-chosen, but the job description sounded very attractive and, knowing from many visits what a lovely city Edinburgh was, I sent off an application. To my surprise I was offered the post without being called for interview. The one drawback was the cost of moving, which was considerable. The University of Otago generously declined my offer to repay some of the cost of bringing us to New Zealand four years previously, but the University of Edinburgh offered me only £60 as their contribution to the cost of transporting myself, my wife, our three children and all our worldly goods from Dunedin — precisely what I would have been offered had we been moving from, say, Dundee or Glasgow. Despite this niggardliness, Hazel and I decided that I should accept the position, and we managed to reduce the cost a little by travelling on a cargo ship — the *Empire Star* — in which I had a free passage as ship's surgeon. There were only eleven passengers including Hazel and the children, and my main duties seemed to be to accompany the Captain on his daily tour of inspection and then drink a gin and tonic — the only aperitif he permitted — with him before lunch. As things turned out, however, I think I earned my passage.

My first problem arose when the ship was about midway between Wellington and Panama, and the Captain developed severe toothache. He had a grossly carious wisdom tooth, and the only thing to do seemed to be to extract it. I was a little nervous, the patient very much more so, and there is no doubt that I used a good deal more local anaesthetic than was really necessary, but I managed to extract the tooth, the whole of the tooth (albeit in fragments), and nothing but the tooth, and we both lived to tell the tale.

As a *quid pro quo* I asked the captain if I could come up to the bridge when we were passing through the Panama Canal. 'Doc.', he said, 'the bridge is yours; I won't be there.' I was puzzled, but when the day came I found that during the passage the pilot is not simply an adviser, as in other parts of the world, but assumes command of the ship. Our captain hated this, and it was his custom to descend from his lofty perch and spend the day with his passengers, leaving the mate as his representative on the bridge. So why not the doctor as well?

The pilot, an American citizen, was an interesting man who clearly knew his job. For the time being he was taking ships from the Pacific to the Atlantic and returning by train; half of his colleagues did the same, and the others took ships in the opposite direction. For entering and leaving the locks we had lines fore and aft on each side to locomotives, termed mules, that ran on rails, and with the help of these, and the engines running dead slow, the whole manoeuvre went very smoothly indeed. The pilot never raised his voice; he occasionally spoke softly to the quartermaster at the wheel, or to one of the sailors manning the engine room telegraphs, and gave hand signals to the men driving the mules. I have always enjoyed watching, or listening to, people doing a difficult job expertly — Donald Bradman batting, Alfred Brendel playing the piano or Marcel Dupré the organ, Richard Sweet performing an oesophagectomy, a pilot landing a jumbo jet when the runway is only just long enough as at Hong Kong or Gibraltar, an expert gardener cutting a hedge, and so on — irrespective of whether or not I know enough about what they are doing to appreciate the difficulties. This was no exception.

The second problem arose some days later when the ship ran out of tonic water. The Captain felt very deprived; and what had been a happy ship was plunged in gloom. The Chief Steward, who seemed in imminent danger of being made to walk the plank, appealed to me for help, though without much hope that it would be forthcoming. Remember John Hunter's admonition, *Don't think, try the experiment,* I retired to my surgery and, an hour or two later, had managed to produce a solution of sugar and quinine sulphate which, when added in the right proportion to soda water, of which the ship had plenty, made it taste, and indeed look, remarkably like tonic water. Tell the Captain, I advised the Chief Steward, that after an intensive search you have found a couple of cases of tonic that had somehow been overlooked, and when you pour his drink put a teaspoonful of my additive in his gin before filling up his glass with soda water. This was more successful than we had dared to hope, and once again we had a happy ship. We did not tell the Captain what had happened until we were just off Beachy Head. His initial reaction was one of indignation at having been deceived in this way, but he quickly got over this and told me that I was the best doctor who had ever sailed with him.

After picking up the Channel Pilot the ship continued on its way to Dunkirk, where the French dock workers unloaded in twenty-four hours a cargo of wool and chilled meat that it had taken three weeks to load in Wellington. The next day we disembarked in Tilbury.

Taking root in Edinburgh

We were met at Tilbury by my cousin, Patrick Burgin, and received a rousing welcome in London from relatives on both sides of the family. I stayed in London at the Athenaeum for a few days, and then went north by train to reconnoitre the situation in Edinburgh, particularly as regards housing and schools for the children, and in the Medical School.

I had written to my colleague-to-be, John Bruce, to appraise him of our arrival. He seemed surprised that my letter should have been written from the Athenaeum, of which he was not then a member. There were, I fear, some more surprises in store for him, but he and his wife, Molly, gave me a very warm welcome. My recollection of my first few days in Edinburgh is rather hazy; the impression that predominates is that of a delightful, but rather alcoholic, party, which moved between the Bruce's house in Moray Place, the house of Sir Walter and Lady Mercer in Murrayfield, and the New Club.

Our first priority, after ensuring that we had a roof over our heads, was to arrange schooling for the children. Our intention was to send them initially to day schools in Edinburgh, and to move the boys, and possibly also Margaret, to boarding schools in England later.

We sent Margaret, who was only five, to an old-fashioned kindergarten-cum-primary school, St Mungo's, run by Miss Christine Lovell in Currie. It proved to be an excellent choice, and Margaret stayed there until she obtained a place as a day girl at St George's School for Girls in Murrayfield. The boys went to the junior school at George Watson's College but later we moved them to a boarding preparatory school, Drumtochty Castle.

From there Keith went to Bootham School and Geoffrey to Sedbergh.

My reconnaissance of Edinburgh Medical School was far from reassuring. I had been promised two wards in the Edinburgh Royal Infirmary, and a free-standing building, named after Sir David Wilkie, in the Medical School to house my academic department and provide laboratory accommodation, including facilities for animal experiments.

It seemed reasonable that my wards [13/14] should have been taken over temporarily by two surgeons on the staff of the Infirmary, J. R. (Derrick) Cameron and James Ross; what was disconcerting was that neither showed signs of being prepared to move out now that I had arrived. But I had the backing of both the Hospital Board and the University, and had by this time considerable experience of dealing with passive resistance in various forms. Mr Cameron moved out within a week or two; Mr Ross, although of the same age as I was, became my Assistant Surgeon, and a valued colleague. Both in due course served as President of the Royal College of Surgeons of Edinburgh, and both became firm friends.

The situation as regards my academic department was more difficult to resolve. When, on the retirement of Sir James Learmonth, the University decided, as my colleague John Bruce aptly put it, to revert to having 'two surgical chairs instead of the professorial sofa', it had assumed that the new Regius Professor of Clinical Surgery would somehow find all his office accommodation, and any laboratory space he needed, in the Royal Infirmary, but had not suggested how this might be done. Bruce and I were appointed on the same day, but he was already installed in Edinburgh whereas I had to give six months notice before leaving Dunedin. It is scarcely surprising therefore that when I arrived a substantial part of the Wilkie building was occupied by the Department of Clinical Surgery; what made the situation even more difficult was that the rest was occupied by people appointed by my predecessor. One of these, E. J. Delorme, joined my MRC Group (*v. infra*); another, Professor J. W. McLeod, FRS, a distinguished retired microbiologist, posed more of a problem. He had been a widower but recently remarried and showed no signs of being ready to move; indeed, the McLeods looked as if they might well outlive the Woodruffs.

McLeod was a delightful man and was doing useful work, but I needed the space for my department and was very relieved when room was found for him in the Department of Microbiology. In retrospect these manoeuvrings have their amusing side, but at the time they were very disturbing. Fortunately I enjoyed the wise counsel and firm support of the Principal, Sir Edward Appleton, the Dean of the Faculty of Medicine, Professor George Montgomery, the Secretary of the University, Mr Charles Stewart, and many colleagues.

The name given to my chair did not indicate its real scope, and I was delighted when, on the retirement of Sir John Bruce from the Regius Chair of Clinical Surgery, the University agreed to rename it the *University Chair of Surgery.* But what mattered at the time, as I said in my Inaugural Lecture,[1] was whether or not it provided 'a favourable opportunity for a surgeon with some interest in fundamental biological problems to contribute to the progress of surgery and to help extend the frontiers of knowledge'. I argued that it did, and cited examples of how biology has contributed to surgical progress, beginning with the work of Pasteur and Lister, and also of how surgeons have made observations of fundamental biological importance in the fields of tissue transplantation and cancer.

One of the uncertainties facing a newly appointed clinical professor is the extent to which his own particular clinical interests are already well catered for by existing members of the hospital staff. Here I was very fortunate. In New Zealand I had become interested in peripheral vascular surgery, and in Edinburgh I inherited the peripheral vascular unit that Sir James Learmonth had established. Dr C. C. Burt held an appointment as full-time physician in this unit, and proved to be a delightful and extremely able colleague. A. I. S. MacPherson — his name was known to me before I came to Edinburgh as a cricketer who had scored a famous century against a team called *The Triflers* that my cousin, John Brown, once ran — had an unofficial attachment to the unit, and access to some of my beds, until he obtained beds of his own in another ward and we were able to divide the peripheral vascular surgery of the hospital between us. As in other surgical charges in the Royal Infirmary we had a full load of general surgery in a broad sense, including responsibility for the treatment of fractures and urology, as well as surgery of the gastrointestinal tract, the breast and the neck, and this situation was slower to change in Edinburgh than in many other teaching centres.

The house staff in Wards 13/14 had been appointed by Sir James Learmonth. It is remarkable that one of the House Surgeons, Gordon Clunie, later became Professor of Surgery in Melbourne; the other, Alan Langlands, became Professor of Radiotherapy in Sydney, and the Senior House Officer, Gerald Milton, became Professor of Surgery in Sydney. My first Registrar was J. E. Newsam, who was later appointed a Consultant Urologist at the Western General Hospital. I appointed as Lecturer/Senior Registrar Bruce Torrance, who became a Consultant Surgeon on the staff of the Manchester Royal Infirmary, and he was succeeded by Bernard Nolan, who became closely associated with the development of renal transplantation in Edinburgh and in due course became the senior surgeon in wards 13/14 (Fig 15).

Designing a new clinical department was a challenging and exciting task. I felt that every doctor working in my wards should feel part of the department, irrespective of whether he or she was employed by the National Health Service or by the University; there should, on the other hand, be room in the department for at least two senior scientists who were not surgeons, and who need not necessarily be medically qualified, who could devote their whole time to research. To produce research of world quality we would have to define fairly closely the area in which we were going to work; initially this was to be tissue and organ transplantation, but was extended later to include the interaction of cancer and host when we became aware of the many ways in which this resembles the interaction between normal tissue transplants and their hosts. In those days shortage of money was not the serious limitation that it is today, and the university agreed to my proposals. I felt nevertheless that it would be appropriate to try to obtain some independent financial support from the Medical Research Council, and suggested to the Secretary, Sir Harold Himsworth, that the Council should set up an MRC Research Group on Transplantation in my department under my chairmanship. After a site visit the Council agreed, and we were in business.

The first person appointed to this group was Dr Norman Anderson. He was an Edinburgh graduate and had been house surgeon to Tom Gibson, the Glasgow plastic surgeon who had collaborated with Peter Medawar in the experiments that established the immunological nature of allograft rejection.[2] Soon afterwards Donald Michie and James Howard were appointed non-clinical senior lecturers and became honorary members of the group. Donald Michie had taken a first in classics at Oxford. One of his hobbies was breeding mice, and he became intrigued by the coat colours of the offspring in relation to those of the parents. Someone advised him to ask Professor R. A. Fisher about this so he made a pilgrimage to Rothamstead Agricultural Experimental Station to see Fisher, and decided then and there to become a geneticist. He came to my department from the Royal Veterinary College, London, where he had been working with Professor Amoroso. He was a brilliant man, but apt to become bored with what he was doing and move on to something else. He was interested in designing machines to play games and, after disposing of the elementary problem of making a machine that could not be beaten at noughts and crosses if allowed to move first, developed a chess playing machine that attracted some attention. After he had been in my department for some years he was invited to go to Stanford University as Visiting Professor of Electrical Engineering to develop this interest, and later returned as Edinburgh's first Professor of Machine Intelligence and Perception. James Howard had qualified in Medicine at the Middlesex Hospital and then embarked on a career in cellular immunology. After some years in Edinburgh, first in my department and then in the Department of Zoology, and a year in Paris with Bernard Halpern, he moved to the Wellcome Foundation. He was elected a fellow of the Royal Society in 1984.

Surgery is a demanding occupation and, in my view, one should not practise surgery at all unless one is prepared to devote at least half one's working time to seeing and treating patients. In principle, I do not think it matters if a university physician or surgeon gains his clinical experience exclusively in public hospitals like those in the British National Health Service or in organizations like American University Hospitals which charge fees; nor, in my view, does it matter whether the doctor is employed full time or is allowed to earn part of his income from private fees, provided that the time taken up by private practice is not so great as to prevent him from meeting his other responsibilities. In so far as university physicians and surgeons do engage in private practice, private patients gain access to people with special skills which they would otherwise be denied, and the doctors concerned have access to a wider range of patients. Moreover, the university gains financially, both directly, and indirectly as the result of gifts from grateful patients. In practice, however, the proviso is difficult or impossible to meet unless private patients can be treated in the teaching hospitals, and when I came to Edinburgh the only facilities for private patients in the teaching hospitals were for those needing neurosurgery or X-ray therapy.

Financially, the disadvantage of being full-time was compensated for to a considerable extent by the system of Distinction Awards that was built into the structure of the National Health Service at its inception. There were four grades of award; these were made on the recommendation of a national committee that took evidence *in camera* from consultants in each region, and experience both as a recipient and, later, as a person called on to advise about others, convinced me that the system was effective, and about as just as it is humanly possible to be. Being full-time did, however, involve other disadvantages of a less material kind.

In particular, in a National Health Service Hospital, a consultant is apt to be surrounded by a considerable number of highly competent junior colleagues, many of whom would, and some of whom could, assume most of his responsibilities if they were allowed to do so, and he is in consequence in danger of becoming isolated from his patients. I tried to overcome this by assuming personal responsibility for the day-to-day care of a proportion of the patients in my wards, and delegating this responsibility in respect of others to various of my juniors.

What criteria should one use in allocating patients in this way? First and foremost, of course, on the basis of the gravity of the case and the competence of the doctor. But it is important for any consultant to deal personally with a proportion of cases of a not so serious kind — in my case, for example, to operate on some patients with an uncomplicated inguinal hernia or varicose veins, and not only on those with, say, an aortic aneurism or a cancer of the colon. One could allocate these less serious cases randomly, but I chose to deal myself with those who came with

27. Therapist I on trailer.

28. Therapist I with her spinnaker up.

a letter from their doctor addressed to me by name as distinct from those addressed 'Dear Doctor'.

How can a professor of surgery find enough time for teaching, administration and research? The answer is that he cannot unless there are people in his department competent and willing to share in these activities; when this is not the case it is invariably research that is neglected. But what is the point in accepting a university post in surgery, or indeed in any other discipline, unless one can do research?

For me the great attraction of the chair I came to in Edinburgh was that it did allow time for research because my responsibility in respect of undergraduate teaching was little more than that of my surgical colleagues in the health service, and I had able and enthusiastic scientific and clinical colleagues in the department, and very good secretarial and technical assistance. I seldom attended meetings of the Senatus Academicus, which entrusted its important decisions to a small executive committee, but I did share fully in the work of the Faculty of Medicine which, at that time, consisted of the professorial heads of departments in the medical school. Today this arrangement would be regarded as unacceptably undemocratic, but it enabled business to be transacted quickly and the decisions reached were, I believe, often the same as, and rarely if ever less satisfactory than, those which would have been reached, albeit in a much longer time, by today's greatly enlarged faculty.

I was, *ex officio*, an examiner in surgery in the final MB, BS examination in Edinburgh, and served as external examiner to various other British universities in turn, and, as discussed later, to one overseas university. I particularly enjoyed examining in Cambridge (Fig 16); partly because Cambridge is such a lovely place, but also because the university expected students sitting their final MB, ChB examination to know quite a lot about surgery, and also about human anatomy. This had been the case also in London when I examined there, but the situation had since deteriorated; in many other universities the standard required in surgery was even lower, and the amount of anatomy one needed to remember to pass had declined almost to vanishing point.

I was able to do a fair amount of postgraduate teaching and was an examiner for the Royal College of Surgeons of Edinburgh; I also served for some years on the Council of the College (Fig 17).

Laboratory research in my department was concerned with four main topics:

1. Specific immunological tolerance of allografts and xenografts, and related phenomena.[3]

2. The effect on allograft survival of administration of antilymphocyte globulin and drainage of lymph from the thoracic duct.[4]

3. Congenital autoimmune haemolytic anaemia in a particular strain (NZB) of inbred mice.[5]

4. Cancer in animals, with particular reference to the loss of antigen from cancer cells;[6] treatment by systemic[7] or local[8] administration of an immunopotentiating agent, *Corynebacterium parvum*, or injection of specific antisera[9] or immunologically competent cells;[10] and the incidence of tumours in T-cell deficient mice.[11] This work provided the starting point for research on cancer undertaken after I retired from the Chair of Surgery, which is discussed in Chapter 15.

The main topics in our clinical research programme were as follows:

1. Transplantation of the kidney from identical twins[12] and other living relatives,[13] or unrelated cadavers.[13]

2. Autotransplantation of the kidney for the treatment of arterial hypertension due to narrowing of the renal artery.[14]

3. Transplantation of bone marrow and foetal liver for the treatment of aplastic anaemia.[15]

4. Transplantation of the lung.[16]

5. Transplantation of skin between twins showing blood chimaerism.[17]

6. Treatment of autoimmune haemolytic anaemia.[18]

7. Residual cancer. Treatment of cancer by infusion of human lymphocytes, administration of *C. Parvum*, and other immunological procedures.[19]

A short account of the transplantation work follows; this is addressed to the general reader. It is based on a chapter I wrote for a recent book on the history of transplantation.[20] A discussion of work on the treatment of cancer, and of why this treatment is not more effective, will be found in Chapter 15. Publications concerned with metaphysical and ethical questions are discussed in chapters 15 and 16.

For a newcomer to have any chance of getting renal transplantation off the ground in conservative Edinburgh it was important that our first case should be a resounding success. To ensure this we decided to wait until we had a patient in desperate need of a transplant who had a healthy identical twin who was willing to donate a kidney, because immunosuppression, which then involved the hazardous procedure of exposing the whole body to a high dose of X-rays, would not be necessary. Our wait ended in 1960 when a middle aged man with advanced renal failure was asked — initially, it is said, by a candidate in the examination for Membership of the Royal College of Physicians of Edinburgh who had heard me lecture on transplantation — if he had a twin, and replied that he had a twin brother. The appearance of the twins, allowing for the fact that one of them was very ill while the other was in good health, and various tests, including fingerprinting and interchange of skin grafts between them, made it almost certain that they were identical, so that we decided to go ahead with the transplantation. A garbled account in the press stated that the twins' fingerprints were indistinguishable, and this greatly alarmed the police, who envisaged the possibility of suspected criminals claiming that fingerprints that appeared to be theirs must be those of a long lost twin. They were greatly relieved when I told them that, while the prints showed areas of great similarity, there were other areas where one print was the mirror image of the other, and others again that were markedly different.

The operation presented some technical problems because the donor kidney had two arteries, and the arteries to which I would like to have anastomosed them in the host were obliterated as the result of arterial disease, but we managed to cope with the problem satisfactorily. The transplanted kidney functioned well, and the donor and the recipient both recovered quickly from the operation. They remained well for six years, when the donor suddenly collapsed and died in the street. At autospy the cause of death was clearly coronary thrombosis, but he had in addition a small cancer of the stomach. Some weeks later the recipient was also found to have cancer of the stomach, but this was inoperable, and he died soon after it was discovered. It is now known that the incidence of some forms of cancer is higher than normal in patients who have been given immunosuppressive therapy following an organ transplant from a non-twin donor, but in this case no immunosuppression was used and it seems almost certain that both twins had an inherited predisposition to stomach cancer.[21]

Our second patient, who received a kidney from her brother and was treated by whole body irradiation, died as the result of infection while her graft was functioning well. We decided not to persist with this method of treatment and were delighted when the immunosuppressive drug *azathioprine* became available in time for our next patient, a boy aged eleven, who in 1962 received a kidney from his father.[22] Three months before this, Dr. J. E. Murray from the Peter Bent Brigham Hospital in Boston had visited my department and had told me about research on immunosuppressive drugs that was being undertaken in Boston, in which an English surgeon, Mr (later Sir) Roy Calne had played a leading role, and in particular about their latest drug, now called *azathioprine*, which was then known by the code name BW322. Murray was subsequently my guest at a meeting of the Association of Surgeons of Great Britain and Ireland, and when we checked in our coats at the meeting I received a tag which, to our amazement, bore the number 322. This must be a good omen, he said, I'll send you some 322 to try. He was as good as his word, and a good omen indeed it proved to be, for the patient is still alive today (Fig 18). A rejection crisis occurred when we tried to stop immunotherapy after the transplant had been in place and functioning well for five years, but full function was gradually regained after treatment was resumed and the transplant continued to function satisfactorily for another twenty years; it then failed and was replaced by a cadaver kidney by my successor, Professor G. D. Chisholm. Though we did not know it until some years after the original operation, the donor and the recipient were what is termed *HLA identical*. The technical explanation of how this came about is that the boy's father and mother happened to have an HLA haplotype in common, and the boy had inherited this common haplotype from his mother. This may well have contributed to the long survival of the transplant, but the rejection crisis that occurred when we tried to withdraw immunosuppression shows also that the so-called minor (i.e. non-HLA) histocompatibility antigens may, in their totality, be of major importance.

Our first patient to receive a kidney from a cadaver had had one kidney removed because of cancer some years earlier and now had cancer in his remaining kidney. This kidney was still functioning so, to avoid putting him on dialysis, I performed the transplantation first and removed the cancerous kidney a few days later. The tumour, which was enormous, was growing along the renal vein, and I did not think the patient would live very long, but he survived for five years, during which time he played golf summer and winter on the Old Course at St Andrews. His account of his golfing exploits was so remarkable that my Senior Registrar, Michael Middleton, who was a good golfer, challenged him to a game at Muirfield. The movie we took of the contest shows two contrasting figures: one, bronzed and athletic looking, the other looking pale and rather tired, but the athletic figure is the patient. He was not quite as expert a golfer as he had led us to believe, but he acquitted himself well nevertheless. He continued to play golf until, one day, he began to feel poorly, and was found to have tumour metastases in both lungs. He died soon afterwards, but he had enjoyed five years of active, happy life as the result of his transplant.[22]

Between 1960 and 1976, 127 patients with end-stage renal failure were treated by kidney transplantation in Edinburgh. These were reviewed shortly before I retired from surgery (Fig 19).[23] A considerable number of them were operated on by my colleague, Bernard Nolan. For immuno-suppression we used azathioprine and steroids (except in case No. 2 and in two cases where the donor was an identical twin), and eleven patients received antilymphocytic globulin (ALG) in addition.

In 1968 I became involved in a case of lung transplantation,[24] though the operation was performed by my colleague, Mr Andrew Logan. The patient, a boy aged fifteen, had swallowed a mouthful of the weedkiller *paraquat* that was in a bottle labelled 'Kola' at his parents' home. This substance causes damage to the lungs if it is ingested and the patient gradually developed severe respiratory distress, despite attempts to eliminate the poison by a procedure known as forced diuresis. Six days after swallowing the poison he was desperately ill, and his left lung, which in the chest X-ray showed more severe damage than the right was removed and replaced by a lung from a cadaver. Immuno-suppression with azathioprine and steroids followed the pattern we were then using in renal transplant recipients. The transplant functioned well for a week, after which the patient developed severe respiratory distress and cyanosis despite assisted respira-tion, and he died thirteen days after the operation. At autopsy the pathological changes in the transplant were similar to those in the patient's own lung, and were thought to be due to residual paraquat in the circulation rather than to rejection. Today, treatment might have taken the form of immediate haemodialysis to eliminate the poison as quickly as possible, followed, if necessary, by transplantation of both lungs and the heart, but there was no precedent for this at the time. This tragic case vividly illustrates the terrible danger of keeping poison in unla-belled, or incorrectly labelled, bottles and of leaving it within reach of children.

Clinical trial of ALG in Edinburgh[23] was rather disappoint-ing, but suggested that it might be useful for treating episodes of rejection, and that, when ALG was given in association with azathioprine and prednisone for routine immunosuppression, it might be possible to reduce the dose of prednisone to a level that would be safer than the dose currently used. The Medical Research Council agreed to my proposal that a multicentre trial should be set up to investigate the matter further, using ALG prepared by the Wellcome Foundation. Unfortunately, the material they produced was certainly no more immuno-suppressive, and decidedly more toxic, than the material we prepared, and the trial was abandoned. Interest in ALG waned, but has been rekindled by the development of monoclonal antibodies specific for particular kinds of T-lymphocyte, and these, I believe, may play an important role in attempts to make a person needing a transplant immunologically tolerant of the tissues of the transplant donor.

Recognition by one's friends and colleagues is heartwarming. I was elated when, in 1967, Peter Medawar wrote to say that he and various other people wanted to propose me for Fellowship of the Royal Society of London, and agreeably surprised when I was elected the following year. I was even more surprised later that year when I received a letter from Downing Street saying that 'The Prime Minister [then Mr Harold Wilson] has it in mind, on the occasion of the forthcoming list of New Year Honours, to submit your name to The Queen with a recommendation that Her Majesty may be graciously pleased to approve that the Honour of Knighthood be conferred on you.' A little later, when this was a *fait accompli*, I received a characteristic letter from Peter Medawar, part of which was as follows:

> My dear Michael,
>
> Everyone here is extremely pleased about the honour a Grateful Sovereign has just showered on you. One feels a proper Charlie at first, of course, but quite soon one gets a sort of congenital feeling about it. It sounds well on you, too ('Let us — ah — seek Sir Michael's guidance on this problem') ... As far as I can make out, recommendations for Knighthood are made by a well-established series of coteries who have a rough rationing system, so that a knighthood ... is actually a strong vote of confidence from the professional fraternity: the time had come (one is entitled to feel) when not even your professional colleagues can obstruct your worldly advancement ... Jean joins me in felicitations, and please give our warmest greetings to Hazel; tell her that after the Accolade (for which woollen underclothing is a Must) nothing will meet the case except a smashing lunch with Champagne at the Mirabelle or the Caprice.
>
> All the very best,
>
> Peter

In the event, the ceremony took place at The Palace of Holyroodhouse (Fig 20) and not, as I had expected, at Buckingham Palace. It was a glorious spring day and there was no need for woollen underwear. I might have been a bit disappointed about the venue, but for the fact that five years previously I had been one of eight guests at an informal luncheon at Buckingham Palace, which was a much more intimate affair than the Investiture. A fellow guest on that occasion was General Sir John Hackett, an Australian by birth, who had been at Geelong Grammar School when I was at Wesley College. He was distinguished both as a soldier and as an academic, and later became Principal of King's College, London. I very much enjoyed talking to him before lunch, and was delighted to have the opportunity of continuing our conversation when he kindly took me back to the Athenaeum afterwards.

Various learned societies at home and overseas invited me to join them in an honorary capacity. I thus became *Associé Etranger* of the French *Académie de Chirurgie* (1964); Honorary Member of The American Surgical Society (1965); *Korrespondierenden Mitglied* of the *Deutsche Gesellschaft für Chirurgie* (1967); Honorary Fellow of the American College of Surgeons (1975); Honorary Member of the British Society for Immunology (1982); and Honorary Fellow of the Royal College of Physicians of Edinburgh (1982). In 1969 I was awarded the *Premio Internaziole, La Madonina,* by the Carlo Erba Foundation in Milan (Fig 21), and in 1970 the Lister Medal by the Royal College of Surgeons of England, and in the same year inaugurated the Edwin Stevens Lectures for the Laity at the Royal Society of Medicine.[25] In 1977 I received a rare honour for a general surgeon, the St Peter's Medal of the British Association of Urological Surgeons, and in 1981 shared the Alan Newton Prize of the Royal Australasian College of Surgeons with my friend Robert Burton, who was Professor of Surgical Science in The University of Newcastle, New South Wales.

In 1970 an old friend of mine, Patrick Forrest (later Sir Patrick) was appointed Regius Professor of Clinical Surgery in Edinburgh in succession to Sir John Bruce. The relationship between the two surgical departments became much closer, because we were both determined to make it so, but I had already come to the conclusion that, with the proliferation of surgical specialties, the time was approaching, if indeed it had not arrived already, when the chairs should be filled by people working in different fields of surgery. I thought it entirely appropriate, therefore, that when I retired five years later my chair should be filled by a urologist, Geoffrey Chisholm.

Soon after we came to Edinburgh we bought a Victorian, stone-built house called *The Bield* (a Scottish name meaning *Shelter*), set in half an acre of garden in the village of Juniper Green (Fig 22), some five miles from the centre of the city, with a splendid outlook over, and ready access to, the Pentland hills (Fig 23). A big attraction was the grass tennis court, though we had to extend this to get sufficient space beyond the limits of the playing area for serious tennis. The house had belonged to a doctor, who had recently died, and seems to have been a happy home for him and his family, as it proved to be for us. There were three floors. The top floor had four bedrooms, one of which we made into a bathroom, and was given over to the children; it now houses grandchildren and their parents when they come to visit us. Other bedrooms, a bathroom and our drawing room, were on the middle floor; while on the ground floor we had the dining room, pantry and kitchen, and studies for Hazel and myself. There was also a cellar which, in addition to fulfilling the usual function of a cellar, provided me with an excellent workshop.

We had brought most of our furniture from New Zealand, but not our piano. Hazel's father very generously offered to give us one, and we chose a Blüthner boudoir grand that Sidney Newman, the Reid Professor of Music, kindly vetted for us. I wondered whether it could be got up the stairs to the drawing room, but Rae MacIntosh Ltd, the vendors, assured me, after a site visit, that it could be done, and they proved to be right, though only just. As we had bought the house for less than we had expected to pay, we were able to afford various alterations, including replacing the lead water pipes with copper pipes, electrical rewiring, and installation of state-of-the-art oil-fired central heating that has served us well ever since. The heating was installed by Edmunds, Epping Ltd, a firm that had been founded by Hazel's uncle, Martin Edmunds, and was then owned by her cousins, Frank and John Edmunds. Efficient domestic central heating was rare in Edinburgh at the time, and some of our new acquaintances seemed to regard it as sinful to be comfortably warm.

After Keith left school he read Civil Engineering at Sheffield University, where Bill Eastwood was Dean of the Faculty of Engineering; a few years after taking his degree he became a Member of the Institute of Civil Engineers, and later a Fellow. Geoffrey went to University College, London, where he took an Honours BSc in Physiology; he then went on to qualify in Medicine at University College Hospital, where my father had been a student some sixty years earlier, and in due course became a house surgeon there. He is now a consultant ophthalmologist in Leicester. Margaret took an Honours BSc in Botany at Sheffield — the Department in which Hazel had worked when we lived in Sheffield just after World War II.

My father, who felt very lonely after the death of my step-mother, came to stay with us in 1958, but returned to Australia a year later. He came again in 1962, but again felt rather restless, and stayed only six months. He would, I think, have settled down happily if we had been living in England, especially in his native Yorkshire, but never really felt that Scotland was home. But he returned again towards the end of 1963, and stayed until he died in 1966 at the age of eighty-nine. One of the happiest features of this period was the extraordinarily close and loving relationship that developed between him and Hazel. They had got on well ever since Hazel and I became engaged, but this went even deeper.

For as long as I can remember truth was paramount for him — indeed I always think of him as Mr Valiant for Truth. He had become totally convinced of the wisdom and power and love of God, and never seemed to waver in this belief as so many of us are apt to do. Two of the hymns sung at a Memorial Service held for him in Melbourne, one by Joseph Addison and the other by Martin Luther, reflect his faith so well that I feel impelled to quote a verse of each:[26,27]

> The spacious firmament on high,
> With all the blue ethereal sky,
> And spangled heavens, a shining frame,
> Their great Original proclaim.
> The unwearied sun, from day to day,
> Doth his Creator's power display;
> And publishes to every land
> The work of an almighty hand.
>
> All praise and thanks to God
> The Father now be given,
> The Son, and him who reigns
> With Them in highest heaven:
> The one, eternal God,
> Whom earth and heaven adore;
> For thus it was, is now,
> And shall be evermore.

Hazel and I, and the children, greatly enjoyed our new home — the first, and indeed the last, we have owned. Hazel, like her father, was a keen and expert gardener; she became also a highly skilled painter and decorator, and a formidable clerk of works when it came to dealing with builders. I turned my engineering training to good account in such matters as laying concrete and dealing with electrical equipment, and undertook some of the less skilled work in the garden as time permitted. We both derived much pleasure from the tennis court, but were driven to conclude that a grass court does not really suit the Edinburgh climate. After some years we joined the Colinton Lawn Tennis Club, where Hazel had the opportunity of playing competitive tennis. We continued to use our own court, weather permitting, though much less after the Colinton courts were resurfaced with all-weather porous concrete (replaced later by artificial grass). Lights were also installed at Colinton, so hardy people could play outdoor tennis in winter, but this did not appeal to us. There were very few indoor tennis courts available in the city, so we played badminton instead in the winter, Hazel again playing in a team.

In 1957, after attending a congress in Paris, Hazel and I spent a short holiday in Nice at the Hotel D'Armenonville, that had been recommended to us by a lecturer in French at Edinburgh University. There could not have been a more fortunate choice. Our next two summer holidays were spent with the children at Guéthary, near Biarritz, and it was here that we met Yvonne Perissé who, with her husband, Yannick, was to become a close friend. The following year we divided our time between a comfortable 'camp' on the Giens peninsula, near Hyères, and the Hotel D'Armenonville, and in 1961 we spent our whole holiday at the Hotel D'Armenonville. As the hotel did not have a restaurant we were able to shop around for our evening meal, and found, with the help of the *Guide Michelin*, a remarkably good restaurant, *Le Père Auguste*, which gave us a good dinner for around ten francs each. Also staying in the hotel were John and Diana Tyler, who were on their honeymoon. They were keen sailors, and reawakened my interest in sailing — which had lain dormant since our holiday on the Norfolk Broads in 1948 — to such an extent that when we got home I bought a boat and joined the Royal Forth Yacht Club, and from this time on sailing has played such a part in our lives that it needs a chapter to itself.

One of the many privileges of living in Edinburgh was that we were able to become members of the French Institute (*L'Institut Français d'Ecosse*). In Australia, when Hazel and I were at school, French was taught like Latin, as a dead language. We learned the grammar, but not how to speak everyday French properly, and the lessons I had had during my holiday in Paris, when my father was working at the Pasteur Institute, had not been enough to make good the deficiency. The French Institute, which was staffed by French people, greatly improved our ability to speak, and understand, conversational French, and aroused our interest in *la civilisation française*. This enabled us to enjoy French radio and films, and helped us to make friends with many interesting people we met when we were on holiday in France.

Besides my father, many relatives and close friends stayed with us at the Bield. They included Hazel's father, Keith Ashby, and stepmother, Bess, and her sisters, Enid and Beth; and my brother, Philip, and his wife, Lyndsay. It was a sad blow for me as well as for Hazel when Keith Ashby died in Australia in December 1971. He was a kind and generous man, a committed member of the Society of Friends who was for a long time Clerk of the Adelaide Meeting, a good farmer, and a good sportsman. He continued playing village cricket into his sixties, and could always beat me easily at tennis.

Other visitors came from all over the world, sometimes just for dinner but quite often to stay for a few days. The countries they represented included (in alphabetical order) Australia, Belgium, Burma, Canada, Czechoslovakia, Denmark, Egypt, France, Germany, Ghana, Greece, Holland, Hong Kong, Hungary, India, Iraq, Israel, Italy, Jugoslavia, Kuwait, Malta, Malaysia, New Zealand, Norway, Pakistan, Poland, Portugal, Roumania, Singapore, South Africa, Sri Lanka, Sweden, Switzerland, the USA, and the USSR. Among these visitors were seven winners of the Nobel Prize for Medicine.

Between 1957 and 1976, while I occupied my Chair in Edinburgh, I visited many of these countries as a scientific adviser, external examiner or visiting professor, or to attend conferences and to observe or participate in research, or simply as a tourist, and some of these trips merit brief description.

My scientifically-orientated travels in Europe included visits to Geneva at the invitation of the World Health Organization (WHO); to Paris, The Hague and Rome to participate in congresses of the Transplantation Society; and to various places, large and small, to participate in other scientific meetings.

In 1961 I was invited to Geneva to take part in a small meeting on the diagnosis and treatment of radiation injuries,[28] sponsored jointly by WHO and the International Atomic Energy Authority. My interest in this subject arose from the use of X-irradiation in high dosage, followed by a rescue procedure, to prevent the rejection of allogeneic organ grafts and for the treatment of advanced cancer. I was invited to Geneva again the following year to chair a small Scientific Group on *Tissue Antigens and Transplantation*,[29] at which I got to know Nils Jerne, then Head of the Section of Immunology of WHO, who shared the Nobel Prize for Medicine in 1984 for his contributions to our understanding of antibody formation, and I returned yet again in 1964 to a meeting of representatives of several WHO groups concerned with immunology. Later still I served for ten years as an Expert Adviser to the WHO Panel on Immunology.

The first international congress of the recently formed Transplantation Society was held in Paris in 1967, under the chairmanship of Peter Medawar, and I gave two papers: one on antilymphocyte globulin (ALG),[30] and the other on ethical problems in organ transplantation.[31] The second congress was held the following year in the United States. The third congress was held at The Hague in 1970, under the presidency of Jean Hamburger.[32] Unhappily his first duty was to remind us that there was *un grand absent* in the person of Peter Medawar, who had suffered a massive cerebral haemorrhage the previous year. The papers were again of high quality, and there were two social functions I remember with particular pleasure: a reception for members of the council of the society given by Queen Juliana of the Netherlands (Fig 24), and an elegant reception at the French Embassy.

Other scientific meetings I took part in included meetings concerned with tissue and organ transplantation in general (Paris 1957; Liège 1959; Padua 1963; Bad Homburg 1966; and Florence 1971); specific immunological tolerance (Prague 1961); the immunosuppressive properties of antilymphocyte globulin (Lyon 1969; Versailles 1970); and the antitumour properties of *Corynebacterium parvum* (Paris 1974).

The meeting in Paris[33] in 1957 was organized by the *Centre National de la Recherche Scientifique*, and almost everyone then working in the field of transplantation was there (Fig 25). Two years later many of the same people, together with others including Joseph Murray, whose work earned him, rather belatedly, a share of the Nobel Prize for Medicine in 1990, met in Liège.[34] Much the same group met yet again in 1961 at Liblice,[35] near Prague, in a house that had once belonged to Casanova. This was a good meeting scientifically but I found Prague depressing. It still retained some of the beauty that Mozart must have enjoyed when he was there, but the people seemed gloomy and frightened, and my unhappiness was not lightened by an afternoon expedition on which we were taken to a former Nazi concentration camp in which the gas extermination chambers and other horrors had been carefully preserved.

The meeting on *C. parvum* was organized by Bernard Halpern. I had first met him when he visited my department in Edinburgh in 1969, and I paid a return visit to him at the *Collège de France* shortly afterwards. It was through him that I became interested in the ability of a killed bacterial culture of *C. parvum* to stimulate the reticuloendothelial system, and decided to see whether administration of this material might inhibit the growth of tumours.[36] Halpern was born in Russia in 1904, and after unimaginable adventures arrived in France at the age of nineteen, passed his baccalauréat at Nancy, and subsequently studied both science and medicine in Paris. He worked for a time in the pharmaceutical industry, then at the Hôpital Broussais under Professor Valery-Radot, and finally was appointed to the prestigious Chaire Claude Bernard at the *Collège de France*. He died in 1978.

Another meeting I attended in Paris in 1974, held at the Sorbonne, was on the subject of *Biologie et devenir de l'homme*. The closing session was addressed by the President of the Republic, M. Valerie Giscard d'Estain. He was expected to speak for only a few minutes, but spoke most impressively for over half an hour on the subject of the conference. It was a most interesting meeting, but open to the criticism that every one present was middle aged, if not elderly. Students who waylaid us in the Boulevard St Michel when we left the Sorbonne were not slow to ask how one could have a conference on the future of mankind from which younger people were excluded.

In the summer of 1961 I spent a month as external examiner in surgery in the University of Baghdad, at the invitation of

Professor Selman Faik. It was extremely hot in the middle of the day — usually at least 115°F in the shade — but fortunately the humidity was very low. The examination began each day at 7 a.m. and we adjourned at noon for lunch followed by a long siesta. This regime was by no means unpleasant, provided one did not get into, or even touch, a car parked in the sun. Teaching was in English, as were the patients' case notes. The clinical examination followed the same pattern as in Britain, but the spectrum of disease in the hospital was very different. One day I visited Babylon, in company with three Iraqi surgeons. The first thing we saw as we approached the site was a large wooden shed painted in bright primary colours, with notices saying 'Drink Coca-cola', *Buvez Coca-Cola*, and the equivalent in Arabic. While we were contemplating this monstrosity we became surrounded by people offering to sell us 'genuine antiques'. Having been forewarned, I did not buy anything, but one of the Iraqi surgeons, to the amusement of his colleagues, bought a piece of pottery which seemed as if it might be genuine just long enough for the vendor to make good his getaway. The ruins themselves, however, which were being skilfully restored, were impressive.

When in Baghdad I was invited one day to lunch at the British Embassy, and learned much about the country from the Ambassador, Sir Humphrey (later Lord) Trevelyan. I also had a salutary lesson on hygeine from Lady Trevelyan. We were discussing the risk of drinking contaminated water in Baghdad and of putting ice in one's drinks. She told me that at diplomatic parties she accepted a neat ice cube, on the assumption that it was probably made from pure, bottled water, but declined if offered a jagged piece of ice, on the grounds that it might well consist of frozen water from the River Tigris. I stuck to this rule for the rest of my visit, and also avoided eating salads. These precautions proved remarkably effective, and I did not suffer at all from gastroenteritis.

I was due to leave Iraq on a Sunday, and on the preceding Friday — which was, of course, a Moslem holiday — Professor Faik asked me if I had an exit visa. I showed him an entry in Arabic in my passport that had been made when I arrived, and that I had been told was my exit visa, but he said this was valid for only a week and was now out of date. He very kindly located the Foreign Minister of Iraq, who had been a patient of his, took my passport to him, and returned with a valid exit visa written by hand by the Minister himself! My flight was supposed to leave at 10 a.m. but when I got to the airport the terminal building was packed with soldiers and we were told that during the night an attempt had been made to assassinate the Iraqi Head of State, Abdul Karrim Kassim, and that all flights had been cancelled. My special exit visa seemed to command respect, but clearly I was not going to be given a plane to myself. Fortunately, after a delay of more than twelve hours, all the passengers for our flight were allowed to board, and an hour later the plane took off.

In 1965 Hazel and I broke our journey home from Australia to visit Iran, Israel, Jordan and Egypt. Jerusalem at that time was divided into Israeli and Jordanian parts, and to get from one to the other we had to go through the Mandelbaum Gate. We were struck by the difference in attitude of the Moslems and the Israelis to places of interest to Christians. The Israelis were keen to show us the extraordinary progress they were making in agriculture and industrial development, and in education and research, but took much less interest than the Arabs in the places associated with the birth, life and death of Jesus, which the Arabs referred to as 'the holy places', and which Hazel and I wanted to see. Some of these made us sad because of the way they were being exploited commercially, but to visit the Sea of Galilee was a deeply moving experience, made even more so as we recalled words of Whittier that we had often sung:

> O Sabbath rest by Galilee!
> O calm of hills above,
> Where Jesus knelt to share with thee
> The silence of eternity,
> Interpreted by love![37]

I returned to Israel in 1974 to preside over the Fifth International Congress of the Transplantation Society, which was held in Jerusalem, the whole of which was by then entirely under Israeli control. My colleagues on the Council of the Society and I were graciously received by the President of Israel, Professor Kazir, and Mrs Kazir (Fig 26), and the congress was a great success both socially and scientifically. I was filled with admiration for the astonishing material achievements that were appar-

20. Therapist II

30. My 80th birthday party, with Hazel, Geoffrey, Karin, Winston, Margaret, and granddaughters, and the Eastwoods.

ent on all sides, but disturbed that a people that had suffered such terrible persecution as the Jews had, could be so blind to the sufferings of the Palestinians.

I visited the United States twelve times in the period under discussion, alone or with Hazel, though sometimes only for a few days.

In February 1962 I attended a conference on transplantation at the New York Academy of Sciences. The programme included an exciting paper by Jacques Miller on his work on the role of the thymus in transplantation immunity, and another by Roy Calne on work in progress in Boston on the use of immunosuppressive drugs to prevent allograft rejection. I crossed the Atlantic in both directions by sea. The return journey was on the maiden voyage of the *SS France*, and I was lucky enough to have been given a first class ticket. We left New York on a sunny winter's day, with mini-icebergs floating down the Hudson River, and all the New York fireboats, with many other small craft, turned out to wish us *Bon Voyage*.

In February 1964 after another meeting in New York, I went to New Orleans to see a patient of Keith Reemstma's who was alive and well nine months after receiving a kidney transplant from a chimpanzee. Just two months later I was back in the United States, at the invitation of Dr Francis (Frannie) Moore, as 'Surgeon in Chief *pro tempore*' at the Peter Bent Brigham Hospital in Boston. I had many friends at the Brigham in addition to my host and enjoyed my visit enormously, but it was a daunting experience, made more so because Frannie forgot to give me in advance the case summaries of the patients to be presented at the 'Grand Rounds' that I was expected to discuss. At the end of the week I was presented with an autographed copy of David McCord's *The Fabrick of Man*,[38] which gives an account of fifty years of the Peter Bent Brigham Hospital. This bears the inscription:

> From the Board of Trustees and Officers of the Peter Bent Brigham Hospital to Professor Michael Woodruff, whose tenure, *pro tempore*, as Surgeon-in-Chief nourished our House Staff, inspired our Surgeons, and graced the Brigham entire.

From Boston I was taken by Frannie and his wife on a tour of the battlefields of the American Civil War. Such is the greatness of Abraham Lincoln that my admiration for him was undimmed despite the Moores' unremitting hero worship.

In 1965 I went to Philadelphia to attend the annual meeting of the American Surgical Association, at which I was made an Honorary Fellow of the Association — a great honour, as the total number of Honorary Fellows is limited to 45. In addition, I took part in the bicentenary celebrations of the University of Pennsylvania Medical School as a representative of the University of Edinburgh, from where, in 1765, John Morgan had returned to Philadelphia to found the first medical school in the United States — older, indeed, than the nation itself.[39]

In 1967 I went to the University of California, Los Angeles (UCLA) as Visiting Professor of Surgery at the invitation of the Chairman of the Department, Dr William P. Longmire, an able and biologically-orientated surgeon who had done important work on allograft rejection. He had found a place in his department for Dr Paul Terasaki, whose laboratory became a Mecca for people interested in donor-recipient matching. I had known his urologist colleague, Willard Goodwin, since 1959, when Willard spent six months sabbatical leave in my department in Edinburgh. From Los Angeles I flew to New Orleans to give the 1967 Rudolph Matas Memorial Lecture[40] at Tulane University.

In 1971, at the invitation of the Harvey Society of New York, I gave the Harvey Lecture, and chose as my subject *Residual Cancer*.[41] This was another daunting task, as I confessed in my closing words:

> I have read somewhere that the captains of sailing ships circumnavigating Cape Horn used to forbid the helmsman to look astern lest he should be so frightened by what he saw that he lost his nerve, and with it control of the ship. A similar feeling has discouraged me from looking back systematically over the series of previous Harvey Lectures but I have read enough of them to feel some diffidence in presenting to you a clinical problem, the solution of which is still a matter for speculation. I trust you share my belief however that, while science is rightly concerned with the search for truth irrespective of possible applications, scientists have a responsibility also to try to discover ways of promoting human welfare. Of course ... the identification of a particular human need is no guarantee that we will be able to do anything to meet it. The realization that the cancer problem, as

it appears to the clinician, would be solved if we knew how to eliminate residual cancer does not mean, therefore, that a solution is at hand. But it may perhaps take us a step nearer to this goal.

In 1972 Hazel and I went to San Francisco for the Fourth International Congress of the Transplantation Society, at which I was elected President of the Society, and gave a paper on the induction of specific immunological tolerance to heart allografts in rats.[42] On the way we stopped in New Orleans, and met the new Chairman of the Department of Surgery, Ted Drapanis. He was a keen sailor, and took us out in his boat on Lake Ponchartrain. The humidity and temperature were such that we had to consume a lot of fluid and salt to replace what we lost by sweating. We stayed at the Ponchartrain Hotel in a suite in which there was an amazing collection of beautiful antique furniture. Someone who had seen our rooms asked the owner of the hotel, Mr Lyle Ascheffenbourg, who ran it as a hobby, whether he thought it safe to have such valuable furniture in a hotel suite. He said that Conrad Hilton had once asked him the same question, to which he had replied: 'Conrad, we have a different clientele to you.'

In 1975 I returned to California with Hazel to take part in the Clinical Congress of the American College of Surgeons in San Francisco, at which I was admitted as an Honorary Fellow. I was presented by Willard Goodwin, and we spent a few days with the Goodwins in Los Angeles before the meeting. I had to fly from there to San Francisco because of other commitments, but Hazel went with them via Yosemite in the now ancient station wagon they had had in Edinburgh — named 'Trespassers W' after Piglet's house in Winnie the Pooh.[43] It broke down just as they reached San Francisco, and was found to be economically not worth repairing, so Willard bought a new one for their journey home.

In 1962, on a flight to Geneva to attend a meeting of the WHO Group on Research in Immunology, I found myself sitting next to Dr J. H. S. Gear, then Director of the South African Institute for Medical Research in Johannesburg, who was a member of the same group. When he learned of my interest in organ transplantation he invited me to go to the Institute for a month to help his colleagues develop experimental kidney transplantation in monkeys and baboons. It was an interesting experience, though the animals, especially the baboons, were frightening. I think these were the first organ transplants to have been performed in South Africa, and like to think that my experiments, primitive though they were, may have encouraged Bert Myburgh, who later became Professor of Surgery at Witwatersrand, to begin the work in this field for which he is now widely known. At the time of my visit the head of the department was Professor D. J. Du Plessis. He was distinguished both as a surgeon and as an administrator, and later became Vice Chancellor of the University. He had a liberal outlook, and introduced me to his colleague, Dr Suzman, and his wife, Janet, who became known all over the world for her courageous fight against apartheid. Our trip gave us an opportunity to visit Hazel's sister, Beth, and her husband, George Anderson, at White River. They took us on what was to be our first visit to the magnificent Kruger Park. We returned from South Africa with a much better understanding of the complexity and difficulty of the racial problems that exist there.

In April 1965, the University of Edinburgh granted me leave for a term to enable me to go to the University of Adelaide as visiting professor in the Department of Surgery. The head of the department was R. P. (Dick) Jepson. He was the first person to be appointed to a full-time clinical chair in Australia, and there could not have been a better choice. He was an excellent general surgeon, with a particular interest in disorders of the thyroid gland, a good teacher who was interested in research, a fine cricketer who had played several times for the Lancashire first eleven, and a competent tennis player. He and his wife, Mary, soon became very popular in Adelaide, and Dick was in great demand by colleagues and their wives in need of surgical care. Hazel and I were given a comfortable apartment in the Queen Elizabeth Hospital. I quickly became involved in the teaching and research in Jepson's department, and was given charge of beds, first in the Queen Elizabeth Hospital and later in the Royal Adelaide Hospital. It was exciting to be back in the city in which Hazel was born and we were married, and where we had so many relatives and friends. During our visit, Keith and Bess Ashby gave the Ashby family home, Wittunga, with its huge garden planted with Australian native plants, to the City of Adelaide. This gencrous gift has given great pleasure to many thousands of visitors every year, who come not only from Adelaide but from all over Australia, and also from overseas.

In 1975 Hazel and I went to New Zealand, where we were guests of the University of Otago at the celebrations commemorating the hundredth anniversary of the founding of the Medical School. My contribution was to give an address entitled 'The Renaissance of Immunology', in which I discussed discrimination between self and not-self, the generation of diversity in populations of antigen-sensitive cells, the transmission of information between cells, and the manipulation of the immune response for therapeutic purposes.[44] We flew from Christchurch to Melbourne, where I had arranged to work at the Walter and Eliza Hall Institute of Medical Research (WEHI) in collaboration with Neil Warner on the growth of tumours in athymic ('nude') mice. The institute maintained a remarkable collection of inbred mice, and my cousin, Margaret Holmes, who was in charge of mouse production, always managed to provide us with all we needed. We did not manage to complete our experiments in the short time available, but Warner finished them with the help of Robert Burton[45] after I had left.

Professor (later Sir Gustav) Nossal, who had succeeded Sir Macfarlane Burnet as Director of the Institute, and his wife, Lyn, lived at Kew in the house, *Neville*, in which I had spent much of my boyhood, but I was unaware of this when we went to dine with them for the first time. We were staying in the Visitors' Flat at the Royal Melbourne Hospital, and Gus drove us to his home. The terrain became progressively more familiar, but I was dumbfounded when he drove in through the gates of Neville, and reduced almost to tears when I identified in the house a cupboard that I had helped my father build when I was a boy.

In the summer of 1976 I retired from my chair, and from the practice of surgery. I laid down this burden with a will, because major surgery is an athletic pursuit and at sixty-five it is high time to stop. There were, moreover, other things I wanted to do; in particular, to spend more time on research than had been possible hitherto.

Sea fever

For as long as I can remember, I have loved the sea, but until 1961 my experience was limited to travelling as a passenger or serving as doctor in large ships, occasional trips in friends' boats, and swimming from the shore. That year, however, I decided to buy a boat.

After reading a book by Jean Merrien,[1] and knowing that on the Forth many boats in harbour sit on the mud at low tide, we chose a bilge-keeler, and named her *Marahau*, after the place where we had spent several enjoyable holidays in New Zealand. She was a solid little boat, and very good of her kind, but like all bilge-keelers, as I soon found, did not sail well to windward. We sold her in 1966, when I decided to take up handicap racing, and bought an *Invicta*, a twenty-six foot keelboat designed by Van Der Stadt, and moulded by Tylers. We decided to register her but had difficulty in finding a name we liked that was not already in use. Our first choice, which reflected both my interest in research and my admiration for Matthew Flinders,[2] was *Investigator*, but this was not accepted by the Registrar at the Port of Leith because there was a fisheries research vessel bearing this name in Canada. We tried a dozen other names but all were already taken, so decided to invent one. We chose *Therapist* because it aptly described the purpose of the boat. I might have guessed, but did not, that in the Royal Forth Yacht Club the boat would soon become known as *The Rapist*, but this did not prevent us from keeping the name when *Therapist* was replaced by *Therapist II*. Apart from being a good name for a doctor's boat, it had the advantage of being easily grasped by French speaking people — a matter of some importance when asking over the radio for a place in a marina in France, or dealing with the French Customs.

We had towed *Marahau* by car from Edinburgh to the Mediterranean and back three times, but this was not going to be possible with *Therapist*. We decided that when we took possession of her we would sail her from Edinburgh to Calais and then continue south via the French canals. We had an uneventful sail to Calais, but disaster struck when a convoy of six barges came into the basin where we were moored and had just finished taking down the mast with the help of a crane. As they approached they appeared to be dangerously close to our boat and, despite our shouts, the nearest barge crashed into the side of *Therapist*.

There is little doubt that if the boat had been built of timber it would have disintegrated, and Hazel and Margaret, who were on board when the collision occurred, might well have been killed, but fortunately no one was injured. The boat, however, was holed and had to be transported to Tylers for repairs. We decided that when these were completed we would take *Therapist* to Edinburgh by road and therefore bought a secondhand ex-army three-ton truck and a trailer. The truck had been used by the Territorial Army and had done only 8,000 miles. As we paid only £50 for it, and sold it six years later for £200, it was a bargain.

The following year we decided to tow the boat to the Mediterranean for our summer holiday. I had built a hard top on the truck and installed two berths (Fig 27), and the boat provided cooking facilities and more berths, so we would stop for the night in any safe parking place. In those far-off days the Boulevard Périphéque did not exist. We stopped just north of Paris to ask the advice of a truck driver concerning the best way to get round the city. '*Moi, monsieur,*' he said, '*je coupé*'; so we decided to do the same, just as we had done when faced with the same problem in London. The boat on its trailer plus the truck was well over forty feet long, but what was even more important was that our height, inclusive of the mast carried horizontally on the boat, was eleven feet six inches. When we came to a bridge where the headroom was stated to be 3.70 metres I had to make a hasty calculation to see if we would fit under it while cars lined up behind me tooting as only French drivers can toot.

We planned to ask a *chantier* in Arles to lift the boat into the
Rhone and look after the truck and trailer until we came back on
our way home, but found when we got there that the yard was
closed for a month. *Faut de mieux,* we continued south by road
until we reached the commercial harbour of *Port St Louis du
Rhône*, where Hazel found a small boatyard close to the lock
which allows vessels, including petrol tankers, to pass from the
Rhone to the sea and *vice versa.* The owner agreed to lift *Therapist*
into the water and to look after the truck and trailer while we
were sailing. While we were getting the boat ready a passerby,
who seemed to know a lot about boats, came and spoke to us. He
turned out to be the senior customs officer in Port St Louis,
M. Roger Oulion, and a keen member of the local yacht club. He
arranged for us to stay for a day or two in Port Abri, a small yacht
harbour entered from the canal that connects Port St Louis to the
Golfe de Fos, and gave us much valuable advice about the local
hazards for small boats, including the wind called the *mistral,*
which can start to blow hard with little warning and for which
we quickly developed a healthy respect. But it was the mosquitoes, rather than the *mistral,* which discouraged us from staying
long in Port St Louis.

On M. Oulion's advice our first port of call after leaving Port
Abri was Bandol, nearly fifty nautical miles to the west and a little
further south. He felt, rightly I think, that we should postpone
a visit to Marseilles until we had some experience of sailing in
these waters. Thereafter we called at the Porquerolles islands,
St Tropez, St Raphael, La Napoule, Antibes, Nice, and Menton,
before returning to collect the trailer and truck, and make our
way home by road. Subsequent holidays followed a similar
pattern, except that we sometimes extended our cruise into Italy,
until 1970, when we were forced by a strong *mistral* to put into
Toulon on the return journey. We found by chance a small
private yacht harbour, *Mediterranée Plaisance*, and Geoffrey and
I went by bus from there to Port St Louis to collect the trailer and
truck. Thereafter, we used *Mediterranée Plaisance* as the base for
our amphibious operations, and kept our next boat there for
several years.

Back home we did well with *Therapist* in 'round-the-cans'
handicap racing, and also managed, with my friend George
Steedman as mate, to win the two main off-shore races started

from Granton (Fig 28), namely, the Bell Rock Race in 1969, and the North Carr Race in 1972. Hazel came along from time to time. She became a first class crew member, and quite a good helmsman, though inclined to give way unnecessarily in close-quarters situations.

In 1973 we sold *Therapist* and bought an Arpège, built in La Rochelle by Michel Dufour, which we called *Therapist II*. She rated as a 'half tonner', and was faster and much more roomy than *Therapist I*. Fitted with a two-cylinder 25 horsepower diesel engine, she was an excellent fast cruising boat, and also quite exciting to race. I took delivery of her in Hamble, on my way back from a visit to Australia, and with Geoffrey and a friend, and George Steedman, sailed her non-stop to Blythe. We received a very warm welcome from the Royal Northumberland Yacht Club in Blythe. Most of the crew had to leave us there and I took the boat on to Edinburgh with three friends from the Royal Forth YC.

For our first summer holiday with *Therapist II* we decided to visit the west coast of Scotland with two German friends, Hans and Ingrid Hirsch. Hans and I sailed the boat non-stop to Inverness, a distance of 225 nautical miles that we covered at an average speed of 5.0 knots. Here we passed through the sea lock to enter Muirtown basin at the start of the Caledonian canal, where we were joined by Hazel and Ingrid, who had come up from Edinburgh by car. The trip through the canal and Loch Ness took three days, but this included a Sunday, when the locks did not operate. We continued to Oban and up the Sound of Mull to Tobermory, and then had to head for home. A feature of the trip was that Hazel and I were woken every morning (except in Loch Ness) by two splashes, caused by the Hirschs diving in for a swim. Eventually Hazel and I were shamed into joining them, but once was quite enough. Hans and Ingrid left when we got back to the canal, and Hazel and I took the boat on to Inverness. Here Hazel left and I was joined by George Steedman and an American friend for the trip back to Edinburgh. We had a pleasant trip as far as Fraserburgh, but thereafter we had dense fog and no wind all the way home. I was very relieved to see the loom of the light and hear the foghorn, first on the Bell Rock and then on the North Carr lightship, and greatly helped by the radio-beacon on May Island.

The following year we did moderately well in racing, though not as well as with *Therapist I*, partly, no doubt, because our handicap was much less favourable. *Therapist II* was too broad in the beam for us to trail, and we decided to devote two summer holidays to sailing her from Edinburgh to Toulon (Fig 29). Our plan was to go by sea to Bordeaux, thence by the inland waterways to Sète, and then on again by sea.

The first year we went from Edinburgh to La Trinité, with stops at Lowestoft, Newhaven, Salcombe, Morlaix, Aber'vrach, Douarnenez, Audierne and Le Forêt. We anticipated some problems crossing the Thames estuary but did not experience any, though one can never relax here. Much the most exciting part of the trip was passing through the Chenal du Four (between the Island of Ushant and the mainland). Here the tide runs at up to 7 knots, so timing is critical. At our first attempt we encountered dense fog, so returned to Aber'vrach, but next time everything went perfectly. There was not much wind but with the help of the tidal stream and the engine we travelled twenty-six nautical miles in two hours. We arrived at Douarnenez after midnight and continued next day to Audierne. This meant passing through the Raz de Sein, which lies between the Ile de Sein and the Pointe d'Audierne. The passage through the Raz is much shorter than that through the Chenal du Four, but can be very rough and the tidal stream is equally strong. This time we had a brisk breeze from the north west, and again attained a speed of 13 knots over the ground, but without the engine. We had to gybe when we were in the Raz, but this went like clockwork. I had not realised how fast we were going, and we overstood Audierne and had to turn round and go back. Exciting sailing!

When we reached La Trinité we moored to a pontoon, and two days later I had to fly to Israel to preside over the Congress of the Transplantation Society, which was being held in Jerusalem, leaving Hazel alone on board. I rejoined her ten days later in the nick of time.

The weather forecast for the night predicted a Force 11 gale in the Atlantic, and by the evening it was blowing at least Force 6 in the harbour. We knew, moreover, that during the night there would be an exceptionally high spring tide which would deprive the harbour of the normally excellent protection afforded by the extensive oyster beds situated just seaward of the harbour wall. There was a boat alongside us moored to the same pontoon, and with a line also to *Therapist*. The crew were all girls, and they had been competing in the offshore race, the *Coupe des Dames*, but fortunately, as it turned out, several boyfriends had joined them in La Trinité.

During the night the wind increased to gale force, so we got dressed and stayed awake. About 5 a.m. Hazel, who had been looking out of the cabin window, announced that we were at sea. I was initially sceptical, but soon saw that the part of the pontoon to which we were moored had become detached from the rest of the pontoon, and a bizarre raft-life structure consisting of *Therapist*, the girls' boat and about twelve metres of pontoon was indeed adrift in the harbour. I started our engine and we cut our mooring lines, and after milling around for some time we managed to moor to another pontoon further in from the sea wall. We heard later the sad news that while all this was happening Mr Edward Heath's *Morning Cloud*, though not with him aboard, had been lost with her crew in the English Channel.

After a few days, conditions in La Trinité had improved sufficiently for *Therapist* to be lifted out of the water and put on a cradle for the winter. Hazel and I were due to attend a conference in Paris in a few days time and meanwhile visited Carnac by car to see the prehistoric *Alignements* — reminiscent of Stonehenge but for the fact that the stones at Carnac are smaller, more numerous, and, as the name suggests, arranged in straight lines instead of in a circle.

The following year (1975) we went by car to La Trinité, found the boat all ready for us, and resumed our journey south with Hazel and myself, and three friends, among them Yvonne Perissé, on board. After one night at Les Sables d'Olonne we spent two days at St Martin de Ré, a beautiful place despite the fact that it was from here that convicts used to be sent to Devil's Island, as *Papillon*[3] has vividly recounted. We stopped next at La Rochelle, and while there took the opportunity to visit Dufour's boatyard. I had noticed several pits moulded in the floor of the cockpit and the bulkhead between the cockpit and the after locker, and asked M. Dufour what they were for. He explained that they were intended to allow the cabin table to be set up in the cockpit, but that to do this one would need a special fitting that had been designed but never made. He very kindly gave me a copy of the drawing, and from this I was able to make the fitting myself. This has since been coveted by every Arpège owner who has seen it.

Our next stop was Royan, where we took down the mast and secured it in a horizontal position in preparation for our passage through the canals. Next day Yvonne left to return by train to Paris and we continued to Bordeaux. It was desirable to get from there to the Canal Latéral à la Garonne at Castets-en-Dorthe, some twenty nautical miles away, on one flood tide, and this meant leaving at 4 a.m. We reached Castets at 9 a.m. without difficulty, and successfully negotiated the rather formidable entry to the canal. We continued via Agen, where two of our crew left and Jean and Bill Eastwood joined us, to Toulouse. Here we left the Canal Latéral à la Garonne and joined the ancient Canal du Midi, where many of the locks are still oval, like those built by Paul Riquet in the reign of Louis XIV. In most of the locks the gates had to be operated by hand; on one side by the lock keeper, and on the other by a member of the crew — in our case Hazel, who leaped nimbly ashore to do this.

As a rule we found the barges very cooperative; they allowed us to keep in the middle of the canal when they were unladen, and when laden (they carried up to 160 tonnes), when they had to stay in the middle themselves, they passed us very slowly. We did, nevertheless, go aground three times. Twice we had to be towed off; the other time, just before Carcassonne, Bill swam ashore and made fast a line to a tree, and we winched ourselves off.

We reached the end of the canal at Marseillan late on a Sunday evening. Next day I met Paul Budker, a retired Professor of Oceanography, who had a boat in the port. He was a friend of the Capitaine du Port at Sète and arranged that the three lifting bridges we would have to pass under next day to get to the sea would be opened for us. This was a great help, because the men who operate the bridges are reluctant to open them for yachts and one may have to wait for hours until a commercial vessel arrives. In our case, however, a man with binoculars on the first bridge read the name on the boat, waved to us, and the bridge began to open. We passed through triumphantly, followed by a dozen or so other yachts that had been waiting hopefully. The other bridges were opening when we arrived; again we were waved through, followed by all the other yachts, and found a good mooring at Sète in the Vieux Port, near the Yacht Club.

Sète is a picturesque place that has sometimes been called the Venice of France, and was the birthplace of Paul Valéry. Jean and Bill left us there, and Hazel and I sailed the boat alone to Toulon, with stops at La Grande Motte, Port du Bouc, La Pointe Rouge (just after Marseilles), La Ciotat, Bandol, Les Embiez and St Mandrier. We had quite a lot of strong *mistral* on the way; when it reached force 7 we stayed in harbour, but otherwise simply shortened sail.

In Les Embiez we went to see Dr Alain Bombard, to whom we had a letter of introduction from Professor Budker, at the Observatoire de la Mer. I had already read his book, *Naufragé Volontaire*,[4] in which he tells how he became interested in survival at sea when, as an interne in the hospital at Boulogne, he was called on to treat seamen who had been rescued from open boats after their ship was sunk in the Atlantic. He believed that one's chances of surviving on board a life raft or dinghy could be greatly increased by collecting water that condensed as dew and drinking this mixed with fluid pressed from raw fish and a small proportion of sea water, and demonstrated this during the remarkable crossing of the Atlantic described in his book.

At St Mandrier we washed and dried our sails, and motored from there to Mediterranée Plaisance at Toulon, where we had arranged to leave *Therapist* for the winter. We received a warm welcome from the proprietor, M. Jérome, though later on our relations became less cordial. I went by train to Sète to collect our car and, a few days later, we drove home to Edinburgh.

We kept the boat at Toulon for seven years. Our summer cruises took us to places such as Hyères and the Iles d'Hyères (Porquerolles and Port Cros), St Tropez, St Raphael, La Napoule, the Iles des Lérins, Nice, St Jean-Cap Ferrat, Beaulieu, Monaco, Menton, and San Remo. In addition, in 1976, we went to Corsica for ten days with George and Dorothy Steedman on board, stopping at Calvi, Girolata and Ajaccio. The navigation was easy because of the radio beacons both on the mainland and on Corsica, and on the way home we picked up the light on La Garoupe ('2 ev. 10 secs') from forty miles away, but I nevertheless took a few astronomical sights for fun with my new sextant. We experienced strong wind and rough sea, especially on the west coast of Corsica, but the most frightening part of the trip was a bus drive we took into the mountains from Calvi.

We met many interesting people in Toulon or while cruising, because we owned a sailing boat and could speak French reasonably well, and some of them require special mention.

One Sunday morning in 1979 Hazel and I, and George Steedman, were strolling round the harbour at St Jean-Cap Ferrat and offered to help an elderly gentleman who was carrying a heavy sail. His name, we found later, was Frédéric Mercier, and he was aged eighty-two. In his youth he had represented France in many international sailing regattas, mostly in Star class boats. He said that he was going to his boat to participate in the annual ceremony of the blessing of fishing boats and pleasure craft stationed at St Jean, and invited us to go with him. Meanwhile, Mme. Mercier, whom we got to know later by her first name, Marina, had been watching from their house and wondering what kind of people her husband had picked up. She now joined us and we all went on board Frédéric's boat, which was called *Vega*. There was no engine but he sailed out of the crowded harbour with incredible skill; unfortunately, however, when we arrived the ceremony had ended so we had to return unblessed. Fortunately, by this time, Madame Mercier had concluded that we were not as bad as she had feared and invited us to their house for lunch. They gave us drinks in a room crammed with silver cups and other sailing trophies, followed by an excellent lunch, prepared by Marina's cook-cum-maid, Solange, who came from Martinique.

Marina was born in Russia, and in the dining room there was a striking portrait of her father, wearing the uniform of a General in the army of the Tsar; also throughout the house there were many of her own paintings. The Merciers have since become close friends, and we have visited them every year since our first meeting. On occasion we have even persuaded them to come on board *Therapist* for dinner, though in recent years Frédéric has not been able to cope with our rather narrow gangplank.

In 1980, when we were in Toulon, I noticed a slightly built lady trying unsuccessfully to winch her husband up the mast of their boat, *Pollux III*, to make some adjustment to the rigging.

They gratefully accepted my offer of help, and later gave me a beer on board their boat. The man turned out to be M. André Quilichini, a Concord pilot for Air France. Later, after his wife had returned to Paris, M. Quilichini came to dinner on *Therapist*; next day we had lunch with him, after which he drove us to the top of Mont Pharon, from where there is a wonderful view of the Rade de Toulon, Les Embiez, and the Iles d'Hyères.

Soon after this we were invited on board a boat named *Tara*, about the same size as *Therapist*, by the owner, M. Bernard de Courteix, a lawyer from Paris. He was then unmarried and had just returned after sailing single handed to Corsica. He later married a paediatrician practising in Paris, and they bought a holiday apartment in Beaulieu and found a place in the port for *Tara*. Since our move to Beaulieu we have dined with them on several occasions and met Bernard's mother.

Another interesting person we got to know in Toulon was Professor Joseph Comiti, owner of a boat named *Galaxie* that was at one time moored alongside *Therapist*. He was in practice as a surgeon in Marseilles, but had at one time been the French Minister of Health.

Two other friends we got to know well, but not through sailing, were André and Nellie Poirier, who ran a restaurant called *Le Morateur* at St Paul de Vence. They were originally from Lyon, where André's father had been the proprietor of a restaurant of the same name. They had once spent a few days at The Bield in company with some English friends of ours when we were on holiday in France. When they left, Nellie had written in our Visitors Book:

Nous nous sentions un peu comme un Roi et une Reine ici. Il y manquait votre présence — Nous vous attendons un jour à St Paul.

We needed no persuasion to visit St Paul, to enjoy a meal in their restaurant and to visit the splendid Maeght Foundation. It was, however, with considerable trepidation that we invited them later to dinner on *Therapist*. Hazel wisely did not try to compete with André by producing French dishes but prepared one of her curries, and this was a great success.

Towards the end of our last summer in Toulon I went to see the proprietor of Mediterranéc Plaisance about some work to be done on the boat and he had with him an elderly gentleman who turned out to be Admiral (retired) Brasseur-Kermadec. I was told that he was there as interpreter, but I think that he had been invited to intimidate me. If so, the plan came unstuck, because I talked to M. Jérome, as I always did, in French, and chatted with the Admiral in idiomatic English that Jérome did not understand. He was a pleasant and most interesting man, and invited me to come with Hazel that evening for a drink on his beautiful ketch, *Jibeca*, which was moored in the port. When asked what we would like to drink we suggested gin and tonic, to which the admiral replied, 'I am very sorry. I know that British sailors drink only Plymouth gin, and all I have is Gordons.' We settled for Gordons, but were astonished by his remark until we learned that Brasseur-Kermadec had escaped from German-occupied France when he was a sub-lieutenant in the Marine Nationale, and had served for the rest of the war in the Royal Navy, where he had gained the Distinguished Service Cross, before resuming his career in the Marine Nationale. Years later he became Naval Attaché at the French embassy in London, and eventually Commander-in-Chief of the French Mediterranean Fleet.

On 29 July 1981, the day of the Royal Wedding in London, I hoisted the signal: 'U W CHARLES DIANA' (UW being the International Code two letter signal meaning 'I wish you a pleasant voyage'). As we did not have television on the boat we walked around Toulon until we found a shop with a television set in the window showing the ceremony in St Paul's cathedral. The Archbishop of Canterbury was just about to pronounce the couple man and wife when the proprietor of the shop looked at his watch, decided that it was time for his déjeuner, and switched off the set. By the time we had found a café with a set tuned to the same program the ceremony was over!

In 1982 we sailed the boat to Beaulieu, where we had arranged to rent a place in the harbour. Before we left Toulon, Hazel, with a little help from me, painted the hull, using a ladder borrowed from a man who was looking after a Swan 38 with the unusual name of *Helisara*, which was also on a cradle. We found that this boat belonged to the celebrated orchestral conductor, Herbert von Karajan, and that the name of the boat was derived from the first names of von Karajan himself and his wife and daughter. I asked the man looking after the boat whether Herr von Karajan

31. Presenting Sir Edward Dunlop for the Honorary FRCSE.

32. Honorary recipients of the FRCPE, 1982.
Seated (L to R) Sir John McMichael, Lord Home,
Dr John Strong (President), Sir John Richardson,
myself and Sir Cyril Clarke.

listened to recorded music when sailing, and was told that he did not, though he often talked about music.

In recent years we have done mainly day sailing from Beaulieu, with occasional trips to the west to La Napoule, and to the east to Menton or just into Italy, and have lifted the boat out of the water each year at either Antibes or St Jean. A few years ago I fitted a furling genoa, and this has made the boat much easier for us to handle. We have taken to going twice a year when we can, first in June and later towards the end of September, when there are fewer people, the air temperature is lower, and the temperature of the sea is at its highest (25–26°C). We are very close to a pleasant beach, where Hazel swims every morning, whatever the weather, before breakfast. I swim when it is sunny, and the water temperature is at least 20°C.

We have many old friends in the vicinity, and have made many new ones, among them Christian de Smet, a dentist practising in Nice, and his wife, Hélène. They own a thirty-six foot sloop, named *Hiva Oa* after the vessel in which Alain Gerbault had circled the world, and every year they go on a long cruise with their two young daughters, Stephanie and Marianne. By a strange coincidence, Christian had been a boarder for a term at Bootham School in York when our son, Keith, was there.

For many years after we bought our first boat, I learned about seamanship and navigation from friends who were experienced sailors, and from reading books, starting with Peter Heaton's *Sailing*[5] and *Cruising*,[6] and going on to Adlard Coles' *Heavy Weather Sailing*,[7] John Illingworth's *Further Offshore*,[8] and various books on navigation. In 1975, however, I decided that something more was needed, and enrolled in classes at Leith Nautical College. This enabled me to gain my Offshore Yachtmaster Certificate and my Restricted Certificate of Radiotelephony, after which I went on to do a shore-based course on astronavigation. Today, anyone who can afford to buy the necessary equipment should be able to fix his position accurately in most parts of the world by signals from artificial satellites, even if he knows nothing about navigation, but the deeper understanding I gained from my classes has given me great satisfaction.

The attractions of sailing are many and various. High among them for me are the sheer physical pleasure of sailing in fine weather with a 10–15 knot breeze, the satisfaction of making a good landfall (in Jean Merrien's words, *Ça s'arrose, un bon atterrisage*[9]), the excitement of competitive racing, and success in battling with the elements when going is tough.

I gave up racing when we moved *Therapist II* to the Mediterranean, but remained a member of the Royal Forth Yacht Club, and served on the council for three years.

I enjoy reading the accounts of people like Joshua Slocum,[10] Alan Gerbault,[11] Yves Le Toumelin,[12] Ann Davison,[13] Francis Chichester,[14] and Eric Tabarly,[15] who have made adventurous single-handed voyages,[16] especially when I am safely tucked up in bed, or in my bunk. Virtually all my sailing, however, has been done as a member, or as the leader, of a crew, and I would not have wished it otherwise. For the greatest pleasure sailing has brought me has come from meeting interesting people, on board and on shore, many of whom I would otherwise not have met, and from the lasting friendships that have sometimes developed from these meetings. What more could anyone ask for?

It was with sadness that I stopped sailing in 1992 and sold the boat.

Second Innings

I wanted, as I remarked in Chapter 13, when I retired from my Chair, to continue research in the field of cancer, partly because of the great biological interest of cancer, and partly because I had seen so much of the misery caused by cancer to so many people. I believed, moreover, that the conquest of cancer would not be achieved by tumour biologists or clinicians working independently, but would depend on the concerted efforts of biologists and clinicians, and that this collaboration would be facilitated if there were people with a foothold, however precarious, in both camps. But to continue to do research, I would have to find both a suitable place in which to work and adequate financial support.

The University had appointed as my successor Professor Geoffrey Chisholm, a distinguished urologist who was then on the staff of the Postgraduate Medical School in London. I had, of course, played no part in this appointment, but was delighted by it because I had become convinced that, with the growth of the surgical specialties, it was no longer appropriate for both the Regius Chair of Clinical Surgery and the University Chair of Surgery to be filled by general surgeons. As Professor Chisholm would not be able to take up his new appointment until early in 1977, it seemed reasonable for me to continue research in my old department for a term, and sufficient financial support for this short time was available from two research funds that had been established in the department. As a long term solution my friend John Evans, Director of the Medical Research Council Clinical and Population Cytogenetics Unit (now renamed the Human Genetics Unit), generously agreed to provide me with laboratory space and facilities for animal work in his unit when the time came to leave the Department of Surgery, provided that I had the necessary grant support to continue working. For two years this was provided by grants from the Nuffield Foundation and the Melville Trust, and thereafter, for six years, by project grants from the Medical Research Council. These covered the cost of animals and the salaries of a graduate assistant and a technician, and also a small honorarium for me. In addition the Wellcome Trust provided me with a secretary for several years, primarily to help with a clinical trial that had been started just before I retired from the university.

When, in the summer of 1985, my third MRC Project Grant ended I decided to stop doing experimental work (apart from finishing off experiments in progress), but I had several papers to write and was also working on another book, and I continued to receive great help from the Unit Librarian, Sheila Mould, and also from the staff of the Illustration and Photographic Section, headed by Norman Davidson. I was still writing at the time of my eightieth birthday in 1991 (Fig 30).

The Cytogenetics Unit had been established, under the directorship of Dr Michael Court Brown, to study the characteristics of the chromosomes of human cells (termed collectively the *karyotype*), to formulate criteria for identifying individual human chromosomes, and to relate karyotypic abnormalities to congenital and other disorders. This became possible when techniques were developed for making 'spread preparations' of human cells in mitosis, in which individual chromosomes were clearly visible. I had first become acquainted with the unit in 1961 when two members of the staff, Karin Buckton and Patricia Jacobs, helped me to identify human twins who were blood chimeras by chromosomal sexing of blood leucocytes.[1]

In 1969 Professor H. J. (John) Evans succeeded Dr Court Brown as Director of the Unit. Under his leadership the cytological work of the unit continued to develop, and the scope of the unit expanded as biology moved into the molecular era. It was a stimulating environment in which to work. I had a succession of excellent assistants, Valerie Whitehead, Gabrielle Forbes and Sam Hodson; and enjoyed the collaboration of Jonathan Bard, Michael Steel, John Gosden and others in the Unit; and of Spedding Micklem and John Ansell in the University Department of Zoology, and Keith James in the Department of Surgery.

My *posthumous research*, as a colleague dubbed it, generated some twenty-five scientific papers[2] and reviews.[3] It has been summarised and set in a broader context in two books: *The Interaction of Cancer and Host — Its Therapeutic Significance,*[4] and *Cellular Variation and Adaptation in Cancer — Biological Basis and Therapeutic Consequences.*[5] It may be helpful to the general reader to give an outline of their contents here.

Malignant tumours, referred to collectively as cancer, develop as the result of a heritable change in one or more of the cells of the host, animal or human, in which they arise. This change, called *transformation*, usually occurs in several steps. It was customary, until fairly recently, to describe malignant tumours as *autonomous*, and some people still use this term. Its precise meaning is not always clear, but it seems to imply, firstly, that tumours are not influenced by any of the factors that control the growth and equilibrium of normal tissues, and secondly, that no special mechanisms, even of the most rudimentary kind, have evolved for controlling carcinogenesis and tumour growth. Today the dogma of autonomy seems untenable in the light of evidence that malignant tumours occasionally regress, or re-appear suddenly after a long period of dormancy; that some tumours are influenced by the presence or absence of hormonal stimulation, and other factors that influence the growth of normal tissues; and that some tumour cells possess antigens or other surface markers that can trigger resistance mechanisms. But, one may ask, does the host reaction have any decisive effect on the development of a tumour; and, if it does, what are the implications of this with regard to the treatment of cancer?

My first book about cancer, as its name implies, tries to answer these questions. It begins by discussing such topics as mechanisms of carcinogenesis; whether a malignant tumour develops from a single normal cell (in which case it is called *monoclonal*) or from two or more normal cells (in which case it is called *polyclonal*); the spread of cancer by invasion of neighbouring tissues, and by dissemination via the blood stream and other routes; the phenomena of dormancy and the spontaneous regression of metastases; and ways in which the behaviour of cancer is modified by the reaction it evokes, with particular reference to the role of antibodies, sensitized lymphocytes, macrophages and natural killer cells. It then examines the therapeutic implications of the phenomena discussed, in particular the possibility that treatment may weaken the natural resistance of the host, and ways in which this resistance may be increased, and describes the results of attempts to apply this knowledge in treating experimental and clinical cancer.

The second book is concerned with the question of why current methods of treating cancer are not more effective. In recent years there have indeed been some major advances, notably in the treatment of acute lymphoblastic leukaemia, Hodgkin's disease, malignant tumours of the testis, Wilm's tumour, and to a lesser extent osteogenic sarcoma; but, on the other hand, there has not been much improvement in the results of treating cancer of the stomach, small cell cancer of the lung, myelogenous leukaemia, cancer of the breast, and a host of other tumours. The reasons for our treatment failures are multiple and complex. The realization that cancer often becomes disseminated at an early stage provides part of the answer, and prompted the introduction of what was called *adjuvant chemotherapy*, i.e. the use of chemotherapy in addition to surgery in the management of cancer of the breast and other tumours, but, while this is of value in some patients, the early high hopes which accompanied its introduction have not been fulfilled. Why? The writer maintains that two factors of critical importance are the heterogeneous nature of cancer cell populations and their capacity to diversify, and examines the evidence for this, and possible ways of dealing with the problem in the light of advances in nucleic acid chemistry, immunology and molecular biology.

During my 'second innings' I continued to participate in meetings of the British Association for Cancer Research, of which I was President from 1979 to 1982; the British Society for Immunology, of which I was made an Honorary Member in 1982; the British Transplantation Society; the Royal College of Surgeons of Edinburgh, where it was my privilege to present for the Honorary Fellowship two old friends, Sir Edward ('Weary') Dunlop (Fig 31) and Dr Joseph Murray; and various meetings of the Royal Society, where I served on the council from 1977 to 1979, and was a Vice-president in 1978 and 1979. In 1982 I was elected an Honorary Fellow of the Royal College of Physicians of Edinburgh (Fig 32).

Further afield, my travels took me to various European countries, the Middle East, Australia and New Zealand, South Africa, Singapore and Malaysia, and China.

In 1978 I attended the biennial congress of the Transplantation Society in Rome, and gave a paper on the current state of clinical immunotherapy of cancer.[6] Many of the participants attended the first public audience of the recently elected Pope John Paul I, who welcomed us so warmly that the Society reproduced his remarks in the published report of the congress.[7] At the time it was sometimes difficult to obtain permission from members of the family of a recently deceased Roman Catholic to remove organs for transplantation because they believed that this would be contrary to the teaching of their Church, but when shown a copy of the Pope's message they often accepted that this was not the case, and allowed us to proceed. One of the social highlights of the congress was the dinner held in the *Castel del Angelo*, from the balustrade of which, in Puccini's opera, Tosca leaps to her death after the execution of Cavaradossi.

Eight years later Hazel and I went to Helsinki for the XIth Congress of the Society, which was dedicated jointly to Rupert Billingham and myself (Fig 33). We found Helsinki a beautiful, though expensive, city, and admired the way in which the Finns got on with the business of everyday life despite the ever-present threat posed by their powerful Soviet neighbour.

In 1980 Hazel and I went to Gibraltar to spend Christmas with Keith, who was Resident Engineer supervising the construction of an extension to the harbour to take container ships, and his family. The Governor, General Sir William Jackson, who was himself an engineer, took considerable interest in the harbour development, and visited the site regularly. The government of Gibraltar had decided that there would not be a formal opening ceremony when the work was completed, presumably for fear of provoking a protest from Spain, but Keith told the Governor that he and the contractor planned to have their own opening ceremony, and added that if, by any chance, His Excellency happened to be in the vicinity at the time, they would be greatly honoured if he would join them for a glass of champagne. The Governor took the hint, and graciously said a few words at the unofficial ceremony. Later, he and Lady Jackson invited Keith, Sue, Hazel and me to lunch at Government House, in the course of which he told us two memorable stories.

The first was of how, in the days of wooden ships, the Royal Navy destroyed a Spanish man-of-war by attacking it with cannon balls that had been heated until they were red hot. These lodged in the timber of the hull, where they smouldered away and eventually set it on fire, causing the gunpowder in the magazine to explode. The second story concerned the name of the Governor's house and, as Sir William acknowledged, was recounted by Sir Winston Churchill in his history, *The Second World War*.[8] Until 1908 the house was called The Convent, because it had originally been a convent though the nuns had left some 200 years ago, but in that year the Private Secretary to King Edward VII wrote to the Governor to say that it was His Majesty's wish that the name should be changed to Government House. The reason was that, following a recent visit when the King had lunched at the Convent, there had been protests in the British press about the King taking lunch in a Roman Catholic Convent, and apparently also, though Churchill does not mention this, some rather ribald comments. Following a visit by King George VI in 1943, however, the then Governor was told that it was His Majesty's wish that the Governor's residence should resume its old name.

A few months later we were in Lyon for a farewell symposium in honour of Jules Traeger, who was about to retire from the Chair of Medicine. When asked by his colleagues what he would like as a present on his retirement he had suggested that this should take the form of a scientific meeting to which people from various parts of the world might be invited, and this gave great pleasure to his many friends. Our celebration dinner was held in Paul Bocuse's elegant restaurant, and as we arrived the celebrated *orgue mécanique* — it does not remotely do it justice to translate this as *barrel organ* — was playing the triumphal march from Aida. It was a splendid meal, and M. Bocuse was kind enough to autograph my menu. We took part in another celebration in France in 1990, when I presented the Prize established in honour of Bernard Halpern at the Collège de France in Paris. During this visit we lunched with Mme. Halpern in her apartment on the Boulevard St Germain. A fellow guest was Dr Charles Merieux, formerly head of the Lyon-based pharmaceutical firm that bears

his name; he was a good friend of Jules Traeger and had, I
suspect, contributed generously to the cost of his retirement
symposium.

In 1981 I went with Hazel to Kuwait for ten days as Visiting
Professor of Surgery, at the invitation of Professor George
Abouna, who had been a lecturer in my department in Edinburgh and had worked in the Nuffield Transplant Unit. He was
born in Iraq but had lived in Britain since the age of five, and was
a graduate of the University of Durham. He had learned to speak
Arabic as a boy but had forgotten it. Teaching in the medical
school in Kuwait was in English, but Abouna's Kuwaiti colleagues often spoke Arabic among themselves and he wisely
decided to brush up his Arabic so as to understand what they
said. Abouna had begun transplanting kidneys in Kuwait soon
after he arrived, and had persuaded Arthur White, an immunologist who had done much of the tissue typing for the
Nuffield Transplantation Unit in Edinburgh, to join him in
Kuwait to set up tissue typing there. For a long time they were
restricted to using organs from living donors because most
Kuwaiti Moslems felt that it would be contrary to their religion
to remove organs from a dead body. This seemed surprising in
view of the liberal attitude they adopted in other matters —
women, for example, did not have to wear a veil in public and
were allowed to drive motor cars, and in the Medical School they
attended the same classes as men. Abouna tried hard, eventually
with some success, to change this attitude, and was able to quote
a ruling of the Islamic Fatwa Committee assembled by the
Ministry of Islamic Affairs in Kuwait, issued in December 1979,
which authorised removal of organs for transplantation after
death of the donor 'provided there is dire necessity, since the
necessity to save a human life overrides the prohibition of
wounding the dead body'.[9]

To increase the supply of kidneys Abouna often used transplants from apparently unrelated living donors, and found that
these often behaved like transplants from parents or non-twin
siblings, probably because cousin marriages were so common in
Kuwait and the diversity of the HLA genes in the population
had, as a result, become significantly reduced.

We stayed at the Hilton Hotel, and were very happy there
until, one day, the Palestinian leader, Yassir Arafat, arrived in

Kuwait. He stayed at the Royal Palace, but his entourage took over the whole floor of the hotel on which our room was situated. We were given another equally good room, and a card saying that we were staying in the hotel, but it was disconcerting to have to run the gauntlet of men armed with tommy guns every time one entered or left the hotel. We walked very slowly and made sure that both our hands were clearly visible. I was provided with a car and an Arab driver who seldom stopped at a red traffic light but never had an accident. Hazel and I received much generous hospitality, which included a visit to an oil field and a cruise on the Gulf. To say thank you we gave a dinner party at the Tower restaurant, from where we had a superb panoramic view of the city.

We returned to Kuwait in December 1982, to take part in the *First International Middle East Symposium on Organ Transplantation*, that had been organized by Professor Abouna. There were fifteen invited participants from Europe and the United States, most of whom I knew well, and we had an excellent meeting.[10] It fell to me to chair the opening session, contribute to various panel discussions, and to sum up at the end of the symposium. On this occasion we stayed at the Sheraton Hotel, where the meeting took place, and everything was very peaceful.

Hazel and I spent Christmas and New Year 1985/86 in Tunis with Keith and family. He was still with Halcrows and was Resident Engineer for a project which involved cleaning up the Lac de Tunis, that was severely polluted. They rented a pleasant house in Sidi Bou Said, quite near to the ruins of Carthage and the baths of Antoninus Pius. Though the population in Tunisia was predominantly Moslem the attitude towards women was more liberal than it had been in any other Moslem country we had visited, and not only was alcohol tolerated but the country produced some surprisingly good wine. This reflected the strong French influence that still existed in Tunisia. President Bourguiba had been educated in Paris, and French was widely spoken; indeed, on Keith's site it was the main medium of communication. We greatly enjoyed visiting the splendid Bardo museum, the ruins of Carthage and, further away, of the Roman City of Dougga; also Bizerta, Suze, Monastir, and the port of El Kantawi. At El Kantawi we went on board a very convincing-looking Spanish man-of-war that had been specially built for Zefirelli's film *Pirates,* though concealed inside the wooden hull were two powerful diesel engines. Keith told us that one day when they were filming, and there was not enough wind to fill the sails, the problem was solved by putting the engines full astern so that the ship appeared to be sailing though it was actually moving backwards through the water. We saw the film later in Edinburgh but were unable to detect this ingenious subterfuge.

Hazel and I have visited Australia four times since I retired from surgery.

The first occasion, in July and August 1977, was primarily to attend the Third International Congress of Immunology, which was being held in Sydney, at which I had been asked to take part in a *Symposium on the Immunotherapy of Tumours.* I combined this with two weeks as Visiting Fellow at the Kolling Institute of Medical Research, attached to the Royal North Shore Hospital, at the invitation of the Director, Dr David Nelson. The social highlight of the visit to Sydney was a supper party for about a dozen people to meet Dame Joan Sutherland and her husband, Richard Bonynge, after a performance of *Lucrezia Borgia* at the Sydney Opera House. Our hosts were Gustav and Lyn Nossal. Gus had been at school with Bonynge, and with the proprietor of the restaurant in which the supper was held. Joan Sutherland was emotionally drained after singing Lucrezia and did not want to talk very much, but Bonynge, who had been conducting, was in sparkling form. While in Australia we received a cable from New Zealand from Keith announcing his engagement to Sue Nairn, a New Zealand girl we had met in Edinburgh, and telling us that they planned to be married towards the end of the month. We hastily revised our travel plans, and flew to Napier to meet Sue's parents, John and Janet Nairn, who had invited us to stay with them at Amblethorn, their beautiful home, set in a large garden complete with peacocks, surrounded by many acres of lush pasture with grazing sheep. We quickly formed a firm friendship with the Nairns that has deepened over the years. Keith and Sue were married in the local Anglican Church by Canon John Wilson, a close friend of the Nairn family. I had the unusual experience of being our son's best man, because he knew no other men in the vicinity apart from his future father-in-law.

Our next visit to Australia was in 1985, when Hazel and I were official guests at the Centenary of the Adelaide University Medical School, at which I had to deliver a lecture[11] in honour of Howard Florey, the school's most distinguished alumnus. A fellow guest was Sir Zelman Cowen, a former Rhodes Scholar and a distinguished academic lawyer, who had been Professor of Public Law in Melbourne, Vice-Chancellor of the University of Queensland, and Governor General of Australia, and was currently Provost of Oriel College, Oxford.

From Adelaide we flew to Melbourne, where I gave various lectures and seminars. We were taken one day by Dr Ian Mackay, Head of the Clinical Section of the Hall Institute, to Flemington Race Course. I know nothing about horse racing, but in one race there was a mare called *Cap d' Antibes*, which I decided to back simply on account of her name, despite Ian's opinion that she had no chance whatever. To my surprise, and Ian's absolute amazement, she won by several lengths!

We dined one evening in Queen's College with the Master, Owen Parnaby, and his wife. Before dinner I reminded the Master that, when I was in College, the men who held scholarships took it in turn to say the College Latin grace before dinner, and asked whether this custom was still observed. He told me it had lapsed, and that it fell to the senior person dining in Hall to say grace in English, but added that he would be delighted if I would say the Latin grace. I accepted this challenge, and once again, to the astonishment of all the undergraduates present, and most of the people at the High Table, *Domine qui aperis manum tuam* ... (p. 48) resounded through the hall.

Hazel and I wanted very much to revisit the Grampian Mountains in western Victoria, where we had spent our honeymoon, and decided that we could just manage a week there before going to stay with Philip and Lyndsay Woodruff at their country home at Noosa, on Queensland's Gold Coast. Forty years on we were not as sprightly as we had been at the time of our previous visit, but we still managed to climb Mount William, Mount Rosea, and the Pinnacle; explore the Mitchell plateau; and visit the Silverband falls, the McKenzie falls, Lake Wartook, Zumsteins, and Bunjil's cave. The wildflowers were at their best, and we were sorry we could not stay longer. Before heading for home I paid a brief visit to the Australian National University in

Canberra, where I had been invited to give a seminar by Professor Bede Morris, Head of the Department of Immunology. I had not met him previously, but had read with interest two addresses he had recently given. One, entitled *Transplantation and Cannibalism*, began with the proposition that in primitive societies cannibalism was practised in the belief that it enabled one to perpetuate characteristics that were admired in friends or enemies — 'you ate your enemy to acquire his strength and courage, you ate your grandfather to acquire his knowledge and wisdom ...', not to satisfy your hunger or your gourmet tastes. It then went on to compare the ethical problems posed by cannibalism and those raised by modern organ transplantation. The other address, which was entitled 'Unnatural selection and the destiny of humanity', will be discussed in Chapter 16.

We returned to Melbourne in August 1987 in response to two invitations that I found irresistible: to contribute to a symposium that was being organized as part of the celebrations to mark the one hundredth anniversary of the foundation of Queen's College, and to deliver the biennial Halford Oration in the University a week later. We learned subsequently that Keith had accepted an appointment with Maunsell and Partners, a well known firm of consulting engineers based in Melbourne, and that he and his family would be moving to Melbourne a few weeks before we were due to arrive. We revised our plans so as to have as long as possible with them and, incidentally, to enable me to attend the dinner to celebrate the fiftieth anniversary of the graduation of people in my year in Medicine, which was to take place in October.

The Queens' College symposium, which was the brain-child of Sir Halford Cook, was entitled *Options for Humanity*, and there were five invited speakers, all old Queen's men. Professor Geoffrey Blainey, a distinguished Australian historian, opened with a paper entitled 'Is there a future?: A word about war' He argued persuasively, though without convincing all his audience, that a nuclear war on a large scale was unlikely. I followed with a paper entitled 'The choice for mankind in relation to biology and medicine'.[12] Next came a paper from Emeritus Professor the Hon. Joseph Isaac, an academic lawyer who was an authority on industrial relationships in Australia, on the subject of 'Industrial co-operation and industrial conflict'. Professor Colin Williams, who currently occupied a Chair of Theology at Yale University, examined the role of reason, and of faith, in the search for truth. The last paper, entitled 'Law, economics and ethics', was given by the Hon. Sir Richard Eggleston, a former Judge of the Commonwealth Industrial Court. In it, he commented on the preceding papers and added some thoughts of his own concerning the need for more research in the social sciences, the application of the theory of probability to evidence of the kind presented in the courts, and law in relation to trade unions.

The Halford Oration was named in honour of Professor G. B. Halford, the first professor appointed in the medical school. He was a physiologist from University College, London, but was expected to teach anatomy and pathology as well as physiology until chairs were created in these subjects. I spoke about 'The interface between science and medicine', and used the occasion to proclaim my conviction that it is important for people who work on different sides of this interface to be able to communicate with each other, and that such communication is easier if there are some people who work on both sides.[13]

Our next visit to Australia was from November 1989 to January 1990. It was essentially a holiday, the highlight of which was a two-week visit to Tasmania with Keith and family. We visited Port Arthur, on the Tasman Peninsula, and then spent several days in Dover (Port Esperance), where I had spent many of my boyhood holidays. From there we visited the only one of the Hastings Caves that was open to visitors, and climbed Adamson's Peak. A track had been made since I was last there, which made the ascent much easier. We had wondered if the climb would be too much for Jonathan, but for speed and endurance he certainly outclassed his grandfather! From Dover we returned to Hobart, and then went to Lake St Clair, Zeehan and Port Macquarrie, from where we had a wonderful all day trip by launch on the Gordon River. Before we disembarked, the launch took us to the narrow entrance to the Gordon River estuary, and it was easy to understand why so many ships bringing convicts to the penal colony established further upstream were wrecked there.

Towards the end of 1985 we spent ten days in Singapore and Malaysia on our way home from Australia. This was the first time that I had felt able to go there since the war, but I wanted to take

Hazel to some of the places I remembered, and felt that sufficient time had elapsed for this not to be too stressful.

In Singapore we stayed at the Tanglin Club, which granted us temporary honorary membership as members of the Edinburgh New Club. It was very comfortable, and we particularly enjoyed relaxing in the swimming pool. We had letters of introduction from Alan Kerr Grant to three physician friends of his: Professor Cheng Siang and Dr John Tambyah in Singapore, and Dr Lim Kee Jin in Johore Bahru, who were all most hospitable. I was deeply moved by two visits. The first was to Changi gaol with Mrs Tambyah, where we saw the memorial to deceased prisoners of war in the gaol chapel; the second, with Dr Lim Kee Jin, to the allied war memorial and cemetery at Kranji, where I read on the roll of honour the names of many deceased friends and colleagues, including those of the matron of the 10th Australian General Hospital, and seven of the eight nurses in the 4th Australian Casualty Clearing Station (CCS). Crossing the Causeway to Johore on our way to dine with Dr and Mrs Lim Kee Jin also evoked vivid memories, though mercifully they were not so emotionally charged.

We decided to travel from Singapore to Malacca by bus, and stopped on the way at Ayer Hitam, where our CCS had been established for a few days in the course of our retreat down the Malay peninsula. Malacca, with its hospital and club was, to my surprise, very much as I remembered it. We looked for the Suan Kee restaurant, where I had enjoyed many excellent Chinese meals before Japan entered the war but, when we did eventually find it, it looked very run down and we were not tempted to eat there. After a night in Malacca we continued by bus to Kuala Lumpur, which had changed considerably since I was last there, except for its ornate railway station. From 'KL' we went to Fraser's Hill, where we spent a night. It was an interesting drive, but the place had lost most of its former splendour.

We returned to Singapore in 1987 on our way to Australia, and again two years later, when we stopped there on our way to, and also on our return from, Australia. Besides being an interesting place, with excellent hotels, in which one feels perfectly safe to wander round, even at night, one can get a flight from London which arrives there in the evening, and it is dark by the time one is ready to go to bed. This, as I pointed out in a letter to Nature,[14] seems to enable one to reset one's biological clock, and so to recover from jetlag, more quickly than one otherwise would.

The highlight of our travels after I retired from my Chair was a three-week visit to The Peoples Republic of China, arranged under the Scientific Exchange Agreement between the Royal Society and the Chinese Academy of Sciences, in the autumn of 1979.

We flew to Hong Kong, but arrived there a day late because our flight was diverted to Manilla to avoid a hurricane. Next day the airways bus taking us to Manilla airport for our flight to Hong Kong stopped suddenly at a traffic light and was run into by the bus behind. The man sitting next to me, who turned out to be an airline pilot though he was not in uniform, got out to look around, and saw that our petrol (*sic*) tank had been holed but that this had not deterred numerous bystanders from smoking. He got back into the bus and suggested very quietly that we would be more comfortable in the shade of a building a short distance away. He thus managed to get everyone out of the bus without any panic, and we resumed our journey to the airport an hour or two later in another bus. One of our fellow passengers was travelling to Manilla and the airline offered to unload his baggage, but the Manilla authorities insisted that he should go back to Hong Kong with the rest of us and return to Manilla on a scheduled Hong Kong–Manilla flight!

In Hong Kong we went to the Hyatt Regency Hotel in Kowloon, where there was supposed to be a room reserved for us. They had no record of this at the hotel, though they did eventually manage to find us one. This was a foretaste of things to come. We collected our rail tickets for Guangzhou (Canton) from the China Travel Service and caught the train next day. The Royal Society had told us that 'the Chinese Academy of Sciences ... will meet visitors at travel terminals with special cars and provide interpreters during the whole visit'. At Guangzhou station, however, the other foreigners on the train, who were all travelling in organized parties, had someone to meet them, but there was no one to meet us. This was disconcerting, because we did not know the name of our hotel, and could neither read nor speak the language, but eventually the courier for one of the organized parties saw our plight and took us to the Dong Feng Hotel, where we were given a room and later had an excellent,

33. Honoured by the Transplantation Society, with Rupert Billingham, Helsinki, 1986.

34. Received by Deng Xiao Ping in Beijing, with Lord and Lady Todd, Sir Michael and Lady Stoker, and the British Ambassador to China.

and very inexpensive, dinner in a restaurant in which everyone else was Chinese. We were relieved to find that the Guangzhou office of the Chinese Academy of Sciences was located in our hotel, and made contact with a man in the office who spoke quite good English, but the Academy staff insisted that they had never heard of us and it looked as if we would be sent back to Hong Kong. At the time I was on the Council of the Royal Society and one of the Vice-Presidents, and I thought it might be worth trying to pull a little rank. The effect exceeded my wildest expectations. A *Vice-President*, they said, in tones of awe; knowing, as I did not, that in China a Vice-President of anything, including the whole country, may well be far more important than the President. Next day our future interpreter, Miss Ma Xuezheng, and other important people arrived from Beijing (Pekin). They were most apologetic, but said that, although my name was on the list of possible visitors, the CAS had not been told when we were coming. I returned their apologies on behalf of the Royal Society and everyone seemed satisfied that face had been saved. Later, the Academy said that the letter about us had been delayed in the post.

I discussed our itinerary with Miss Ma, and gave her abstracts of the lectures I had prepared. She said that it would simplify matters for the CAS if Hazel and I would accompany Lord Todd, the President of the Royal Society, the Foreign Secretary, Michael Stoker, and their wives, who were due to arrive in China in a few days time, on various official visits and sightseeing trips, in addition to visiting scientific institutions and giving lectures as originally proposed. I replied that we would be delighted to do this provided that Lord Todd agreed. In the event he seems to have been presented with something of a *fait accompli*, which he accepted with characteristic urbanity and kindness.

Meanwhile arrangements were made for me to visit various hospitals and the Institute of Cancer Research in Guangzhou; the Institute of Oncology, Pekin Medical College, and the Academy of Medical Sciences in Beijing; the Cancer Institute and Hospital, and the Institute of Cell Biology, in Shanghai; and, after our return to Ghangzhou, Chung Shan University, and rural medical establishments in the Pearl River Delta. Our hosts were interested to hear that Hazel had been trained in systematic botany, and also arranged visits to the Guangzhou orchid garden, and the South China Botanic Gardens associated with the Institute of Botany. We were told that the Institute was particularly interested in the genetics of rice, including hybridization techniques, and Hazel was rather apprehensive about this visit, but got off to an impressive start when she correctly diagnosed the splendid trees lining the avenue leading to the institute as *Eucalyptus citriodora*. In the herb garden the labels were in Chinese, but the language difficulty was eased when the taxonomist, Dr Chen Tak-Chou, produced a Latin/Chinese catalogue. At the farewell tea ceremony, when asked for her comments, Hazel consolidated her position by suggesting that high priority should be given to the naming of specimens in Chinese characters and in English, stating the plant family and origin, and, if it was of commercial value, what it was used for.

We flew from Guangzhou to Beijing, where we stayed at the Pekin Hotel with the Presidential party. Each day three cars arrived at the hotel: a large one for the Todds, a middle sized one for the Stokers, and a smaller one for Hazel and me, and this cavalcade was sometimes joined by a fourth car carrying the British Ambassador, Mr (later Sir) Percy Craddock. The highlight of the visit was going with the Presidential party and the Ambassador to meet Chinese leaders, including Deng Xiaoping, and the President of the CAS, Fang Yi (Fig 34). Deng was a short, almost dwarf-like man, but he dominated the assembly. He and Lord Todd had an animated conversation through interpreters, while the rest of us listened in silence, after which a photograph was taken of the group, with Deng and the Todds in the centre and the Woodruffs on the periphery.

We also attended a State Banquet in the Great Hall of the People given by Hua Gofeng, Chairman of the Central Committee of the Communist Party of China and Premier of the State Council. Hua Gofeng spoke at some length, not during but before dinner, and we were thoughtfully provided with a written English translation of his speech. We were guests at other, smaller banquets, had lunch one day at the Embassy, and attended the thankyou dinner given by Lord Todd in honour of our Chinese hosts, at which he astonished them by making a speech in Mandarin! I was told later that he had learned this while convalescing after a heart attack. He also knew a little Cantonese, and on another occasion, when our hosts apologised because someone had welcomed him in Cantonese instead of in Mandarin, he thanked them in the same language.

The food on these occasions was invariably excellent, but the same could not be said of what we were offered to drink. I found that beer, when it was available, was the best choice, but this did not help Hazel, who does not care for beer; the wine was often very sweet and the fiery spirit known as *mao tai* was awful. The ambassador told me that the best thing to do was to wait till some ice-cream came along and tip the mao-tai over it, and I gratefully followed this suggestion. Dinner usually ended at about 9 p.m. Certain dishes were served only as a last course, and when one of these appeared one was expected to know that it would soon be time to say goodnight. If one did not take the hint the host would say, 'You must be feeling very tired', and if one still did not take the hint would get up and shake hands. This convention seemed to us to have much to commend it, but we have never dared to try it at home.

From Beijing we flew with the Presidential party to Shanghai, continued a few days later by train to Hangzhou, and then returned by air to Guangzhou, where we said goodbye to them. While we were with the Presidential party we usually went our separate ways so far as visits to laboratories and hospitals were concerned, but remained together for sightseeing and social functions. We had known the Stokers since the day on which Michael Stoker and I were admitted to the Royal Society, but I had only been on formal terms with Lord Todd, and had not previously met Lady Todd, although I knew that she was the daughter of a former President of the Royal Society, Sir Henry Dale. Their unfailing kindness and sense of humour turned what might have been an embarrassing experience into a pure delight.

My scientific visits nearly all conformed to the following pattern: (1) A meeting in the morning in a conference room where one drank tea, listened to members of the staff of the institute describe their work, and commented on this. (2) Return to the hotel by car for lunch. (3) A lecture by the visitor, which was translated sentence by sentence, and lasted at least two hours because people in the audience often challenged the official translation. When the lecture ended there were invariably several minutes silence before anyone asked a question or made a comment, which would have been disconcerting had I not been forewarned, but once discussion started it was usually lively and to the point. Although I managed to get into a few laboratories, the scientists I met preferred to talk about their work rather than demonstrate what they were actually doing, probably because they realised that their laboratories did not come up to western standards. I found that lack of uniformity in the phonetic spelling of Chinese names, and well-meaning but misguided attempts by some Chinese colleagues to help the visitor by reversing the usual Chinese arrangement of writing their surname before their other names, could make it difficult to identify individuals, and even, on occasion, the institution one was visiting. To overcome this I adopted Hazel's suggestion of inviting the people I met to write down their names in Chinese characters, and asked our interpreter later to tell me the phonetic equivalent.

We were received everywhere with great warmth. The posthumous influence of Mao was waning, the gang of four were discredited, and some years were still to elapse before the tragic massacre in Tiananmen Square. This change in outlook is well illustrated by the fact that, instead of having to visit Mao's tomb in Beijing, we were taken from Guanzhou to the birthplace of Sun Yat Sen, where we visited his house, the Memorial Building, and the Sun Yat Sen Memorial Middle School, places at which were competed for by boys and girls from all over China. We were allowed a generous amount of time for sightseeing, especially during the National Holiday. Among the many interesting places we visited were the Great Wall of China and the Ming Tombs; the Winter Palace and the Forbidden City in Beijing; the Bund and the Temple of the Jade Buddha in Shanghai; the West Lake, Dragon Spring Tea Plantation, Ling Yin Temple, Pagoda of the Six Harmonies and Tiger Well in Hangzhou; and a silk factory and craft centre in Fo Chan.

Our last three days in China were spent visiting Chung Shan county in the Pearl River Delta with Professor Tsung Yung-shen, Director of the Canton Institute of Oncology. Having said goodbye to the Todds and the Stokers, and the head of the Foreign Affairs Bureau of the CAS, we set off by car with Tsung and an interpreter for Si Kiu, the capital of Chung Shan county. This was a most interesting journey which involved four car ferry crossings, and gave me a chance to talk at length with Tsung, who spoke excellent English, but had been away when I visited his institute.

We stayed two nights in a hotel in Si Kiu which was crammed with Chinese visitors from places as far afield as Australia, California and Hong Kong. We were welcomed by the member of the county government responsible for foreign visitors, the county Director of Health and Education, and the Director of the County Hospital. They told us that the county had a population of about a million people, living in three towns and twenty-five peoples' communes, and organized into 450 production brigades. Factories in the towns, which were controlled by the county government, manufactured farm machinery, fertiliser, cement and paper; the main agricultural products were rice, sugar cane, silk, pigs, fish, poultry, bananas, peanuts and vegetables. Fish farming was practised on an extensive scale; the excreta and dead chrysalyses of silk worms were tipped into the fish ponds to feed the fish, mud from the ponds was used as a fertilizer round mulberry trees, and leaves from the mulberry trees were used to feed the silkworms. Fortunately there was a high input of solar energy to keep the system going.

Each production brigade and factory had a health centre, and each town and commune a hospital. There was a county hospital for more serious cases, and those requiring still more specialized care were sent to Guangzhou. I gave a talk on the treatment of cancer at the county hospital, which was translated into Mandarin by Tsung, and then into Cantonese by one of the so-called barefoot doctors. This is the name given to men who, after elementary and middle school education, had worked as peasants and then been selected for a year or more of training in medical diagnosis and first aid in the county hospital. All the barefoot doctors we saw seemed remarkably skilful in detecting which of their patients needed to be referred to a qualified doctor at the county hospital. If one was particularly good he would be given further training, and if really exceptional he might be selected for further general education and sent to Medical College to qualify as a full doctor; and in one commune I visited I was told with great pride that one of their barefoot doctors was currently a third-year student at Chung Shan Medical College. If, on the other hand, a barefoot doctor regularly failed to recognize patients with cancer or other diseases requiring investigation he soon reverted to being a full-time peasant.

China, as Mao was wont to remind his compatriots, has a long history; it also covers an enormous area and has a vast population. Judgments based on a three-week visit are therefore apt to be fallacious, but it may be worth restating some of the impressions I formed at the time, particularly in regard to Chinese science and medicine.

We found that there was an age gap of at least ten years between scientists who were established before the cultural revolution and somehow survived, and those who had completed their training subsequently. Both groups shared the determination of their political leaders to catch up with the west in matters of technology. Both also paid lip service to the importance of developing basic research of high quality in China, but with varying degrees of conviction. Many of the scientists I met kept reasonably up to date with their reading of Western scientific journals, but their research often lagged far behind. This was hardly surprising; indeed, it surprised me that so much progress had been made in so short a time.

In the hospitals we visited, Western medicine and traditional Chinese medicine were practised side by side, and patients were often asked which they would prefer. When we asked how an uneducated peasant could be expected to exercise this choice we were met only with polite smiles. The pattern of disease I saw in China differed markedly from that seen in Europe, and also was different in different parts of the country. I was particularly interested in differences in the pattern of neoplastic disease. In Guangzhou, by far the commonest type of cancer was nasopharyngeal carcinoma, with which I was virtually unfamiliar; in Beijing, cancer of the oesophagus was particularly common; and in Shanghai, primary cancer of the liver. Various reasons were suggested to account for this, but none of them sounded convincing, and I felt that the question merited serious investigation.

It seemed likely that if China continued on her present course she would move into a position of leadership in science and industry in the course of a few decades, but I was by no means convinced that this would happen. As I said in my report to the Royal Society: 'My agnosticism in this regard arises from the current habit of attributing the anti-science of the cultural revolution entirely to the gang-of-four. It seems to me incredible that Mao played no part in this, or that intelligent people were really convinced by this convenient interpretation of events. It would clearly be disastrous for the [present] Chinese leaders to acknowledge Mao's responsibility without long and careful preparation, but until they do the possibility of a Maoist counter-counter-revolution will continue to exist.' Seventeen years later this gloomy prophecy looks as if it is in danger of being fulfilled. This prompts two further, and more fundamental, questions. First, can so huge a population as that of China be governed in a democratic way? Secondly, if not, is a solution to be found in subdivision, as is happening in Russia? It is of enormous importance, not only for China but for the whole world, that the right answers to these questions can be found.

The faith of a scientist

Many of us spend much time and effort formulating, and trying to answer, questions about the world in which we live, or, more generally, the universe, of which our world is a minute part. Some of these questions are open to experimental investigation, and thus fall within the domain of science, which can provide provisional answers that may be refined by further investigation; others, though not at present capable of being investigated experimentally, may become so as new techniques of investigation are developed. Even the scientist, however, has to assume, as an act of faith, that what he observes is real, and behaves in a rational way.

What do I mean by *faith*? Clearly not, as some cynics have suggested, pretending to believe what we know to be untrue, but a conviction that is not demonstrably false, and is so strong that, even though there is no formal proof, one is prepared to base one's life on the belief that it is true.

The scope of scientific enquiry, as Hanbury Brown has reminded us in his book, *The Wisdom of Science*,[1] is wider than it is sometimes thought to be, but there are nevertheless questions that lie outside its domain. Different people often give different answers to such questions, and there are no objective tests by which to distinguish those that are true from those that are false, but this does not mean that all such questions are meaningless or unimportant.

In this chapter I propose to examine some of these extra-scientific questions, starting with questions about matters of which we have at least some experience (which I will call retrospective questions), and going on to consider questions about what may lie ahead of us (prospective questions). My answers, as I said in my Edwin Stevens Lectures,[2] are based on a view of the universe that is basically religious, and which I would myself describe as specifically Christian, though more orthodox Christians may disagree. No doubt my upbringing has played a major role in shaping my beliefs; these include, however, the belief that what we are told has to be examined critically before it is accepted.

The notion that, in the words of Jacques Monod,[3] '*l'homme ... est seul dans l'immensité indifférente de l'Univers d'où il a emergé par hasard*', is for me quite incredible. Admittedly, to reject Monod's view and attribute the universe to a divine creator raises, but does not answer, the question of the origin of the creator, but this is a question I am content to live with because it is for us unanswerable. The life and teaching of Jesus, however, is open to examination, and it seems to me irresponsible, to say the least, to ignore it, or not to try to assess its significance.

Ernest Renan[4] ends his *Vie de Jésus* with the words: '*Jésus ne sera pas surpassé ... tous les siècles proclameront qu'entre les fils des hommes, il n'en est pas né de plus grand que Jésus*'. A stupendous claim, but does it go far enough?

For some two thousand years Christian theologians have struggled to reconcile belief in the humanity of Jesus with belief that he was divine. John Polkinghorne, a distinguished theoretical physicist who recently became an ordained priest of the Church of England, has said in his book, *The Way The World Is*,[5] that 'one cannot write about the two natures of Christ ... without being irresistably reminded of the wave-particle duality of light.... Of course, physics found eventual understanding in the beautiful work of Paul Dirac when he created the first example of a quantum field theory.... Christology has not yet found its Dirac. Perhaps it never will'. Perhaps; but I think my mentor, D. K. Picken, got it right in the statement that I quoted earlier (p. 62), but which bears repeating here: 'The apparent paradox of the humanness of Jesus and his unique oneness with God is resolved if we see Jesus as the supreme revelation of God and true manhood, provided that we give the word *supreme* its true value.'[6] For Picken supreme implied not only unsurpassed, but unsurpassable.

The first of the retrospective questions I want to consider is, *Why are things the way they are? In particular, how do we come to be here?*

Today, most cosmologists seem to date the universe from a cataclysmic explosion of a superdense agglomeration of matter, commonly called *the big bang*, that is supposed to have occurred some ten to twenty billion years ago, but if asked what preceded the big bang they say either that they have no idea or that the question lies outside the domain of science. This frankness is refreshing, but does not encourage further investigation. Indeed, as Hanbury Brown has remarked,[1] 'we seem to have reached a point where a modern *Book of Genesis* has nothing to add to *fiat lux.*' Cosmologists are, however, delighted to talk about what they think happened later, starting a few minutes, or even a few milliseconds, after the big bang, and when it comes to the question of the origin of life seem to be generally agreed that this would not have happened unless a number of critical conditions, referred to in their totality as the *anthropic principle*, had been fulfilled. This implies, of course, that had these conditions not been fulfilled we should not be here to discuss the matter, but that does not explain how they were. Conceivably, there are many possible worlds, among them ours, which happen, by chance, to provide the conditions that we need; alternatively, and to me this seems more plausible, our world was created by God to serve this purpose. Whatever the explanation, there is as yet no convincing scientific evidence of the existence of life, let alone life comparable to ours, anywhere except on our little planet, and in cosmological terms life has not existed here for very long. Why? I have no idea.

We are on firmer ground when we ask how, following the appearance of lowly forms of life, higher forms have arisen. The thesis that this was brought about by a process of natural selection, put forward independently by Charles Darwin and A. R. Wallace, aroused furious opposition from orthodox Christians, illustrated by the confrontation between Bishop Wilberforce and T. H. Huxley at the meeting of the British Association in Oxford in 1860, in the course of which Wilberforce is said to have asked Huxley whether it was 'through his grandfather or his grandmother that he claimed descent from a monkey?'[7] I do not doubt the importance of natural selection, but I agree with

Hanbury Brown[1] when he says that 'Wilberforce is commonly underrated; he had something more important, if less amusing, to ask ... He wanted to be shown that there is actively at work in nature, coordinate with the law of competition and with the existence of such favourable variations, a power of accumulating such favourable variations through successive descents.' And, adds Hanbury Brown, 'At the time of the Oxford debate no one could demonstrate such a power, and they didn't know that a Moravian monk, Gregor Mendel, was actively engaged in doing so.'

Mendel's work, published in an obscure journal in 1864 but not widely known until 1900, provided evidence of how heredity works, and molecular genetics has subsequently provided much more, but there are still important questions that remain to be answered.

In recent years, Darwinian and neo-Darwinian views on evolution have been challenged by a number of biologists, among them S. J. Gould and N. Eldridge,[8] on the ground that the fossil record points to long periods of stability, interspersed with short periods of rapid change in which new organisms suddenly appeared, whereas Darwin had envisaged a much more steady and gradual process. In 1981 Sir Andrew Huxley, a grandson of T. H. Huxley, devoted much of his Presidential Address to the Royal Society[9] to countering this challenge, and argued convincingly that the data presented by Gould and Eldridge can be accommodated in a Darwinian framework, but he accepted that there was almost no fossil evidence for the origin of the main divisions of the early animal kingdom, and also, at present, no convincing explanation of the existence of consciousness. One might add that there is also still much to be learned about how the variations on which selection operates arise. These criticisms and counter criticisms are of great scientific importance, but in my view they do not help either to confirm, or to refute, the existence of God.

Another important factor to consider in any discussion of evolution, to which an Australian immunologist, Bede Morris, first drew my attention, is the extent to which man is modifying the evolutionary process.[10] To quote Morris's words; 'We are now witnessing the emergence of man's intellect and creative genius to the extent that human achievements are influencing in a significant way the pattern of evolution by *unnatural selection*. . . . In so far as man remains part of the natural world it can be argued that his effects on it are part of natural selection; but now man has the knowledge and the necessary technology to make, at least to some extent, objective decisions about the evolution of his natural world ... Progressively, over the last few hundred years, many natural selection pressures on human populations have been eliminated by discoveries and developments in medical science. The early achievements ... related to sanitation, water supply and hygiene. More recently vaccines and antibiotics have eliminated most of the infectious plagues; modern surgery and medicine repair genetic disasters and enable naturally disqualifying gene combinations to propagate; the halt and the blind are cared for and the frail supported by the social order. This conservative face of humanity is matched by the carnage on the road, the death and debilitation caused by drugs, and the misery and anguish due to racial and political victimisation. These human achievements ... have no counterparts in other species.' Morris goes on to discuss the implications of advances in nuclear technology, but concludes that 'there is a concatenation of social circumstances and scientific discoveries in biology which have a far greater significance for human civilization than the atom bomb. These discoveries will determine both the short-term prospects and the final destiny of humanity.' In general I agree with this disturbing analysis, though I would emphasise that it is not these discoveries in themselves, but what we do about them, that will determine our fate.

This leads naturally to my second question, which is about freewill. I am unable to treat seriously those who deny that we have freewill, for, if they are right, the fact that they make this statement is itself pre-determined, as is my comment about it. Clearly, our freewill is limited by constraints of various kinds, but we often err in thinking that something is impossible when it is not. When Jesus said to his disciples that if they had faith they could say to a mountain, 'Move from here',[11] and it would move, I do not think he meant this literally, but with proper equipment and sufficient time mountains can indeed be moved. Some 96 million cubic yards of earth were moved in making the Panama Canal;[12] today it would, I am sure, be feasible to level Ben Nevis and dump the soil and rock in the Irish Sea if we really wanted to. And who, when I was a boy, would have thought that in 1969 men would be walking on the moon?

Freewill forces us to make choices. If we believe in one God the best choice we can make is to try to discover His will and surrender our wills to His. George Matheson's hymn, *Make me a captive, Lord*,[13] sums this up so perfectly that I quote the first verse below. Though written by a Christian, and commonly sung by Christians, it could surely be sung also by Jews and Moslems.

> Make me a captive, Lord,
> And then I shall be free;
> Force me to render up my sword,
> And I shall conqueror be.
> I sink in life's alarms
> When by myself I stand;
> Imprison me within thine arms,
> And strong shall be my hand.

Some people, while firmly convinced that they exercise freewill, appear to believe that God, having set the universe in motion, has withdrawn, and is unable, or unwilling, to exercise any control over it. Others go to the opposite extreme, and claim to see divine intervention in all sorts of happenings that scientists seek to explain in other ways. Neither position seems convincing to me. What seems much more plausible is the view that God, in whose image we are made, also exercises freedom that is subject to constraints; though His range of choice is infinitely greater than ours. It may be, as some have suggested, that the constraints to which His will is subjected are self-imposed, but I do not see how we can presume to form a judgment about this.

My third, and last, retrospective question is about pain and suffering. No one, I imagine, and certainly no practising doctor, can be unaware of the widespread existence of suffering, under which label I include both mental anguish and physical pain. Biologically, of course, pain has an important protective function. It is true, also, that much human suffering is the result of man's inhumanity to man, and therefore potentially avoidable; but there is also much which cannot be accounted for in these ways. How are we to explain this?

The life and death of Jesus, of countless of his followers, and of many others who would not call themselves Christians, bear witness to the fact that suffering voluntarily accepted on behalf of other people, or in maintaining some deeply felt conviction, can be a powerful force for good. It is more difficult to know what to say when people have experienced great suffering willy nilly — a child with leukaemia, the parents of a severely handicapped child, bereaved people, soldiers and civilians caught up in a war for which they were not in any way responsible, and so on. People sometimes suggest that suffering is punishment meted out by God. This was clearly in the minds of the disciples when, confronted by a man who had been blind from birth, they asked Jesus whether this was because the man himself or his parents had sinned. Jesus' reply is illuminating: 'It is not that this man or his parents sinned,' he said, 'he was born blind that God's power might be displayed in curing him,'[14] and he went on to restore the man's sight. We must remember also that we can, if we are old enough, choose how we react to unavoidable suffering, and turn it to good effect. The story of Job illustrates this dramatically for those familiar with it, as does St Paul's assertion: 'I have learned in whatsoever state I am therewith to be content,'[15] but almost everyone will remember other examples from his own experience. My experience of the various ways in which prisoners-of-war in Singapore reacted to their captivity, recounted in Chapter 8, is a case in point.

We must recognise, on the other hand, that suffering beyond a certain limit that varies with the individual can be utterly destructive, and for some people the end of their earthly life is not something to be abhorred, but a blessed relief. All who practise medicine are aware of this, but opinions differ about what should be done in such cases. Clearly, much can and should be done to mitigate both physical pain and mental anguish, but short of depriving a patient of all awareness of himself and his surroundings there are limits to what palliative treatment can achieve.[16] Should the patient then be obliged passively to wait for death or is it the right of everyone to decide when his life should be ended, and to obtain help in achieving this objective?'

Some years ago, the Rev. Leslie Weatherhead, in a letter to the Times,[17] argued that euthanasia, or suicide if the doctor was unwilling to cooperate, was justified in such cases, but I am not so sure. I have no doubt about the propriety of switching off life-support machines used to maintain respiration when it is clear that the patient is what is nowadays called brain dead, but that is quite different from deliberately terminating a life that would otherwise continue. To introduce legislation that would permit this would, I believe, open the way to terrible abuses and dangers, though I think it is important for the courts to distinguish between genuine mercy-killing and killing for other reasons, and am glad that some progress has been made in this direction. The moral, as distinct from the legal, problem is inescapably a matter for the conscience of each individual concerned, be he patient, close relative or doctor.

What lies ahead for the universe, including the little bit of it we inhabit, and for us as individuals? I am content to leave it to cosmologists to speculate about cosmological questions. The immensity of the distances, and the time-scale, they talk about have a mind-numbing effect so far as I am concerned. Given that light from the sun takes roughly ten minutes to reach the earth I can form some sort of mental picture of a light year, but distances of millions of light years are, for me, unimaginable; and when told[18] that it has been estimated that the gigantic black holes into which concentrations of matter may contract will decay by black body radiation after $(10^{10})^{76}$ years my mind simply switches off.

The question about what lies ahead for us personally is of more immediate importance, and concerns us all.

Many people believe that when they die they will simply cease to exist. Such a fate seems vastly preferable to enduring the everlasting torment that others believe awaits the unrepentant sinner, or even the prospect of swanning about for ever on a cloud with nothing to do but play the harp, that has been postulated as the fate of the good. Moreover, even if we do not believe in any kind of personal survival, we may share A. A. Milne's belief[19] that 'there is nothing that we do or say but makes its ripple in the everlasting sea. We die, but the world goes on; and for those who come after us Life is different from what it would have been had we never lived... . Life in this world can flow on continuously, for ever; and when we die we become part of its stream, and are at last immortal.'

This is indeed a rational and stoical view of what lies ahead. But we have been told, on the highest authority, that something infinitely better awaits us. We do not know what form this will take, but I believe that our life on earth serves as an apprenticeship for a new life, richer than anything we can imagine.

What have we done to deserve this? Saintly people are prone to answer, 'Nothing', but I do not accept this. Nowhere near enough, certainly, but nothing? I have so often seen people behave towards others with almost unbelievable unselfishness and kindness; and I cannot believe that this counts for nothing, whatever else they may have done. The description of the last judgment in St Matthew's gospel is illuminating here. While it is not, in my opinion, to be taken literally, the significance of the King's answer to those who asked when they had given him sustenance or clothing seems crystal clear: 'I tell you this: anything you did for one of my brethren here, however humble, you did for me.'[20]

It would be absurd, on the other hand, to try to ignore, or make light of, our shortcomings, individual and collective. We do well to ask, like the psalmist: 'O thou Eternal One, our Lord … what is man that thou should'st think of him? What is mortal man that thou should'st heed him?'[21] But for me the answer is clear. We are God's children. Wayward children all too often but, despite our foolish ways, His love never fails.

Notes and references

[A number in square brackets is the number in the list of the author's published papers deposited with the Royal Society, London.]

CHAPTER 1

1. Woodruff, Michael. 'The choice for mankind in relation to biology and medicine.' In *Options for Humanity*. Queen's College, University of Melbourne, 1988. pp. 5–29. [255]
2. Huxley, Andrew. 'Evidence, clues and motive in science.' *New Humanist,* vol. 93, 1977. pp. 61–66.

CHAPTER 3

1. Smith, J. C. *A Book of Verse for Boys and Girls.* Humphrey Milford, Oxford.
2. Wills, Mrs L. M. and others. From the hymn 'Father, hear the prayer we offer'. *Songs of Praise.* Oxford University Press. 1929.
3. Chamberlain, Rt. Hon. Neville. *In Search of Peace. Speeches (1937–1938).* ed. Arthur Bryant. The National Book Association. Hutchison, London. 1939.
4. Woodruff, Philip. *The Men Who Ruled India.* 2 vols. Jonathan Cape, London. 1953.
5. Ball, W. W. Rouse. *Mathematical Recreations and Essays.* Revised by H. S. M. Coxeter. Macmillan, London. 11th edn. 1947.
6. Thompson, Silvanus, P. *Calculus Made Easy.* Macmillan, London. 1910. Many later editions.
7. Whitrow, G. J. 'Newton's Role in the History of Mathematics.' *News and Notes of the Royal Society.* vol. 43, 1989. pp. 71–91.
8. Littlewood, J. E. *A Mathematician's Miscellany.* Methuen, London. 1957. Revised by B. Bolobos. Cambridge University Press. 1986.

9. Hobson, E. W. A. *A Treatise on Plane Trigonometry.* Cambridge University Press. 6th edn. 1925.

10. From *Punch*, London. 17 February 1915.

11. Stuart, Dorothy M. 'Est Deo Gratia. A Song for St George's Day.' From *The Shire.* 29 April 1916.

CHAPTER 4

1. Parnaby, Owen. *Queens' College. University of Melbourne. A Centenary History.* Melbourne University Press. 1990.

2. Watts, Isaac. From the hymn 'There is a Land of Pure Delight'. *Songs of Praise.* Oxford University Press. 1929.

3. *Biographical Memoirs of Fellows of the Royal Society.* vol. 30, London. 1984. pp. 443–511.

4. *Biographical Memoirs of Fellows of the Royal Society.* vol. 14, London. 1968. pp. 117–138.

5. Hardy, G. H. *Pure Mathematics.* Cambridge University Press. 5th edn. 1928.

6. Goursat, E. *Cours d'Analyse Mathématique.* 3 vols. Gauthier-Villars, Paris. 3 ième. ed., 1923.

7. Alexander, John. *David Kennedy Picken. A Personal Memoir.* Ormond College, Melbourne. 1988.

8. Woodruff, Michael. 'D. K. Picken. As I Knew Him.' *Ormond News Letter.* Ormond College, Melbourne. 1989. [256]

9. The Stavisky affair caused a considerable political scandal in France. A vivid picture of Stavisky, and the political background to the scandal, was presented in Alain Resnais's film, *Stavisky*, which has been described by Jorge Semprun (*Le 'Stavisky' d'Alain Resnais.* Gallimard, Paris. 1974. p. 17) as '*une fusion qui établit avec la réalité historique des rapports particuliers, à la fois précis et fabuleux*'.

10. Tossy Spivakowsky was born in Odessa in 1907. He studied the violin, and made his debut, in Berlin. He remained in Australia until 1940, giving concerts and teaching at the University Conservatorium of Music. He then moved to the United States (see Sadie, S. (ed.). *The Grove Concise Dictionary of Music.* Macmillan, London. 1988.

11. Barnes, J. *Ahead of His Time. E. W. Barnes, Bishop of Birmingham.* Collins, London. 1979.

12. Rev. Dr Frank Borland. Cited by Henderson, K. T. in *Prayers of Citizenship.* Longmans, London. 1940.

13. Picken, D. K. *Purpose.* ASCM, Melbourne. 1931.

CHAPTER 5

1. Littlewood, J. E. 'The mathematician's art of work.' *Rockefeller University Review*, vol. 5. pp. 1–7. 1967.

2. See Bell, E. T. *Men of Mathematics*. 2 vols. Penguin Books, London. 1953. pp. 580–611.

3. Gompertz, B. 'On the nature of the function expressive of the law of human mortality, and on a new mode of determining the value of life contingencies.' *Phil. Trans. R. Soc. Lond.*, vol. 115, 1825. pp. 513–585.

4. Gompertz, B. 'A supplement to two papers published in the Transactions of the Royal Society, On the science connected with mortality;' the one published in 1820, and the other in 1825. *Phil. Trans. R. Soc. Lond.*, vol. 152. 1862. pp. 511–559.

5. See, Race, R. R. and Sanger, R. *Blood Groups in Man*. Blackwell Scientific Publications, Oxford. 1950. Ch. 7.

6. See, e.g. Hardy, G. H. and Wright, E. M. *An Introduction to the Theory of Numbers*. 3rd edn. Oxford University Press. 1954.

7. Thompson, Silvanus P. *The Life of William Thompson, Baron Kelvin of Largs*. 2 vols. Macmillan, London. 1910. p. 1139.

8. Weatherburn, C. E. *A First Course in Mathematical Statistics*. 2nd edn. Cambridge University Press. 1949. pp. 65–66.

9. 'God made the Integers; All else is the work of man.' (Kroneker's epigram was, it seems, not intended literally.)

10. Russell, B. *The Principles of Mathematics*. Cambridge University Press. 1903.

11. Russell, B. and Whitehead, A. N. *Principia Mathematica*. 3 vols. Cambridge University Press. 1925, 1927.

12. Carnap, R. *The Logical Syntax of Language*. Kegan Paul, London. 1937.

13. Medawar, P. B. *Memoir of a Thinking Radish*. Oxford University Press. 1986.

14. e.g., Fisher, R. A. *Statistical Methods for Research Workers*. 6th edn. Oliver and Boyd. London. 1936.

15. ibid. Preface. p. ix.

16. Weatherburn, C. E. *A First Course in Mathematical Statistics*. 2nd edn. Cambridge University Press. 1949. This book is based on lectures addressed to students of agriculture, biology, economics, psychology, physics and chemistry. It assumes that the readers will have, in the author's words, 'an average mathematical equipment, including an ordinary knowledge of integral calculus'.

17. Russell, B. 'The study of mathematics.' This essay was written in 1902, and published in 1907 in the *New Quarterly*. It is reprinted

in *Mysticism and Logic*. Penguin Books, London, 1953, where the passage quoted appears on pp. 62–63.

18. Quoted in Bell, E. T. *Men of Mathematics*. Penguin Books, London. 1953. pp. 445–446.

19. ibid. p. 477.

20. Lindemann's proof appeared in *Mathematische Annalen*, vol. 20, 1882. pp. 213–225. Simplified (but still rigorous) proofs will be found in many books. See, e.g., Hobson, E. W. *A Treatise on Plane Trigonometry*. Cambridge University Press. 1925. pp. 305–306; or Hardy, G. H. and Wright, E. M. *An Introduction to the Theory of Numbers*. Oxford University Press. 3rd edn. 1954. pp. 173–176.

21. See reference 6.

22. See Bell, E. T. *Men of Mathematics*. Penguin Books, London. 1953. pp. 235–239.

23. E. T. Bell's book, cited in reference 22, goes some way to meet this need. It gives a vivid account of the lives of great mathematicians, from Zeno and Eudoxus to Riemann, Poincaré and Cantor. There is room for another book which has more to say about their work, and that of more recent mathematicians, but is similarly addressed to those who are not professional mathematicians.

24. See Chapter 3, reference 5.

25. See Chapter 3, reference 8.

26. McCutcheon, J. J. and Forfar, D. O. 'On a certain diophantine equation; or Zink tax, and where it led.' *The Mathematical Gazette*, vol. 70, 1986. pp. 260–262.

27. Personal communication from Professor R. B. Potts, Department of Mathematics, University of Adelaide.

28. My proof is as follows: Let $x^2+y^2/xy+1 = N$. Then:

(1) If $x=y$ the only solution in integers is $x=y=N=1=1^2$

(2) If x does not $=y$, let x be the larger of x and y.
Then $N<x^2$, otherwise xy must be <1.

(3) If $x>Y$, and there is a solution when x and N are +ve integers and y is a +ve or -ve integer or zero, we can exclude the possibility of y being -ve because x^2+y^2 is +ve and, if y is -ve, $xy+1$ is +ve only if $|xy|<1$.

(4) Suppose we have an integral solution when $x=x_1$, $y=y_1$, $N=N_1$, and $x_1>y_1>/=0$. If y_1 and N_1 are kept constant the possible values of x are the roots of the quadratic equation $x^2 - x.N_1y_1+y_1^2 - N_1=0$.
Call these roots a,b. Then $a+b=N_1y_1$ (i); $ab=y_1^2-N_1$ (ii)
It follows from (i) that if a is integral, so is b. We can exclude $a=b=\frac{1}{2}(N_1y_1)$ since from (ii) this would require $N_1^2<4$, i.e. $N_1=1$. Suppose $a>b$, then it follows from (ii) that $b<y_1$, and we can write $x_1=a\geq y_1>b>0$.
So we have another solution $x=b$ (call it x_2) such that x_2^2) such that $x_2^2+y_1^2=N_1(x_2y_1+1)$, where $x_2\leq y_1$. If $x_2=y_1$ we have the solution $N_1=1$.

If not, repeat the process and find $y_2<x_2$, and so on. Eventually, since we are dealing with integers, one of x and y becomes zero, and N equals the square of the other.

29. Herrick, Robert. *To the Virgins, to make much of Time.*

CHAPTER 6

1. See Russell, K. F. *The Melbourne Medical School.* Melbourne University Press. 1977.

2. *Biograhpical Memoirs of Fellows of the Royal Society.* vol. 1, London. 1955. pp. 119–134.

3. Jones, F. Wood. *Aboreal Man.* Edward Arnold, London. 1916.

4. Jones, F. Wood. *The Problem of Man's Ancestry.* Society for the Promotion of Christian Knowledge. London. 1918.

5. Jones, F. Wood. *Man's Place Among the Mammals.* Edward Arnold, London. 1929.

6. Jones, F. Wood. *The Principles of Anatomy as seen in the Hand.* Churchill, London. 1920. (2nd edn. Baillière, Tindall and Cox, London. 1944.)

7. Jones, F. Wood. *Structure and Function as seen in the Foot.* Baillière, Tindall and Cox, London. 1944.

8. Jones, F. Wood and Porteous, S. D. *The Matrix of the Mind.* Edward Arnold, London. 1929.

9. Jones, F. Wood. 'The medico-legal aspect of judicial hanging.' *Proc. Medico-Legal Soc. Victoria.* 1935. p. 1.

10. Jones, F. Wood. *Design and Purpose.* Kegan Paul, Trench, Trubner and Co., London. 1942.

11. Jones, F. Wood. *Habit and Heritage.* Kegan Paul, Trench, Trubner and Co., London. 1943.

12. Jones, F. Wood. *Hallmarks of Humanity.* Baillière, Tindall and Cox, London. 1948.

13. Jones, F. Wood. *Trends of Life.* Edward Arnold, London. 1953.

14. Wills, R. A. *The Spread of Tumours in the Human Body.* Butterworth, London. 1952, 1973.

15. King, E. S. J. *Ovarian Tumours.* Edward Arnold, London. 1928.

16. King, E. S. J. *Localized Rarifying Conditions of Bone.* Edward Arnold, London. 1933.

17. King, E. S. J. *Surgery of the Heart.* Edward Arnold, London. 1938.

18. Souttar, H. S. 'The surgical treatment of mitral stenosis.' Brit. med. J. vol. 2, 1925. pp. 603–606. See also: Cutler, E. C. and Levine,

S. A. 'Cardiotomy and valvulotomy for mitral stenosis. Experimental observations and clinical notes concerning an operated case with recovery.' Boston med. surg.J. vol. 188. 1923. pp. 1023–1027.

19. Lewis, T. *Clinical Disorders of the Heart. A Handbook for Practitioners and Students.* Shaw and Sons, London. 5th edn. 1920.

20. Chamberlain, The Rt. Hon. Neville. *In Search of Peace.* Hutchinson and Co., London. 1939.

21. C. E. M. Joad expressed what many pacificists felt when he wrote, in *What Is At Stake, and Why Not Say So?,* 'It is because I know that this is not a struggle which requires me to hate every man born in Germany because he was born in Germany, but to hate certain ideas that aim at the imprisonment of the minds of men and the destruction of a way of life ... that I have abandoned pacificism ... and thrown in my lot with those who insist that the Nazis must be defeated.'

CHAPTER 7

1. Henderson, K. T. *Prayers of Citizenship.* Longmans, Green and Co., London. 1940.

2. Oldham, J. H. *A Devotional Diary.* Student Christian Movement Press, London. 1925. (11th edn. 1937).

3. Jamieson, E. B. *A Companion to Manuals of Practical Anatomy.* Oxford University Press. 7th edn. 1950.

4. Whittaker, C. R. *Operative Surgery.* E. and S. Livingstone. 5th edn. Edinburgh. 1939.

5. Lt. Col. T. Hamilton. *See* reference 10, p. 35.

6. Wodehouse, P. G. *The Code of the Woosters.* Herbert Jenkins, London. 1938.

7. Letter to Dr Georgina Sweet. 24 September 1941.

8. Letter to Rev. Kenneth Beckett. 26 June 1941.

9. Letter to Mrs H. A. Woodruff. 1 September 1941.

10. Hamilton, T. *Soldier Surgeon in Malaya.* World Distributors (Manchester) Ltd., London. 1959. (Original edition by Angus and Robertson, Melbourne.)

When Dr Hamilton and his wife visited Edinburgh in 1960, he gave me a copy of his book bearing the inscription: 'To one of a happy unit, from the C.O., Tom. Hamilton'. I was glad to see that he agreed that it was a happy unit, though he protested when I said that the most important reason for this was that it had such a splendid C.O. Much of the detailed information in what follows was gleaned from this book.

11. Euripides. *Fragments.*

CHAPTER 8

1. White, J. Glynn. 'Reminiscences: Changi 1942–5.' *Occasional Papers on Medical History in Australia.* Ed. Attwood, H., Forster, F. and Gandevia, B. University of Melbourne. 1984. pp. 35–57.

2. Nelson, H. *Prisoners of War. Australians Under Nippon.* Australian Broadcasting Commission, Melbourne. 1985. p. 20.

3. Lodge, A. B. *Deserter or Hero? The Gordon Bennett Royal Commission.* Centre for Australian Studies, London. 1989.

4. Rollo Edwards-Kerr described his escape in a talk he gave in Monaco in 1985 to *Les Amis du Club 'Les Voisins'.* With five others, including a Dutchman who had become British by naturalisation and was an experienced sailor, he left Singapore early on the morning of 16 February in a nearly derelict yacht they had found at the Singapore Yacht Club. They sailed through a minefield but were saved by their shallow draught, and after various near-disasters arrived at Tanjong Pinang. Here they abandoned their boat, which was now quite unseaworthy, but managed to persuade the Dutch authorites to lend them a Government launch, which took them to Rengat, in Sumatra, and from there they made their way by road and a narrow guage railway to Padang. Here they joined a party of British and Australians and embarked on the SS *Domayer Van Twist,* which took them to Perth.

5. *See* Bowden, T. (Ed.) *Changi Photographer. George Aspinall's Record of Captivity.* ABC Enterprises and The MacMillan Co. of Australia. 1989. pp. 82–93.

6. Smith, D. A. and Woodruff, M. F. A. *Deficiency Diseases in Japanese Prison Camps.* Medical Research Council, London. Special Report Series No. 274. 1951.

My part of this book is based on a report I submitted to the Director General of Medical Services, Australian Military Forces, in 1946.

7. This section is based on an address I gave for the Australian Broadcasting Commission, which was broadcast on 6 January 1946 in the Spirit of Man series, organized by K. T. Henderson.

8. See, for example, Sir Ernest Dunlop's *The War Diaries of Weary Dunlop.* Viking Books, London. 1987.

9. Maingot, R. *Postgraduate Surgery.* London. 1936.

10. Frazer, Sir James, G. *The Golden Bough.* 1 Vol. London. 1922.

11. Whittaker, E. T. and Watson, G. N. *Modern Analysis.* Cambridge University Press. 1915.

12. Carnap, R. *The Logical Syntax of Language.* Kegan Paul, Trench, Trubner & Co., London. 1937.

13. Lewis, C. I. and Langford, C. H. *Symbolic Logic.* The Century Co., New York. 1932.

14. Weber, H. (Trans. Thilly, F.) and Perry, R. B. *History of Philosophy.* Charles Scribner's Sons. New York. 1925.

15. Trotter, Wilfred. 'The herd instinct in peace and war.' In *Collected Papers of Wilfred Trotter FRS.* Oxford University Press, London. 1941.

16. Markowitz is the author of a remarkable book, *Experimental Surgery,* first published in 1937 by Williams and Wilkins, Baltimore.

17. Maugham, W. S. 'The Pool.' *collected Short Stories.* Vol. I. Penguin Books, London. 1963.

18. Woodruff, M. F. A. and Sampimon, R. L. H. 'Some observations concerning the use of hypnosis as a substitute for anaesthesia.' *Med. J. Aust.* vol. 1, 1946. pp. 393–395. [2]

CHAPTER 9

1. Smith, D. A. and Woodruff, M. F. A. *Deficiency Diseases in Japanese Prison Camps.* Medical Research Council, London. Special Report Series No. 274. 1951.

CHAPTER 10

1. Woodruff, M. F. A. *Surgery for Dental Students.* Blackwell Scientific Publications, Oxford. 1954. (4th edn. with Hedley Berry. 1984).

2. Krebs, Hans. *Reminiscences and Reflections.* Clarendon Press, Oxford. 1981.

3. Woodruff, M. F. A. and Woodruff, H. G. 'The transplantation of normal tissues: with special reference to auto- and homotransplants of thyroid and spleen in the anterior chamber of the eye, and subcutaneously, in guinea pigs.' Phil. Trans. Roy. Soc. Lond. vol. 234. 1950. pp. 559–582. [5]

CHAPTER 11

1. I use the current term *allograft* though at the time the term used was *homograft.*

2. Murphy, James B. *The Lymphocyte in Resistance to Tissue Grafting, Malignant Disease, and Tuberculous Infection.* Monographs of the Rockefeller Institute for Medical Research. No. 21. 1926.

3. Chew, W. B. and Lawrence, J. S. 'Antilymphocytic serum.' J. Immunol. vol. 33. 1937. pp. 271–278.

4. Burnet, F. M. and Fenner, F. *The Production of Antibodies.* 2nd edn. McMillan, Melbourne. 1949.

5. Billingham, R. B., Brent, L. and Medawar, P. B. 'Actively acquired tolerance of foreign cells.' *Nature* vol. 172, 1953. pp. 603–60.

6. Woodruff, M. F. A. 'Some impressions of medical schools in the USA.' *Zodiac* vol. 2. 1951. pp. 111–112. [6]

7. *See* Clapesaddle, H. *The Doctors Mayo.* Pocket Books, New York. 1956. (First publ. Univ. Minnesota, 1941.)

8. *See* Chapter 8.

9. Woodruff, M. F. A. *The One and the Many.* Edwin Stevens Lectures for the Laity. Republished in Woodruff, Michael. *On Science and Surgery.* Edinburgh University Press. 1977.

10. Huggins, C. 'Endocrine induced regression of cancer.' *Science* vol. 156. 1967. pp. 1050–1054.

11. *See* Chapter 10, ref. 3.

12. *See* Dobell, A. R. C. 'Surgery in the era of technology: Recollections of a Gibbon resident.' *Bull. Amer. Coll. Surg.* vol. 75. 1990. pp. 6–12.

13. Woodruff, M. F. A. *The Transplantation of Tissues and Organs.* Charles C. Thomas. Springfield, USA. 1960.

14. Woodruff, M. F. A. and Allen, T. M. 'Blood groups and the homograft problem.' *Brit. J. Plastic Surg.* vol. 5. 1953. pp. 238–242. [17]

15. Woodruff, M. F. A. 'Hunterian Lecture — The transplantation of homologous tissue and its surgical applications.' *Ann. R. Coll. Surg. Engl* vol. 11. 1952. pp. 173–194. [12]

16. *See* Chapter 5, ref. 6.

17. Jones, R. V. *Most Secret War. British Scientific Intelligence 1939–1943.* Hamish Hamilton, London. 1978.

18. Moberley, W. *Crisis in the University.* SCM Press, London. 1949.

19. *See* Woodruff, H. and Woodruff, M. 'Don's Swanwick.' *The Australian Intercollegian.* April 1949. pp. 29–30.

CHAPTER 12

1. Rame, D. *Wine of Good Hope.* Collins, London. 1939.

2. Woodruff, M. F. A. 'The university and surgery.' *Lancet* vol. 2, 1953. pp. 1–11. [16] Reprinted in Woodruff, M. F. A. *On Science and Surgery.* Edinburgh University Press. 1977. pp. 1–12.

3. Newman, John Henry, Cardinal. *The Idea of a University.* Reprinted. Ed. C. F. Harrold. Longmans, Green and Co., London. 1947.

4. John Milton. 'Hymn on the morning of Christ's nativity.'

5. Publication. [50]

6. The numbers of the publications in the appendix relating to work done in Dunedin are in the range [15] to [50].

7. Publications [51] and [198].

8. Publications [35] and [44].

9. Publication [46].

10. *See* Smith, C. V. *From N to Z.* Hicks, Smith and Co., Wellington, NZ. 1947. Revised 1954. This is an amusing, perceptive, critical and affectionate account of many aspects of New Zealand life by a business man who was a member of the Council of Otago University.

CHAPTER 13

1. Woodruff, M. F. A. 'Surgical science.' *Univ. Edinb.J.* vol. 19. 1958. pp. 14–21. [49]

2. Gibson, T. and Medawar, P. B. 'The fate of skin homografts in man.' J.Anat., Lond. vol. 77. 1943. pp. 299–310.

3. Publications [51, 54, 61, 63, 64, 66, 72–74, 79, 99, 163, 174, 186].

4. Publications [87, 95, 113, 117, 119, 123, 124, 126–129, 131, 132, 135, 138, 140, 144, 146, 147, 154, 155, 159, 160, 161, 162, 168, 170, 172, 175].

5. Publications [97, 103, 121, 130].

6. Publication [75].

7. Publications [105, 141, 176, 179, 185, 187–190, 194–197].

8. Publication [200].

9. Publications [157, 168, 176, 179].

10. Publications [76, 79, 82, 88, 98].

11. Publications [187, 216].

12. Publication [62, 150].

13. Publications [70, 89, 94, 100, 101, 112, 115, 116, 133, 137, 149, 150, 171, 178, 193, 198, 204].

14. Publication [104].

15. Publication [60].

16. Publication [142].

17. Publications [52, 69].

18. Publication [81].

19. Publications [60, 65, 83, 93, 120, 152, 153, 165, 180, 184, 192, 201, 202, 205, 206].

20. Terasaki, P. I. (Ed.) *History of Transplantation: 35 Personal Recollections.* UCLA Tissue Typing Laboratory, Los Angeles. 1991.

21. Woodruff, M. F. A., Robson, J. S., Ross, J. A., Nolan, B. and Lambie, A. T. 'Transplantation of a kidney from an identical twin.' *Lancet*. vol. i, 1961. pp. 1245–1249. [62].

22. Woodruff, M. F. A., Nolan, B., Robson, J. S. and MacDonald, M. K. 'Renal transplantation in man. Experience of 35 cases.' *Lancet* vol. i, 1969. pp. 6–12. [150]

23. Woodruff, M. F. A., Nolan, B., Anderton, J. L., Abouna, G. M., Morton, J. B. and Jenkins, A. McL. 'Long survival after renal transplantation in man.' *Brit. J. Surg.* vol. 63, 1976. pp. 85–101. [204].

24. Matthew, H., Logan, A., Woodruff, M. F. A. and Heard, B. 'Paraquat poisoning — Lung transplantation.' *Brit. med. J.* vol. 3. 1968. pp. 759–763. [142]

25. Woodruff, M. F. A. *The One and the Many*. The Edwin Stevens Lectures for the Laity. Royal Society of Medicine. London. 1970.

26. Addison, Joseph. In *Songs of Praise*, Oxford University Press. 1931, and many other hymnals.

27. Luther, Martin. *ibid.*

28. World Health Organization. *Diagnosis and Treatment of Acute Radiation Injury*. WHO, Geneva. 1961.

29. World Health Organization Technical Report Series, No. 286. *Research in Immunology*. Geneva. 1964.

30. Anderson, N. F., Clark, J. G., James, K., Reid, B. L. and Woodruff, M. F. A. 'Biological properties of antilymphocytic antibody and antibody fragments.' In Dausset, J., Hamburger, J. and Mathé, G. (Eds.). *Advance in Transplantation*. Munksgaard, Copenhagen. 1968. pp. 103–106. [131]

31. Woodruff, M. F. A. 'Ethical problems.' ibid. pp 723–724. [145]

32. *Transpl. Proc.* vol. III, No. 1, 1971.

33. *Colloque Internationale sur la Biologie des Homogreffes*. CNRS Paris. 1957.

34. Biological Problems of Grafting. *Les Congrès et Colloques de l'Université de Liège*. Liège. 1959.

35. Mechanisms of Immunological Tolerance. *Proceedings of a Symposium held at Liblice near Prague, November 1961*. Czechoslovak Academy of Sciences. Prague.

36. Halpern, B. (Ed.). *Corynebacterium parvum. Applications in Experimental and Clinical Oncology*. Plenum Press, London. 1975.

37. Whittier, J. G. From the hymn 'Dear Lord and Father of mankind.' *Songs of Praise*. Oxford University Press. 1932.

38. McCord, G. *The Fabric of Man. Fifty Years of the Peter Bent Brigham*. Published for the Hospital by the Fiftieth Anniversary Celebration Committee. Boston. 1963.

39. Corner, G. W. *Two Centuries of Medicine. A History of the School of Medicine, University of Pennsylvania.* J. B. Lippincott Co. Philadelphia. 1965.

40. Woodruff, M. F. A. 'Immunological considerations in the treatment of cancer.' (20th Rudolph Matas Memorial Lecture.) *Bull. Tulane Medical Faculty* vol. 26. 1967. pp. 231–238. [120]

41. Woodruff, M. F. A. 'Residual cancer.' *Harvey Lectures.* Series 66. 1972. pp. 161–176. [180]

42. Jenkins, A. McL. and Woodruff, M. F. A. 'Specific immunosuppression of cardiac allograft rejection in rats.' *Transplant. Proc.* vol. 5. pp. 727–732. 1973. [186]

43. Milne, A. A. *Winnie The Pooh.* Methuen. London. 1926. p. 32.

44. Woodruff, M. F. A. 'The renaissance of immunology.' *New Zealand Med. J.* vol. 83, pp. 1–4. 1976. [203]

45. Warner, N. L., Woodruff, M. F. A. and Burton, R. C. 'Inhibition of the growth of lymphoid tumours in syngeneic athymic (nude) mice.' *Internat. J. Cancer.* vol. 20. pp. 146–155. 1977. [216]

CHAPTER 14

1. Merrien, J. *Plaisir de la Mer.* Denoel, Paris. 6th edn. 1962.

2. See: Austin, K. A. *The voyage of the Investigator. 1801–1803. Captain Matthews Flinders, R. N.* Seal Books. Rugby. 1968.

3. Charrière. H. *Papillon.* Robert Laffont, Paris. 1969.

4. Bombard, A. *Naufragé Volontaire.* Editions de Paris. 1953.

5. Heaton, P. *Sailing.* Penguin Books, Harmondsworth. Revised Edn. 1962.

6. Heaton, P. *Cruising.* Penguin Books, Harmondsworth. 1959.

7. Coles, K. Adlard. *Heavy Weather Sailing.* Granada Publishing, London. 3rd edn. 1980.

8. Illingworth, J. *Further Offshore.* Adlard Coles, London. 6th edn. 1969.

9. Merrien, J. *L'Art du Large.* Robert Laffont, Paris. 1962. p. 84.

10. Slocum, J. *Sailing Alone Around the World.* The Chaucer Press, Bungay. Reprinted 1986.

11. Gerbault, A. *A la Poursuite de Soleil.* Grasset, Paris. 1929.

12. Le Toumelin, Y. *Kurun Autour du Monde.* Flammarion. Paris. 1953.

13. Davison, Ann. *My Ship is so Small.* Davies, London. 1954.

14. Chichester, F. *Gipsy Moth Circles the World.* Hodder and Stoughton, London. 1967.

15. Tabarly, E. *Victoire en Solitaire.* Arthaud, Paris. 1964.

16. Merrien, J. *Les Navigateurs Solitaires.* Denoel, Paris. 1965.

CHAPTER 15

1. Woodruff, M. F. A., Fox, M., Buckton, K. A. and Jacobs, P. A. 'The recognition of human blood chimeras.' *Lancet.* vol. i. pp. 3–8. 1962. [69]

2. Publications [212, 216, 219, 220, 226–229, 232, 237–239, 242, 243, 245, 248, 250]

3. Publications [217, 218, 221–223, 230, 234, 236, 246, 247]

4. Woodruff, M. F. A. *The Interaction of Cancer and Host. Its Therapeutic Significance.* Grune and Stratton. New York. 1980.

5. Woodruff, M. F. A. *Cellular Variation and Adaptation in Cancer. Biological Basis and Therapeutic Consequences.* Oxford University Press. 1990.

6. Publication [222]

7. *Transplantation Proceedings* vol. XI. p. xxxiii. 1979.

8. Churchill, Winston S. *The Second World War. Volume IV. The Hinge of Fate.* Cassell. London. 1951. p. 728.

9. See ref. 10, pp. xi–xii.

10. Abouna, G. M. (Ed.) *Current Status of Clinical Organ Transplantation.* Martinus Nijhoff. The Hague. 1984.

11. Woodruff, M. F. A. 'What's going on in the cancer patient?' *Pathology.* vol. 18. pp. 175–180. 1986. [246]

12. Woodruff, M. F. A. 'The choice for mankind in relation to biology and medicine.' In *Options for Humanity. The Sir Douglas Wright Symposium.* Queen's College, University of Melbourne. 1987. pp. 5–29.

13. Woodruff, M. F. A. 'The interface between science and medicine. The Halford Oration, University of Melbourne.' *Chiron.* vol. 3. 1988. pp. 4–10.

14. Woodruff, M. F. A. 'Jetlag.' *Nature.* vol. 331. 1988. p. 6153. [260]

CHAPTER 16

1. Brown, R. Hanbury. *The Wisdom of Science.* Cambridge University Press. 1986.

2. Woodruff, M. F. A. *The One and the Many.* Edwin Stevens Lectures for the Laity. Royal Society of Medicine. 1970. Reprinted in Woodruff, Michael. *On Science and Surgery.* Edinburgh University Press. 1977.

3. Monod, J. *Le Hazard et la Necessité.* Editions du Seuil. Paris. 1970.

4. Renan, E. *Vie de Jésus.* Nelson. Paris. 1863.

5. Polkinghorne, J. *The Way the World Is.* Triangle. SPCK, London. 1983.

6. Picken, D. K. *Purpose.* ASCM. Melbourne. 1931.

7. Wilberforce, S. Cited in ref. 1, p. 64.

8. Gould, S. J. and Eldridge, N. 'Punctuated equilibria: the tempo and mode of evolution reconsidered.' *Paleobiology.* vol. 3. 1977. pp. 115–151.

9. Huxley, A. 'Address of the President.' *Proc. Roy. Soc. B.* vol. 214. 1982. pp. 137–152.

10. Morris, B. 'Unnatural selection and the destiny of humanity.' Unpublished address. 1985.

11. Matthew, Ch. 17. verse 20. *The New English Bible.* Oxford and Cambridge University Presses. 1961.

12. Cited in Theroux, P. *The Old Patagonian Express.* Penguin Books, London. 1980. p. 241.

13. *The Church Hymnary.* 3rd edn. No. 445. Oxford Univ. Press (and many other hymnbooks).

14. John, Ch. 9. vv. 3–4. *The New English Bible.* Oxford and Cambridge Univ. Presses.

15. Philippians, Ch. 4. v. 11. *Bible, Authorised Version.* Oxford University Press.

16. Woodruff, M. F. A. *On Science and Surgery.* Edinburgh Univ. Press. 1977. p. 115.

17. Weatherhead, L. Letter to the Editor. *The Times.* 17 April 1970.

18. Polkinghorne, J. *The Way the World Is.* Triangle. SPCK. London. 1983. p. 9.

19. Cited in Thwaite, A. *A. A. Milne. His Life.* Faber and Faber. London. 1990. p. 344.

20. Matthew, Ch. 25, v. 40. *The New English Bible.* Oxford and Cambridge University Presses. 1961.

21. Psalm 8. v. 4. Moffatt, J. *A New Translation of the Bible.* Hodder and Stoughton, London. 1926.

Index